Blog Design

FOR DUMMIES®
A Wiley Brand

by Melissa Culbertson

FOR DUMMIES®
A Wiley Brand

Blog Design For Dummies®

Published by:
John Wiley & Sons, Inc.,
111 River Street,
Hoboken, NJ 07030-5774,
www.wiley.com

For general information on our other products and services, please contact our Customer Care Department within the U.S. at 877-762-2974, outside the U.S. at 317-572-3993, or fax 317-572-4002. For technical support, please visit www.wiley.com/techsupport.

Wiley publishes in a variety of print and electronic formats and by print-on-demand. Some material included with standard print versions of this book may not be included in e-books or in print-on-demand. If this book refers to media such as a CD or DVD that is not included in the version you purchased, you may download this material at http://booksupport.wiley.com. For more information about Wiley products, visit www.wiley.com.

Library of Congress Control Number: 2013936849

ISBN 978-1-118-55480-7 (pbk); ISBN 978-1-118-55499-9 (ebk); ISBN 978-1-118-55478-4 (ebk)

Manufactured in the United States of America

10 9 8 7 6 5 4 3 2 1

Contents at a Glance

Table of Contents

Chapter 18: Ten Well-Designed Blogs

Introduction

*T*he average person spends roughly three seconds on a website before deciding whether to stay. That's not enough time to read your latest blog post and know your blog is awesome. Instead, design impacts that decision. If the visitor does happen to stay, you want to keep them around with a blog that just plain makes sense to use.

This book seeks to help you improve your blog design, whether you're starting from scratch, redesigning an existing blog, or simply tinkering with your current design. I cover blog design in ways you might expect — design principles, colors, and fonts — and in ways you might not know are actually part of design — navigation, usability, and shareability. This book breaks all that down in an approachable, easy-to-use format so you can design a blog that encourages readers to stick around.

About This Book

Think of this book as a design guide for the average (and awesome) blogger. Most bloggers don't have experience with design or coding. You simply have a voice you want to share through your blog. Whether you design a blog yourself, hire someone, or purchase pre-made design elements, this book gives you to tools to understand what makes a blog successful from a design and navigation standpoint.

This book is geared towards bloggers of all skill levels, although if you've been blogging for a while you may already know some of these tips or techniques. But not so fast! You may have been blogging for a long time but never knew underlying design principles, basic color theory, or exactly how to do a particular technique I mention. That means everyone learns something from this book.

By the end of this book, you'll know:

- What constitutes good blog design and why design matters in the first place
- How to ensure your blog design syncs with your blog goals, your audience, and your content
- Ways to customize your blog design, from headers to footers and everything in between
- How to design your blog to be easy to navigate and use
- Ways to create design-friendly content to improve readability

You can work through this book page by page or completely out of order. You'll find value either way. In typical *For Dummies* fashion, this book makes it easy to find what you're looking for with clearly outlined parts, chapter intros that spell out what you'll learn, and a detailed index to find your way to something specific.

Finally, this book isn't meant to intimidate you when it comes to blog design. In fact, my goal is to empower you to take control of your blog design and feel confident about it. Even when your design is complete, use this book as your design guide when you need help with a specific piece of your design or just want to browse through examples of great blog design.

Foolish Assumptions

Forgive me, but I'm about to make some assumptions about your blogging knowledge. I expect that if you picked up this book, you know some of the basics of blogging such as uploading a photo, publishing a blog post, and installing plug-ins. I assume that most bloggers who buy this book already have a blog, but if you don't then you can still find value in this book. It just won't cover the beginning steps of how to set up a blog and get things rolling.

The majority of this book is not geared towards any specific blog platform; however, when I show you steps, they are typically for the WordPress.org platform because it's the most popular one. The majority of plug-ins that I mention are also for WordPress, although some plug-ins can be used on multiple blog platforms. When possible, I mention options for Blogger, Tumblr, and a few other platforms, too. I also assume that you aren't a developer or professional blog designer. I wrote this book to make good blog design achievable for the masses, so my advice won't always be the most complex or require you to dig deep into your code. However, it will always be geared toward helping bloggers without a design or technical background achieve a blog design they can be proud to show their friends and fellow bloggers.

What I don't assume is the type of blogger you are. The information in this book isn't just for a parent blogger or a food blogger or any other type of blogger. I wrote this book with all bloggers in mind and with oodles of full-color examples of great blogs on the Web. In fact, pay special attention to those blog designs outside your niche because you might discover cool ideas you don't see within your own blogging circles.

Conventions Used in This Book

Throughout this book, I use a few basic conventions over and over to make the information I present easy to understand:

✔ If you see text in **bold**, you're meant to type just as it appears in the book. A little exception though: when you work through a steps list, then each step is bold to make the steps easier to follow. In those cases, the text to type isn't bold.

✔ If you see text in italics, this means I'm introducing a word or phrase you might or might not know, then defining it.

✔ Web addresses and code appear in `monofont`. If you're reading a digital version of this book on a device connected to the Internet, note that you can click the web address to visit that website. Nice!

✔ When you need to select an option in a menu, I use a little arrow (⤵) to let you know the path to take, such as Dashboard⤵Appearance.

Icons Used in This Book

This book features little icons like these to point out special points of interest:

The Tip icon marks tips (well, duh!) and extra ideas that you can use to make your blog design even better. Consider these the make-designing-your-blog-easier icons.

When you see the Remember icon, store this information in the back of your mind for future use. This icon marks things I want to reinforce as super important.

Red alert! Red alert! This little gem marks important information that may alert you to design pitfalls or save you a headache or two. I don't use this one often so pay special attention when I do.

Information tagged as Technical Stuff means extra geeky stuff that you can normally skip over. Unless, of course, you love getting technical.

Beyond the Book

Blog Design For Dummies isn't just what you see within the book you're holding. Here's a glimpse at this book's companion content, which you can reference online at anytime:

✔ **Cheat Sheet:** Whether you want to know the meaning of a term or refresh your memory about main design principles, you have those answers and more in this book's online Cheat Sheet (`www.dummies.com/cheatsheet/blogdesign`). Consider this Cheat Sheet your handy reference guide for content you use again and again. It also includes a list of links for all the plug-ins covered in this book.

✒ **Extras:** There's so much about blog design to share that I even wrote four more pieces of content that couldn't fit inside this book. Be sure not to pass over the extras for Parts II through V. In each of those parts, I include a link to an online article that extends beyond what I cover in this book. You'll find how to create a favicon, ideas for using navigation to drive traffic to your blog pages, clever ways to greet new visitors, and ten great websites for design inspiration. Discover these extras at www. dummies.com/extras/blogdesign.

✒ **Updates:** The tech world is fast-moving so sometimes information published in a printed book does change. When substantial changes impact the accuracy in this book, we let you know. You can find these updates at www.dummies.com/go/blogdesignupdates.

Where to Go from Here

You don't have to start this book by flipping the page to Chapter 1 and reading chapter by chapter until you get to the Appendix. But, hey, you can if you want! Start anywhere your burning questions take you, whether you're dying to know how to select colors or fonts (Chapter 6) or ways to make your content easy to find (Chapter 12). However, consider the first few chapters mandatory. They provide you a basic foundation not only in design, but in understanding your blog. These basics will undoubtedly lead to a stronger blog design.

If you have a question or want more tips on blog design (or blogging in general), find me on my blog Momcomm (www.momcomm.com), Twitter (www. twitter.com/MelACulbertson), or Facebook (www.facebook.com/ momcomm).

For additional blog design inspiration, take a peek at my Pinterest boards (www.pinterest.com/melaculbertson). I have boards dedicated solely to blog design goodness from color combinations to even more blog design tips.

Part I
Getting Started with Blog Design

In this part. . .

- ✔ Gain an understanding of why blog design matters and learn how visitors typically travel through online content.

- ✔ Learn what you need to start a blog design.

- ✔ Explore the foundation of great design by learning four core design principles and how to apply them.

- ✔ Examine your own blog's goals, content, and audience to make impactful blog design decisions.

- ✔ Get tips on building blog design guidelines so your blog remains consistent in both design and content.

1

Recognizing Components of a Well-Designed Blog

*B*logging introduces a way for people to have a platform for sharing their words with anyone in the world. Along with that opportunity comes the chance to build a blog design that complements your words and leaves a lasting impression.

When you think of blog design, the first things that come to mind might be colors, fonts, or an overall blog layout. However, blog design goes deeper than that. In fact, this quote from Apple founder Steve Jobs pretty much sums it up: "Design is not just what it looks like and feels like. Design is how it works."

The main purpose of this book is to teach design to bloggers who aren't designers. Few things about design are required because designing a blog is more like part art and part science. We all have different tastes and styles, but in the end, design should function to give a visitor a positive experience.

In this chapter, I introduce you to how good blog design benefits your blog. You also get a glimpse at how web users generally look at websites — and blogs in particular. Then I tackle foundations of good blog design so you can recognize good design and understand why it's good. Additionally, this chapter introduces a few tools to help you start designing (or re-designing) your blog.

Knowing Why Blog Design Matters

I'm sure this has happened to you: You're hungry, so you search online for local restaurants and click a result that sounds interesting. The restaurant's website has shockingly ugly colors, auto-playing music, and flashing graphics. The menu is at the bottom of the last page you'd look for it and offers no descriptions, no prices, and no pictures. And even if you wanted to go to this restaurant at this point, the address is nowhere to be found. This restaurant may be the best one in town, but you just formed an impression of the food solely from its website.

Great blog design matters in the same way that restaurant's website does. When your design looks polished and professional, and is straight-forward to use, readers automatically trust that you also have good content. Good design also implies that you're committed not only to keeping your content fresh but committed to your readers as well.

So, does design matter more than content? Nope. If you had walked into that restaurant from the street, ate there, and loved it, you probably wouldn't care what its website looks like because you know the "content" is solid. But without an appealing blog design, a reader may never take a minute to actually read your content. After all, if your design is bad, why would your content be any better?

Good blog design reinforces the idea that your content is awesome. The ins and outs of your design keep your new visitors exploring your content, help you meet your blog goals, and draw attention to your blog's most important asset: your content.

Communicating with design

In the face-to-face world, facial expressions and body language often speak more than the words coming from someone's mouth. Your blog's design communicates in the same way, speaking even before your content does. The colors you use, the fonts you select, the images you showcase, and even the layout you choose all communicate something to the reader.

Design should reinforce the personality of your blog or help convey what your blog is about. A powerful image in your header can communicate emotion or a single design element can give readers a clearer picture of your blog's message. Even text can make a bold statement, serving as a graphical element to attract a reader's eye.

On my blog Momcomm (www.momcomm.com), I write about blogging and social media. I want my blog to be perceived as fun and approachable as well as communicate that this blog makes even complex topics easy to understand. As you can see in Figure 1-1, my blog design features a smiley face in the header and a prominent *Welcome!* in the sidebar to make readers feel welcome. In addition, I use plenty of formatting in my blog posts to make them easy to follow.

Figure 1-1: My blog uses design to communicate my message of being approachable and welcoming.

In addition, the placement of certain blog elements within your design can communicate what you want a reader to do. For example, an e-mail subscription's prominent location at the top of the page communicates its importance.

In Chapter 3, I talk a lot about how to showcase your voice, determine your tone, and more to help build a strong, purposeful design.

Orienting users with navigation design

When people think about blog design, they usually think of colors, fonts, and images first. But design also includes navigation design, which is design centered around how visitors move through your blog.

Your navigation design should always be focused around helping blog visitors find their way around your site in the simplest, most logical way possible. Part III of this book is entirely devoted to making your blog easy to navigate and to use.

However, navigation design can also mean offering your readers little (or big) surprises that go above and beyond the basics. For example, the blog From Away (www.fromaway.com) focuses on cooking and eating in Maine, with a page called Our Favorite Places in Portland (www.fromaway.com/our-favorites) that covers Portland's best breakfast sandwiches, pizzas, lobster rolls, and more.

In Figure 1-2, you can see the breakfast sandwich section, where a visitor can navigate to each restaurant's website, see a map of those restaurants, and click a link to go to reviews of those sandwiches. Plus, each sandwich is clearly numbered and represented by a close-up image. The result is a useful tool that readers will return to when they want to eat in Portland. An image toward the bottom of their homepage calls attention to the page, and it's also linked from their main navigation menu.

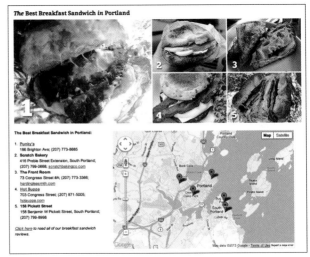

© FromAway.com

Figure 1-2: This blog gives visitors useful content with a friendly design.

After you get the basics out of the way on your own blog's navigation design, consider ways you can add bonuses like this to get readers deeper into your content or other useful content elsewhere.

Discovering How Readers Visually Travel Your Blog

Humans may be diverse and dynamic, but we typically surf through web pages in a similar way. Images, color, and fonts attract attention, serving as little marks on a road map that pull you through a website's or blog's design.

This section covers a couple of ways to recognize how blog visitors typically behave when they land on a blog.

Exploring how visitors click through websites

Just as humans are diverse, we're also creatures of habit. We do things in similar ways and feel more comfortable when things are a certain way and in a certain order. Certain web and blog designs work because they follow the way most people work through websites.

Many studies show that visitors spend more time looking at the left side of a web page than the right. In fact, one study from Nielsen Norman Group (www.nngroup.com/articles/horizontal-attention-leans-left/) showed that web users spent 69 percent of their viewing time looking at the left half of a page — and because (in this Western culture) we read from left to right, this makes sense. Due to this convention, you probably notice that many blog designs have a header and navigation menu at the top, a main column of content on the left, and a sidebar on the right.

Many well-designed blogs use other layout types successfully (see Chapter 7 for some examples) by using attention-grabbing design elements to pull readers to other parts of the blog design.

In addition, website visitors spend about 80 percent of their time on the part of a web page that's above the fold (what's viewable on a page before the visitor has to scroll down), according to another study from Nielsen Norman Group (www.nngroup.com/articles/scrolling-and-attention/).

Although you can stick with conventions like these to help with your blog design, the web's ever-changing nature means that conventions can change over time. The only sure-fire way to see how visitors behave on your own blog is to track mouse clicks. You can track mouse clicks using heat maps. A *heat map* is a visual representation of website traffic that uses color-spot intensity to show how readers click through a website.

For example, I tracked my blog's clicks for a period of time to see what results I'd get. With a color spectrum where blue means fewer clicks and red means more clicks, I noticed that my About page tab on the top left of the page and my Twitter icon in my sidebar got the strongest amount of clicks (see Figure 1-3). In addition, some of my navigation tabs — Online Course & E-book, Page Critiques, and Find a Designer — were clicked more often than my Advertising and Contact tabs, as denoted by the green spots on those tabs.

Figure 1-3: This heat map shows that most visitors click my About page.

If you want to try out heat mapping to see how your blog design performs, you can try

- **Crazy Egg:** www.crazyegg.com
- **Clicky:** www.clicky.com
- **Mouseflow:** http://mouseflow.com
- **ClickTale:** www.clicktale.com

All the preceding websites except Crazy Egg offer a limited, free plan as well as pay versions. With mouse tracking services like these, you can see exactly where visitors click, even when they click an area that isn't clickable — meaning that you could discover people are clicking a design element that isn't linking to anywhere but should be.

Recognizing that people are skimmers

Come on, admit it. You skim, too! Think about all the content out there to consume: blogs, news sites, social media sites, and so on. With so much to read, you can easily get overwhelmed. In fact, I know you won't read this entire book word for word. But don't worry — I'm not offended!

People skim through blogs because time is limited, they're searching for something specific, or both. It doesn't mean they don't like your content (although they may skim to get a feel for your blog). It does mean, though, that you have to account for the fact people skim when you work on your blog design.

The goal in designing with skimmers in mind isn't necessarily to make people change their skimming ways but rather to account for the fact that some people just have time to skim and to also acknowledge that others you may convince to stop and take action.

In your actual blog post, consider adding subheadings that stand out from your main text. For visitors who are skimming, subheadings give them your key points. If something catches their eye, they might stop to read your entire post.

In your sidebar, think about using a pop of color on your e-mail signup form that gets the reader to stop and take action. Purposeful design like this might entice a visitor to stop and sign up for your newsletter.

Using Design Elements That Complement Your Message

You started your blog for a reason. Maybe you have funny stories about life to tell or helpful tips to share. Maybe you have a passion for inspiring others or encouraging people to do something. Every blogger has a message to share. Good blog design reinforces that message.

Communicating your brand through design

Good branding is the reason you know you get an amazing quality if you buy your favorite name-brand product. Branding is also the reason you first think *safety* or *luxury* when someone says a car manufacturer's name, rather than just thinking *car manufacturer.*

Even if you never really thought about what your brand is, you still have one. Your brand is how people perceive your blog. Blogs with strong brands make emotional connections with their readers and are consistent both in their design and their voice, even if they blog about many different topics.

Your blog readers probably don't think that much about the ins and outs of your blog's brand, but branding works for that very reason. Good branding makes you devoted to a product, an evangelist for a service, or a fan of a blog, mostly for reasons people don't think too hard about. It's that emotional connection and that consistency that keeps them coming back.

If you're unsure just what your brand is or should be, just ask yourself this: *What do I want my blog to be known for?* Then list a few things that come to mind. Your design should support the things you jot down.

Colors, fonts, and images are obvious ways to infuse a brand into your blog design, but branding extends into the way you format your posts, too. For example, if you write quick-witted, punchy blog posts, your paragraphs should be short and punchy as well.

To what extent you (yes, you!) become part of your blog's brand depends on your blog's goals. For example, Brittany Van der Linden's lifestyle blog That's Vandy (www.thatsvandy.com), shown in Figure 1-4, is a play off her last name. Because her blog is about making life awesome "the Vandy way," her blog's header design signifies her as part of the brand. A pink circle around her headshot makes the connection that Vandy relates to her, while the bold blue tagline unmistakably lets readers know what to expect from her blog.

© That's Vandy, www.thatsvandy.com

Figure 1-4: This blog brand uses an image of the author in the header.

Acknowledging the importance of images

The usage of imagery can make or break any blog design. Great images command attention, and poor quality images lessen an image's ability to make a positive impression. In fact, images are so crucial to a blog's design that I devote all of Chapter 15 to using images in your blog. When using images for your blog design, use those that help tell your story or support your blog's message.

The header design from the Pile O' Fabric (www.pileofabric.com) blog rotates close-up images of fabric (see Figure 1-5). These colorful images make a vibrant impact to reinforce what the blog is about.

Figure 1-5: Pile O' Fabric rotates a few bright and colorful images in the blog header.

Applying enough formatting

Formatting often gets overlooked when it comes to blog design. I mean, colors and fonts are way more fun, right? But formatting your content in a way that's easily readable can be the difference between someone actually reading or sharing your blog post or page and someone just hitting their browser's back button, never to return.

Even if you aren't a designer, keep in mind that even text should be visually appealing. If you're writing a tutorial to make something easy to understand, your tutorial layout should be easy to follow with clearly marked steps and possibly images to support certain steps.

Think about it. What's easier to read: long paragraphs that say "First you do this. Next you do this." Or a numbered list of steps? Of course, the clear list of steps is a better way because that makes each step distinct and easy to follow along. Otherwise, your readers may get lost in the instructions.

In Chapter 16, I get into ways that you can make your content easy to digest, from using lists to including subheadings.

Creating a Great-Looking Blog (When You Aren't a Designer)

Good designers don't slap a design together. They think critically about each element that goes into the complete design, from the overall layout down to the colors.

This book isn't meant to make you a full-fledged blog design expert, but you don't have to be a design expert to whip up a nice-looking blog. Sure, you might want to know how to do this and that. The more you learn, though, the more you can add to your blog design over time, whether you're enhancing the design or the functionality. These next sections cover a few key tips that I want to stick into your mind like superglue as you go through the rest of this book.

Striving for simplicity

What's the sure sign of amateur designers? Overkill. Too many colors, too many fonts, too many different-sized thingamabobbers. Confident designers know that a blog design with minimal design elements can make a big statement.

As you work through your blog design, do a few self-checks periodically to ensure your design isn't becoming too busy.

The blog In Jennie's Kitchen (www.injennieskitchen.com) presents a perfect example of a simple, clean, and effective blog design (see Figure 1-6). The blog header uses only a warm, neutral color with a small blue line under her blog name. The small blog header size allows more of the photo from the most recent blog post to show, drawing your attention down into the content.

Building a blog that's intuitive

When you turn a doorknob, you instinctively know to turn it to the right. Because of this, you might be a little confused if you tried to open a door with a doorknob that turned to the left. Intuitive design means that your blog works in a way that most people expect it to, much like that doorknob.

For example, if a piece of text within a blog post is underlined, then most readers would try to click that text, expecting that it was a hyperlink that takes you to another page. A visitor looking to search for content on a blog looks for a search field, not a link or button that leads to a separate page to begin a search — or worse yet, they find no search box at all.

Figure 1-6: A small header size gives more prominence to blog post images.

An intuitive blog design works so that visitors don't need an instruction manual to get around the blog and find content that interests them. Part of achieving this means designing with website conventions in mind, like when to use underlined text, which signifies a link. The other part of ensuring an intuitive design revolves around putting items visitors need within easy reach so they don't have to dig too far, like a search box or a drop-down list of your categories.

Of course, you can't ensure that every single person never has any problems navigating through your blog. However, you can find out a lot about your specific blog visitors through your blog analytics. Use Chapter 5 for help with understanding how your blog analytics can help improve your design.

Keeping design balanced

Is your blog header really "heavy" with design elements or text on one side but sparse on the other? *Balance* helps tie elements together so the design is more evenly weighted. The two types of balance are symmetrical and asymmetrical:

- ✔ **Symmetrical balance:** *Symmetry* in design happens when a design is nearly the same on both sides of a central point. I say "nearly" because sometimes the symmetry is exact, and other times it's not. If you were to take a circle and fold it in half, each side is exactly the same. However, I might have a design with a square on one side of a center line and a circle on the other side. That's still symmetry. Symmetry in design can provide a sense of stability, harmony, and order.

➼ **Asymmetrical balance:** *Asymmetry* just means the absence of symmetry. An asymmetrical design might have three design elements on one side and a large block of text on the other. Asymmetrical design creates interest and provides contrast. However, you don't want a lopsided design, with several design elements on one side of your blog header and none on the other side.

You see asymmetrical blog designs more often than symmetrical, but both work when done well. In Figure 1-7, these two header layouts show how balance can work in design. The layout on the top creates balance with a symmetrical design. On the bottom, the layout shifts the diamond to the left but provides balance with a large block of text beside the diamond.

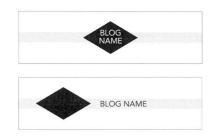

Figure 1-7: Examples of balanced symmetrical and asymmetrical design.

Staying away from clutter

Think about that section of your house where papers, bills, and other things pile up. (I know you have one.) Wouldn't it be easier to find that water bill if you had only 4 things sitting there and not 20?

One goal of good blog design is to draw attention to important parts of your blog, whether you want readers to notice an e-mail signup box or just your actual blog post. Think of clutter as attention's arch-nemesis. Too much clutter scatters your reader's attention all over the place; so, not only can that reader not home in on something, but he also has a harder time finding something he is looking for. And because most blog readers are skimmers, there's only so much attention to go around.

When tweaking your blog design, you might find yourself adding "things" — especially to those sidebars. An affiliate banner ad there, a cool widget down there, a link to your most popular post over there, and so on. Next thing you know, your sidebar is stuffed with, well, stuff.

Sidebars are the main offenders, but clutter can be anywhere — in your blog header, your footer, or anywhere else you might want to add elements. This kind of clutter comes in the form of jumbling together too many design elements. For example, the individual design elements that make up a blog header might be well designed, but together they present no clear focus to make those elements work together.

The solution? Be ruthless in limiting what to add to your blog design. Good designers know that each element needs a purpose. You need a filter for what to include and what to remove. To help you filter, ask yourself these questions before adding new things to your blog design:

- ✔ Does this design element solve a problem, like add balance to your design?
- ✔ Are you adding a design element just to fill up space?
- ✔ Does your overall design maintain a focal point when you add a new design element?

If you're considering adding a functional element to your blog design, such as a special button or grouping of links, consider these questions:

- ✔ How does this element fit into the purpose of my blog?
- ✔ Does this element support one of my blog goals?
- ✔ Is there a more effective place for this?

When you become deliberate in your design, you see that not everything deserves a spot in your blog design. Your design will be stronger for it!

In Chapter 11, I dive more into ways to steer clear of sidebar clutter.

Looking at Available Tools

When you work on your blog design, you'll find a few tools are helpful from the start. Okay, so you can't really start a blog design without a blogging platform and an image editor. Those two are mandatory! Themes, templates, widgets, and plug-ins make your path to a rocking blog design that much easier. I introduce them all in the following sections.

Selecting a blogging platform

If you already have a blog set up, you can go ahead and skip over this section. If you're starting from scratch, though, you need to choose a blog platform before you can start working on your blog design.

Choosing a blog platform isn't an easy decision because blog platforms come in many different flavors. I include a list of the most commonly used platforms in Table 1-1 to get you started. The main difference to consider is whether you want a blog that's hosted or self-hosted:

✔ *Hosted* means that the blog software and your content live on the blog platform's own web servers. Hosted blog platforms take the responsibility of managing the software, data, and web-hosting so you don't have to. Many bloggers start off with a hosted platform and eventually switch to a self-hosted platform to have more control over their blog design. However, many bloggers are completely happy sticking with hosted platforms. The most popular hosted blog platform is Blogger.

✔ *Self-hosted* means that you install the blogging software on your own web server. You can pay for server space through a hosting company like Hostgator or Dreamhost. You have more control over your blog (and blog design) with a self-hosted site, but you also have more maintenance and responsibility over your blog when something goes wrong. The most popular self-hosting blog platform is WordPress.org.

Many bloggers start out with hosted blog software because it is generally (but not always) free, whereas self-hosted blogs may mean you must pay for web hosting, domain names, and other Internet services. In Table 1-1, I include costs for the software, but not for hosting and other services, which will vary depending on which providers and services you choose.

Table 1-1	Popular Blogging Platforms	
Platform	**Hosted or Self-Hosted**	**Free or Paid**
Blogger www.blogger.com	Hosted	Free
Moveable Type www.movabletype.com	Self-Hosted	Software is free for non-business blogs; you pay hosting fees to hosting company
Squarespace www.squarespace.com	Hosted	$8–$24/month
Typepad www.typepad.com	Hosted	$8.95–$29.95/month (slightly more if billed monthly instead of yearly)
Tumblr www.tumblr.com	Hosted	Free
WordPress.com http://wordpress.com	Hosted	Free (for more design control, Custom Design upgrade available for $30/year)
WordPress.org http://wordpress.org	Self-hosted	Software is free; you pay hosting fees to hosting company

The majority of this book offers advice and tips for blog design regardless of the platform. However, I often talk about plug-ins that work only for WordPress.org, because it's the most flexible platform for customizing and designing your blog.

Finding an image-editing program

To design your blog, you need at least one tool that lets you create design elements to place into your blogging platform. With an image-editing program, you can create a blog header, design elements for your sidebar, and edit images for your blog.

Many bloggers use photo-editing programs, such as the following:

- ✔ **PicMonkey:** Free. www.picmonkey.com
- ✔ **Photoshop:** Subscription fee. www.adobe.com/products/photoshop.html
- ✔ **Photoshop Elements:** $99.99. www.adobe.com/products/photoshop-elements.html

Some programs, like PicMonkey, you can use straight from the web and don't need to install any additional software. Other programs, like Photoshop, need to be purchased or subscribed to and then downloaded onto your computer. In Chapter 15, I share these and many other options to suit a range of needs.

Using themes and templates

Regardless of your platform, themes and templates are a great place to start building your blog design. Themes and templates both provide a design framework to display the content of your blog. The terms *theme* and *template* are sometimes used interchangeably, but themes are typically more robust, including functionality that improves your ability to customize the theme more easily.

Hosted blog platforms have their own templates to choose from. For some hosted platforms like Tumblr, you can use one of its designs or use one created by someone else.

Because WordPress.org has the most design options, I cover the platform's blog themes options in more detail in Chapter 7. I also give you some websites to find WordPress.org themes as well as Blogger templates.

Exploring the importance of widgets and plug-ins

When it comes to blog design, you can add a lot of features to your blog without really coding anything. Each blogging platform varies in the ability to customize the design and functionality of your blog.

Widgets are little applications that you can install to run within your blog. WordPress comes with many built-in widgets to do things like display your recent posts, a search form, or a drop-down of categories. (Blogger calls widgets "gadgets.") Widgets are limited mainly to displaying things in your header, sidebar, or footer.

Some widgets and gadgets are built into the platform, and some widgets can be used in all types of platforms. In Chapter 11, I cover some social media widgets (such as a Facebook Like box) that work anywhere you can add HTML code.

Plug-ins are pieces of software that give additional functionality to a larger software application like WordPress. Widgets are a type of plug-in, but plug-ins can do things beyond what widgets can do. Plug-ins can give your blog a commenting platform, a way for readers to share blog posts, or an entire e-commerce store. The plug-ins discussed in this book are for WordPress.org; however, some of them can be used for other blogging platforms.

2

Applying Core Design Principles

*J*ust like art, blog design is subjective. My taste may not be your taste and vice versa. And that's okay. The world would be quite boring if everyone had the same tastes. Despite our own personal tastes, good design applies overarching design principles to make someone's blog pleasing to the eye and easy to navigate.

As part of human nature, your readers make split-second judgments based on looks alone. That means your blog design speaks before your words ever do. Then when someone goes deeper and actually starts navigating your blog, truer opinions start forming around your overall blog design.

In this chapter, I cover four foundational design principles that leave a lasting impression: proximity, repetition, contrast, and alignment. These design principles originally related to print design, but as the digital world has evolved, they work just the same for web design.

Regardless of whether you design your blog yourself or hire someone to design it for you, recognizing the key design principles will make you realize why you like certain blog designs and not others. The designs you like probably follow these principles. Throughout the chapter, you see how proximity, repetition, contrast, and alignment work to make a great blog design.

Providing Structure with Proximity

The principle of *proximity* in design refers to the way you place design elements in relation to one another. You can apply this principle to your blog design to emphasize relationships between certain elements and thus affect the overall user experience by providing structure.

When considering how to use proximity, think of your entire blog design as well as specific parts of your design.

Thinking of your blog design as a whole, placing certain elements in close proximity to your header suggests that they warrant attention. When you visit a blog, you notice the header first because it's at the top of the page and usually the largest visual element on the page. With that in mind, if you have your social media buttons at the top of a sidebar or within your header, you're subtly telling the reader, "Hey! These social media buttons are important!" When buttons are placed near or within your header, they become one of first things a new blog visitor sees on your blog, like these social media icons in Figure 2-1 at the top of the blog Tidy Mom (`www.tidymom.net`). Newspapers use proximity in this same way, placing major headlines and teasers leading to other important content above the fold.

© Cheryl Sousan, TidyMom.net

Figure 2-1: Social media buttons appear at the top of the sidebar so visitors find them easily.

When it comes to various blog elements, applying the principle of proximity means placing similar or related elements near one another while ensuring that unrelated elements live somewhere else on a page. You can best implement this by grouping related content and by effectively using white space.

Grouping related content

For your blog layout to feel comfortable for your reader, using proximity can save the day. Plus, placing related content or design elements near one another allows your blog visitor to get to the important sections of your site quickly and efficiently. Think about the inside of your car. Sure would be harder to use your stereo if the controls weren't all together. And the same thing goes with blog design. When items are grouped logically, your overall blog design just makes more sense.

For example, by organizing your navigation design with proximity in mind, you create associations in the visitor's mind that make it easier to explore your blog.

Some parts of your navigation logically fit together, such as

✔ Social media buttons (Facebook, Twitter, LinkedIn, Pinterest)

✔ Subscription methods (RSS, e-mail)

✔ Ways to find content (search box, categories, popular posts)

On Dear Crissy's blog (www.dearcrissy.com), Crissy groups her search box, recent blog posts, categories, and archives together on her sidebar, as shown in Figure 2-2.

In addition, creating proximity in navigation can be something as simple as placing similar blog pages together in your navigation menu. If you have a food blog, for example, having a Recipes tab and Favorite Cooking Tools tab placed beside each other makes more sense than if you put a Contact page between them.

Applying the principle of proximity also suggests relationships between items grouped together. As an example, grouping a blog name and tagline together emphasizes the relationship between the two. This especially comes in handy if your tagline doesn't make as much sense without the context of your blog name. As an example, if your blog name was A Slice of Life and the tagline was "Taking bites of the good stuff," then the tagline becomes more effective placed close to the blog name. I cover taglines in more depth in Chapter 8.

However, you can't adequately create groups of design elements or content without a designer's best friend: white space.

© DearCrissy.com, blog design by PurrDesign.com

Figure 2-2: Group options to find blog content.

Defining white space

White space refers to absence of text or graphics within a design. Contrary to how it sounds, white space isn't necessarily white, though. White space not only provides balance to your blog design, but it also becomes critical to implementing the principle of proximity.

 The proper use of white space can also shape your blog design in other different ways. For example, white space makes text on your blog more legible. Design elements surrounded by white space reinforce those elements' proximity to one another, attracting attention to that part of your blog. And white space can also guide the readers' eyes in a certain direction, like to focus on an area you want to highlight. Large areas of white space can even communicate an air of sophistication and openness.

In Figure 2-3, the white space on the right side of Lee La La's header (`http://leelala.net`) allows you to notice the dandelion seeds floating down. Their path leads your eyes to the social media buttons. If that white space were filled with graphics, your eyes wouldn't have been led down to the buttons as smoothly because other graphics would interrupt that flow.

© Lindsay Roberts, leelala.net

Figure 2-3: White space guides a reader's eyes along a path.

 Using white space in blog design often intimidates beginning designers, so they make the mistake of covering an entire image with design elements or spreading design elements out just to fill up the space. Instead, give graphics and words room to breathe and resist the urge to fill up every virtual nook and cranny.

 When designing elements of your blog, be careful not to trap white space. *Trapped white space* refers to the space awkwardly boxed in between two or more design elements. Figure 2-4 illustrates how white space can get trapped within a blog header design. Trapped white space hinders the flow of design.

Figure 2-4: Trapped white space to the left of the tagline.

The best fix is to adjust the other design elements in a way that eliminates bounded white space.

Using Repetition

Humans expect repetition. You see repetition in nature, such as a giraffe's spots or a flower's petals. You also see repetition in the man-made pieces of the world: Think of street sign shapes or windows on a high-rise building.

In design, *repetition* means using the same or similar elements throughout your design. If you were to spread out all the elements of your blog design onto a (virtual) table, you want all those pieces to look like they're parts of a greater whole.

Repetition enhances flow of your blog design by connecting different design elements to one another. In Figure 2-5, you can see how the blog Running with Penguins (`http://runningwithpenguins.com`) uses repetition. The penguins and clouds are repeated within the header. Also using the penguin in the sidebar keeps the reader moving through the blog design.

© Dean Schuster

Figure 2-5: Repetition creates a unified look in a blog's design.

These are elements of your blog design where you can apply repetition:

- ✔ Fonts
- ✔ Color schemes
- ✔ Images or icons
- ✔ Font size, colors, or images
- ✔ Blog post and sidebar headings
- ✔ Blog page layout structure

Creating consistency

Just like consistency is important in branding, consistency also plays an important role in blog design. Could you imagine if every single blog post looked like they were from different blogs? Or if your blog sidebar looked like it came from a completely different site than your header?

Repeating some of your design elements consistently through your blog not only eliminates confusion, but the repetition also creates continuity and rhythm in your blog design.

As shown in Figure 2-6, Money Saving Mom (`http://moneysavingmom.com`) illustrates consistency by repeating the script font from the header throughout the graphical elements in the sidebar on the right.

© *Money Saving Mom, LLC*

Figure 2-6: Repeating a font through a blog creates a consistent blog design.

Using repetition without being boring

Although repetition contributes to a strong blog design, using too much repetition can lead to a boring and stale look. Thinking back to a giraffe's spots, each spot on a giraffe isn't exactly the same. They vary in size and shape, making the animal even more beautiful.

One of my favorite blog designs is from Simply Vintagegirl (`www.simply vintagegirl.com/blog`). In Figure 2-7, you can see three distinct parts of Simply Vintagegirl's overall design unified by repetition. Emily Rose uses the bird image from her blog header in the sidebar and to the left of each blog post title. However, she varies the bird in each instance by applying color, changing the size and adjusting the orientation.

© Emily Rose Brookshire, SimplyVintagegirl.com

Figure 2-7: Repetitive design elements don't have to look exactly the same.

Repetition can also suggest that items are related to one another. In my blog's social media buttons shown earlier in Figure 2-1, they all are blue circles, even though what's in the center signifies the social media platform they link to.

When you vary repeated elements in your blog design, make the variation subtle. That way, your design still looks unified. The birds from Simply Vintagegirl's blog wouldn't connect her blog together the same way if all the birds were completely different.

Creating Contrast

Contrast in blog design occurs when two or more elements are different from one another. The more difference between the elements, the greater the contrast. Your blog design can benefit from contrast in a few ways:

- ✔ **Contrast can provide visual interest.** Our eyes are drawn to contrasting things, such as a pale moon against a black sky or a tall building surrounded by others a fraction of its size. In blog design, contrast can keep a blog pleasing to look at instead of being bland and uninteresting.

- ✔ **Contrast can make an element jump off the page and encourage the reader to take action.** If you want to highlight a button that links to your new e-book, you can use contrast so the button stands out while still fitting into your overall design.

Pat Flynn's blog Smart Passive Income (www.smartpassiveincome.com) uses light green boxes with a dark green border to make important areas of his blog design stand out. In Figure 2-8, the "Don't know where to start?" and eBook Guide boxes contrast with the black video and e-book image to make those elements pop off the page and drive interest in his blog.

© Smart Passive Income

Figure 2-8: Using different colors can help you achieve good contrast in your design.

✔ **Contrast makes text easy to read.** Have you ever been to a blog where you couldn't read an actual blog post because the background color and text color were too similar? Yeah, me too. Contrast needs to exist for blog post readability to entice your visitors to actually stay and read your posts. A white background with black or dark gray text is always a safe choice for main areas of content like a blog post.

Exploring methods to create contrast

You can apply contrast to your blog design in a few ways. Here are some common ones, which you can see in Figure 2-9:

Figure 2-9: Four ways to provide contrast.

✔ **Color:** Probably the most common way to apply contrast is through color. You can use contrasting colors of the same shade (such as black with a light gray) or two colors on opposite ends of the color wheel (orange and blue). You can even use a single color to make a certain blog element stand out, such as how the red Free Instant Access button stands out against a pale green background in Figure 2-8. (Read more about color in Chapter 6.)

✔ **Fonts:** Using two different fonts that complement each other can also create contrast in your text. For example, pairing a script font with a sans-serif font provides visual interest. (See more about fonts in Chapter 6.)

You can also apply contrast with the same font by applying bold and italics. Just use either in moderation. Also, avoid underlining text because most online visitors would assume that an underlined word is a hyperlink.

✔ **Size:** Having two or more design elements of different sizes also creates contrast. For example, most all blog designs use a blog post title that's larger than the subheadings within the post's content.

✔ **Images within your blog content:** Adding images to your blog content provides contrast by breaking up large passages of text and drawing the reader further down into your blog.

After you understand these ways to apply contrast, you can start combining them to add even greater contrast, such as using two different fonts with two different colors.

Applying the right amount of contrast

Contrast in blog design can be tricky. More contrast doesn't always equal better contrast. And sometimes you might not want to apply enough contrast for fear of taking it too far.

Too much contrast can be jarring to the reader or hinder your blog's readability. For example, using white text on a black background is a frequently cited example of too much contrast. Although it may work in small doses, reading paragraph after paragraph becomes tiring because your eyes have to work harder to read the text. It also produces *halation,* the tendency of white characters or text to "glow" when on a black background.

Although not necessarily jarring, too little contrast can also make your blog hard to read. For example, creating subheadings in your blog post by just bolding text may not make the subheadings stand out enough for someone skimming your blog post. (Most people skim.) In this example, using a different font and a different color (as shown in Figure 2-10) adds enough contrast for the way people will likely interact with your blog's content.

Pinterest is full of ooooh pretties and ohhhhh cools. But it's also a landmine full of aaahhh craps. Pins that aren't quite what they seem. Pretty on the outside... but annoying (and potentially harmful) on the inside.

But let's wade through it together, shall we? Here are five types of pins you shouldn't re-pin:

1. Pins that Don't Go To a Permalink

There are few Pinteresty things more maddening than finding a great recipe, how-to or what not, then clicking on it and having it go to someone's home page. Ugh! Whaaaa? Now you're telling me I have to search around a website to actually find the image in that pretty picture?

If it's an omg-gotta-have-that-pin type of pin then I might bother to search for the post on their site. If I'm lazy, I'll just go back and be annoyed at the person who pinned it that way.

Of course, if you're just pinning an overall website (like if you had a board of blogs you like), then by all means, have at it. But if you're pinning a recipe, then by golly PIN THE RECIPE POST, not the website. You'll be happy with yourself too when you go back to try out the recipe and can actually find it.

2. Pins that Give Away Too Much

You're a blogger. I'm a blogger. And us bloggers like traffic. So how would you like if someone described the entire point of your post in the pin description? Doesn't give someone much incentive to actually click through to the post if all the juicy details are right on Pinterest, ya know?

Figure 2-10: Using a different font and color for blog post subheadings.

When you're deciding how elements should contrast, keep in mind the following questions:

- ✐ **What are the most important and second most important actions you want blog visitors to take?** Add contrast to highlight the areas of your blog where readers will take those actions (such as the Free Instant Access button example mentioned earlier).

- ✐ **How can contrast make this content easily accessible to blog visitors?** Sometimes, breaking up text with photos is ideal. For example, a how-to post full of photos that show the steps is the most efficient and easy-to-skim way to present that information and break up the text. If your content is more conceptual than visual, breaking text into subheadings as shown in Figure 2-10 may be a better choice.

Aligning Design Elements

Alignment refers to lining up elements or text within a design. Even if you've never designed anything before, you've used alignment in a word processing program when selecting left, center, right, or justified alignment for your paragraphs.

Proper alignment makes various design elements or text appear as if they were connected through a visible line. I'd say that alignment is the most subtle of the core design principles, mainly because unless you're aware of this design principle, you may not be able to pinpoint why a design looks "off." Despite the subtlety, alignment is a key principle of blog design, because alignment gives a blog design a clean and polished look.

You can align design elements both on a vertical or horizontal axis.

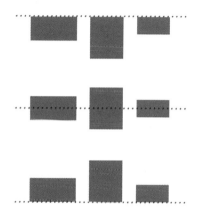

- ✔ **On a vertical axis,** you could align left, center, or right. Aligning a blog post's text is an example of vertical alignment.

- ✔ **On a horizontal axis,** you align design elements to the top, center or baseline. Figure 2-11 illustrates ways to align differently shaped rectangles. Despite the type of alignment, the rectangles look as if they were connected by a visible line, which I've added for you as a dashed line.

Figure 2-11: Examples of top, center, and baseline alignment on a horizontal axis.

Creating order through alignment

Aligning various elements on your blog or within a design element gives your design order and improves readability.

When talking about alignment as it relates to blog design, here are some common elements where you can apply alignment:

- ✔ Components of the blog header
- ✔ Sidebar buttons or badges
- ✔ Text within your post or sidebar
- ✔ Images within your post or sidebar

You can also take a more bird's-eye view of your blog design and look at how separate blog elements align to one another. For example, in Figure 2-12, I added a dashed line so that you can see how the blog name, tagline, blog post title, and post content all align to the left.

Using grids or lines to aid in placement

If you're designing your own blog, you're most likely using a theme or framework that already takes alignment into consideration. However, if you're designing your blog header or other components that make up your overall blog design, grids or lines can help ensure that parts of your design line up.

Figure 2-12: Alignment of various components of a home page.

Using a grid system provides you with a guide so your design elements don't look like they were haphazardly placed here and there. Some design programs like Adobe Illustrator or Photoshop have settings to show grids and the capability to add guiding lines. In Adobe Photoshop, design with a grid by choosing View➪Show➪Grid. In Photoshop Elements 11, you choose View➪Grid.

When it comes to aligning text within your actual blog posts, you don't have to worry too much. Blogging platforms such as WordPress default to aligning your text to the left, but you can change this by simply clicking the icons that adjust your alignment to the right, center, or full (justified).

3

Getting to Know Your Blog (Even Better)

. . . .

In This Chapter

▶ Understanding how goals affect blog design

▶ Pinpoint your voice and tone

▶ Exploring ways to get to know your audience

. . . .

*B*efore you embark on designing your blog, you and your blog need to sit down and have a little chat. Get to know one another. Maybe even have some coffee together.

Kidding aside, to design a blog that reflects who you are and what you blog about, you need to take a closer look at your blog. I assume that you've already defined your purpose for blogging. If you still scratch your head over that, start there and determine what made you start a blog in the first place. As Darren Rowse from the popular blog Problogger once said: "If you're fuzzy on what your blog is about, it's unlikely that anyone else will have much of an idea either."

This chapter goes beyond your blog's purpose. I help you go deeper by giving you some ways to take a closer look at your blog. That way, you really, truly understand it. In this chapter, I show you how to create goals, get to know your audience, and even hone in on the voice and tone you want to shine through in your blog design.

Creating Goals for a Strong Design

If you're serious about growing your blog and creating a strong design, move setting goals to the top of your blog design to-do list. Think of them as the skeleton of your blog. From design to navigation to content, every decision you make about your blog should move you toward putting meat on that skeleton's bones.

Without goals, you might find yourself veering off track with your blog design. Sure, your design may look nice, but it might not mesh with what you want to accomplish in your blogging. And if you weren't blogging to accomplish something, you probably wouldn't have invested in this book to improve your blog design.

Pinpointing what you want to accomplish

If the thought of setting goals makes your mind go blank, try one of the easiest, most common ways to set goals: the SMART method. SMART is a mnemonic device that has been used in project management for decades. The letters in SMART can stand for different things, depending on who you talk to, but here's what I stick with:

- **Specific:** Say exactly what you're looking to achieve. Generic goals may be easy to think up, but they don't move you toward an achievable goal in the same way specific goals do. "I want to make money blogging" isn't specific enough. "I want to earn $500 a month through advertising" is specific.

- **Measurable:** Quantify your goal with numbers. Say you gained 500 e-mail subscribers last year. That's less than 50 per month. So, shoot for 75 new subscribers a month. Or 100. Just try not to fall into the trap about obsessing about numbers.

  Other measurables you can strive for could be publishing three times per week, increasing subscribers by 30 percent, or earning a certain amount of money from blogging.

- **Actionable:** When setting goals, stick with action words. Even better? Imperative verbs. Start your goals with words like *increase, create,* and *grow.* All these cut to the chase, driving action on your part.

- **Realistic:** Being realistic means setting goals that are challenging but doable. Also avoid claiming that you want to be the best, funniest, and so on. I'm not saying you can't ever be *the* best, but there are plenty of steps you'll need to take to get there — so make *those* your goals.

   Try not to make your goals too difficult or too easy. If you aren't sure whether your goal is realistic, you can always adjust it later.

- **Timely:** I don't know about you, but my inner procrastinator doesn't work without a timeframe to complete something. Why? There's no urgency to light my fire. Add timeframes to your goals to keep that fire lit.

To start writing out your goals, think about your blog's bigger purpose as well as more specific things you want to accomplish. Then brainstorm goals that can help you meet that ultimate achievement, select the most burning ideas, and then start adding measurements and timeframes.

How many goals you create really depends on you. Too many can overwhelm you, but too few can make achieving them too easy. Start with two to five goals and then adjust if you need.

Set a reminder on your phone or calendar to review your goals at regular intervals. Blogs change over time, and you might need to rearrange your blog design layout to help meet those goals.

Drawing attention to goal-oriented design elements

After you write out your goals, put them in a place where you see them often — whether that means you type them on a desktop sticky note or scribble them on a real sticky note. Keep your goals top of mind because they form the basis for many decisions about where to place your design elements.

The ways that design can support your goals may surprise you. As you build your blog design, take a look at your goals and think about how elements of your design, layout, and navigation can be used to meet your goals.

Say you want to increase your e-mail subscriber list by 15 percent in three months. The following design decisions can help you meet this goal:

- ✏ Promote your e-mail offering in a conspicuous space on your home page.

- ✏ Create an e-mail subscriber box that asks only for an e-mail address instead of a first and last name plus an e-mail address. This would make subscribing as easy as possible.

- ✏ Place a subscription box elsewhere on your blog. Perhaps you add the subscription box at the bottom of each blog post, to your About page, or in your footer.

Carrie with Children (www.carriewithchildren.com) is an example of how to adjust your design layout if one of your goals is to bring awareness to a certain topic. Carrie writes about many topics but wants to give special attention to Down syndrome. To do that, she includes a Down Syndrome tab to the right of the popular About tab and features a separate section for Down Syndrome posts prominently on her home page (as shown in Figure 3-1).

Figure 3-1: Use blog design to steer attention to a certain topic.

If you can't think of how you can use design to meet your goals, don't worry just yet! Keep your goals handy as you go through this book. You'll have many "aha moments"!

Defining Your Writing

Although this book covers aspects of blog design, your writing and your blog design need to be in sync. Everything that surrounds your words affects how readers perceive those words.

When you define your writing, blog design choices become easier. I talk about all these design elements further into the book, but your niche, voice, and tone all influence blog design elements, including

✔ Font choice and size

✔ Blog colors

✔ Imagery you use

When it comes to defining your niche, voice, and tone, you might find these next sections easy, especially if you've blogged for a while.

Sometimes even experienced bloggers have a hard time describing what they write about because they just write what's top-of-mind and then click the Publish button. Even if that's part of your shtick (say, you're known for your amazing randomness), you should still have an underlying voice and tone to your writing. For example, you make even the most mundane parts of life sound hysterical.

Carving out a niche (or not)

A *niche* simply means the topic that you write about. In the blogging world, you find two camps: those who believe you must have a niche to be successful, and those who think you can be successful without one.

Having a niche can seem more manageable because you have a tighter focus and you don't have to meet the needs of many different audiences. Because niche blogging really digs into a specific topic, it's easier to be seen as an expert or a thought leader about your topic. You may also attract more readers because niche blogs can generate more traffic from search engines.

Not having a niche might give you more flexibility, though, especially if you're passionate about more than one topic but lack the time to run multiple blogs. Parent bloggers are a perfect example of this. A mom blogger may share stories about her children, write about family-friendly recipes, share the latest fashion trends, and document a weight loss journey all in one blog.

One great example of blogging without a niche is the blog Jenny on the Spot (http://www.jennyonthespot.com), as shown in Figure 3-2. Jenny writes about everything from parenting to style to health. She places some of her blog's main topics within easy sight in the navigation menu. Then her home page segments her latest blog posts around those topics and more. Even though she writes about many things, her blog design and content tie together.

On the other hand, not having a niche can hinder your ability to stand out as an expert or a leader. Without a niche, you may have a harder time branding yourself because you blog design has to encompass the many topics you want to write about.

Figure 3-2: The Jenny on the Spot blog covers a range of topics.

Even if you decide you don't need a niche for your blog, you still need to establish your voice and tone. Think about your favorite magazine. That magazine may write about many different topics, but one section doesn't sound like a completely different magazine than another section because the voice and tone are consistent.

Showcasing your voice

Voice refers to the distinct personality of your writing. Voice combines attitude, style, and your personal character to give your blog a certain "feel." If your audience could read two very different articles from you and still know they're both written by you, then you've mastered your voice.

Defining your voice comes more naturally for some bloggers than others. And that's perfectly okay. More than likely, your voice will also develop as you do as a writer. To better define your voice, ask yourself these three questions:

> ✔ Who are you writing for?
>
> ✔ Why are you writing?
>
> ✔ What do you want readers to "get" about you through your writing?

Voice is an integral part to your brand so by answering these questions, your voice becomes more apparent and defined. Spend some time with these questions because the blog design decisions you make should take your voice into consideration.

Readers see your design before they have time to read the content. However, your blog design should *feel* like your voice. For example, if your writing is sarcastic and dry, your blog shouldn't be whimsical or flowery.

You can also emphasize voice in your blog design by how you actually format your blog posts. Word choice and sentence structure are part of writing but they are visual, too. I dig more into that in Chapter 16.

If you don't have a niche, really understanding and developing your voice and tone becomes even more critical.

Determining your tone

Tone is your blog's mood or attitude. When you write, do you sound snarky, kind, serious, fun, sarcastic, reassuring, helpful, earnest? We lose nonverbal communication when we write — your audience doesn't have the benefit of understanding your words through facial expressions, gestures, or the pitch of your voice. You have just one thing: tone.

People often confuse tone with voice, but tone is actually *part* of your voice. You've likely heard the phrase "tone of voice." While your voice may be humorous, your tone might be sarcastic. The tone of your writing can vary a little from post to post, but your voice should remain consistent.

Tone can also vary depending on your target audience or their feelings. Think about how you would share big news with an adult friend versus a child. You'd probably use different words and inflect your voice differently. Or if you were sharing big news with someone who thought might object, you might vary your tone again to keep in mind their feelings.

Look over blog posts you've written and write down adjectives to describe the overall tone in your writing. Then think about what those adjectives do and don't mean. You can see how I did this for my own blog (Momcomm) in Table 3-1.

Table 3-1	Tone for My Blog	
Tone Attribute	**What It Means**	**What It Doesn't Mean**
Approachable	Write like I'm helping a friend; don't sound like a know-it-all; don't be intimidating.	I invite readers to let me give them extensive feedback via e-mail or social media. (I limit extensive feedback to my published weekly critiques.)
Casual	Use contractions; write like I'm talking to one person playful writing (like using "yo!" or "y'all")	I don't use improper grammar or most "text-speak" (I might use OMG but not *"prolly"* for probably)
Simple	Avoid jargon; explain without fluffy words ("use" not "utilize")	Content is "dumbed down"

No matter what your tone, make sure it's authentic and doesn't feel forced.

For a really slick look at how a company uses tone to adapt to their audience's feelings, check out the MailChimp site Voice and Tone (`http://voiceandtone.com`).

Understanding Your Audience

Like voice and tone, your blog design also depends on knowing who your audience is and what they want. The more you understand your audience, the easier time you'll have making design decisions (like those I go through in Chapter 5). Your audience has an especially strong impact on the following design elements:

- **Navigation:** When you know your audience, you can organize your blog navigation tools so your readers can easily find the content they want.

- **Home page and overall layout:** Your audience can impact the visual hierarchy of where content belongs on your blog, particularly your home page. For example, if you know your audience enjoys your craft tutorials the most, then you could place a button that links to those tutorials near the top of your sidebar or always include your latest craft tutorials in a rotating gallery towards the top of your home page. You can also start applying those core design principles that I talk about in Chapter 2.

When getting to know your audience better, you want to look at both your current audience and the type of audience you want to attract.

Knowing your audience can benefit your design

Understanding your audience means that you can design a blog that makes them feel comfortable. Your design and layout should not only focus on their interests, but also align with your tone and goals.

Here are things you can learn from your audience that benefit your blog design:

- **How much content they consume about your topic:** If your audience wants multiple posts a day (and you have that capacity on your own or with contributors), you may choose a different blog layout than someone who posts twice weekly. A perfect example would be a deal blogger whose readers expect to know about the latest sales and coupons.

- **What answers they're seeking:** Your audience's content preferences can help you decide how often to write about a certain topic. You can also build a popular topic into your blog design. If your audience likes your video tutorials, you might design a blog page just for those. If your audience wants basics about sewing, create a sidebar image that links to a page dedicated to sewing for beginners.

- **What platforms or communities they belong to:** If your audience heavily uses Pinterest (a social media site for bookmarking and sharing links via images), you want the functionality in your blog design to be Pinterest-friendly. That means good image titles and easily visible PinIt buttons. If they are big Twitter users, you might consider a widget that shows your latest tweets.

- **Their basic demographic make-up:** If your audience is mostly males in their 20s, your site design should look a lot different than a blog whose audience is women in their 50s. While you can assume you know your audience, you might be surprised by the results. Even though my blog name has "mom" in it (Momcomm.com), my site isn't read by only moms.

- **Tech-savvyness:** Do your readers have smart phones, tablets, or the latest gadgets? Or do they use their computers just for web surfing and e-mail? If most of your readers aren't bloggers, maybe you don't need the CommentLuv plug-in that automatically pulls that commenter's latest blog post. It might be confusing and inhibit someone from leaving a comment. If your blog readers are heavy smartphone users, they'll appreciate a mobile version of your site or even a special mobile phone app.

Resist the urge to think that your blog is for anyone and everyone. Without a target audience, you water down your writing and make it harder to design your blog.

Finding out who they are and what they want

After you understand how knowing your audience can make your design friendlier, you need some ways to actually gather that information. The best place to start in defining your audience is talking to your existing readers. You can then look at people who don't necessarily read your blog but who you want as readers.

You might be surprised at the ways you can collect information about your audience. Sure, companies pay big bucks for massive surveys, focus groups, and other sorts of research. As a blogger, though, you don't need such in-depth and precise surveys to find out what your audience wants. Here are a few tools to gather information about your audience:

- ✓ **Facebook** (www.facebook.com):

    Ask a valuable question to your fans, friends or group members. Depending on the relevance of your topic, ask your fans, Friends, or group members a question.

    Don't hound anyone with multiple questions. Ask sparingly and make sure your question really gets to what you want to accomplish.

    Look at the user profiles of some of your fans. Check out the About description and see what other fan pages they like. This might seem a little like spying at first, but remember you're looking at only what that person made publicly available.

- ✓ **Twitter** (https://twitter.com):

    Do a search for a hashtag (#topic) or keyword related to your blog topics. Within that hashtag or keyword, study the conversations that happen within the hashtag, note where these Twitter users link to content, and look at their Twitter profiles.

    Peek at your own followers. No, you don't need to stalk anyone. Just take a look at their bio, visit their blogs (if they have one), and get a sense of their interests.

- ✓ **Quantcast** (www.quantcast.com):

    See your site's demographics. After you set up Quantcast on your site (it's free), you can view your profile to see age range, gender, and other demographics about your audience.

    If you know of blogs in a similar niche as yours (or they write about similar topics), you can look up their profiles on Quantcast using the search feature. If they don't use Quantcast, they won't have a profile. It's also worth mentioning that a profile also displays web site traffic but most bloggers claim Quantcast doesn't report traffic very accurately.

In addition to using the tools in the preceding list, you can get more in-depth knowledge about your audience from your audience themselves. Here are a couple of techniques to dig deeper into your audience's opinions and preferences:

✔ **Interview a few blog readers.** Ask them to describe your blog and see whether readers' perceptions align with your own. Ask them whether they can find content on your site easily. Find out the types of things they will want to see on your blog.

✔ **Survey your audience.** Ask questions about content and how your site works. Be careful not to ask directly about your blog design. (You're the one who best knows your goals, voice, and audience. Asking your entire readership about colors or fonts can lead to subjective answers that make your decision even harder.) You can use these tools to create your survey:

- *SurveyMonkey* (`www.surveymonkey.com`): SurveyMonkey is the leader in web-based surveys and for good reason: It makes creating surveys a cinch. With a free account, you get basic reports, 10 questions per survey, and 100 responses per survey. You can actually embed the survey in a blog post or blog page, too.

- *Polldaddy* (`http://polldaddy.com`): Polldaddy comes from the same company that created Wordpress.com. With a free account, you get 10 questions per survey and 200 responses per month. You can even survey people from an iPhone or iPad (cool idea if you were at an event or conference) and also embed the survey on your blog.

- *Google Drive* (`https://drive.google.com`): Through Google Drive, you can create a form that drops answers into a spreadsheet for you to analyze. You can also embed the form into a blog post or a blog page. While you can easily create a form with questions, Google Drive doesn't turn multiple choice answers into quantifiable data. For example, if you want to find out what percentage of those surveyed answered *a. Excellent* to your first question, then you have to do the math yourself using the spreadsheet formulas. For this reason, Google Drive works best for surveys when you ask open-ended questions that don't need to be quantified.

You might think I'm missing an obvious place to gain insight into your audience: blog analytics, such as Google Analytics. But don't worry — I devote an entire section to it in Chapter 5.

What your readers answer on certain survey questions may contradict with what your analytics program tells you about your most popular types of posts or topics. For example, your analytics may show your most popular posts are on a topic readers don't rank as one of their favorite topics. Because some of your traffic may be from visitors who come from search engines but don't turn into regular readers, be sure to compare survey results with your traffic patterns. That way, you'll gather a more complete picture of what your audience and potential audience both want.

Creating a user persona

After you have a solid understanding of who your target audience is, consider developing user personas to paint an ever clearer picture. A *user persona* is a short profile that describes a segment of your audience.

Think of personas as your "fake real people." Even if your target audience seems pretty straightforward, you might have different segments within your audience. For example, if you write a blog about photography, you might have a nonprofessional looking for tips on taking better photos or an amateur photographer looking to build a photography business. Personas bring to life these segments by creating a fake name, picture, and description of these different audience segments.

Sometimes people think that building personas means that you're stereotyping your audience. However, think about personas more like archetypes rather than stereotypes. Archetypes seek to create a general model of a personality or behavior, whereas stereotypes seek to demean a type of person by emphasizing clichéd or predictable behavior.

Personas can help you make better decisions about your blog. Every time you launch an e-mail, start to create a promotion, or have a brilliant idea for a new blog post series, pull out your personas. Does that "thing" resonate with one of them — or better yet, a few of them?

Then, after you understand your audience more thoroughly, you can move to making decisions for your blog design.

Establishing a Style Guide

*W*ouldn't It be great to have one place you could refer to regarding all the design and content decisions you make for your blog? Well, that's where a style guide comes in.

Both print and web designers have long used style guides. A company might have an editorial style guide that lays out their content's voice and tone. They might also have a branding style guide or brand book that provides detailed information about their brand's core message along with branding do's and don'ts. I once saw a large company's guide that was nearly 100 pages long!

As a blogger, you don't have to go that crazy. You can combine everything into a simple style guide for your blog. This chapter explores why you should create a style guide and what to potentially include in yours. I also show you how easy it is to create a simple style guide. Finally, I walk you through special considerations for blogs with multiple contributors.

Exploring the Benefits of a Style Guide

You might think that spending time on creating a style guide seems like a complicated process that only bigger blogs need. Or that such a guide just adds to your to-do list. The truth is any blogger can benefit from a style guide — and it's really easy to create one.

As your blog grows, you'll find yourself looking for ways to be more productive. Having a style guide saves you time so you aren't pouring through your blog or your design files trying to remember what exact shade of blue you use in your header or whether you capitalize a certain word. You can peek at your style guide for the answer — and then quickly get to work.

If you build your guide bit by bit as you work through your blog design, you'll hardly feel like you did any extra work at all. I'm not kidding!

Building a foundation of reference material

As you start redesigning your blog — or even build a design from scratch — you make decisions that guide how you want your blog to look and your content formatted. However, as time goes on, you might find you don't remember to always use the guides you created in the first place.

Luckily, you don't have to remember everything because (wait for it) a style guide remembers for you. By building a style guide as a foundation, you have just one file to reference versus searching for something in a design file, your blog, or somewhere else altogether.

Plus, if you decide to extend your blog's design into other places — say, custom graphics for your Facebook page or for a business card (see Chapter 17) — you'll pat yourself on the back for having all your blog's styles in one place.

Your style guide is an excellent resource if you ever collaborate with someone on a project for your blog. For example, if you work with a designer to help you create a custom Twitter background, you can share your style guide with the designer, so he or she knows exactly what colors your blog design uses. If anyone writes a guest post for your blog, you can share a modified version of your guide (or paste it into an e-mail) to outline how you capitalize your post titles, what size the post images should be, and other post guidelines.

Creating consistency throughout your blog

As I mention in Chapter 2, consistency is one of the core design principles of good design and branding. Consistency gives your blog a polished, professional look.

Blog readers often subconsciously notice inconsistencies in blog design and content, such as the difference in two shades of blue or the fact that you wrote *USA* and *U.S.A.* in the same blog post. Although these inconsistencies most likely won't deter a reader from returning to your blog, the inconsistencies do add up and take their toll in the following ways:

- From a writing perspective, inconsistencies within blog posts are like little speed bumps, slowing down your reader and hindering concentration.
- From a blog design perspective, inconsistencies can give your blog a sloppy feel, even if your reader can't quite place exactly why.

✔ Good marketing and public relations representatives you may want to partner with do notice consistency. Your blog writing and design are, in a way, your personal brand. If you pay attention to the details in your blog, you have a better chance of attracting partners who value a similar attention to detail and standards for quality.

A style guide gives you an easy way to maintain consistency because your design and content decisions all live in one document. When you have a guide to reference, you make it easier on yourself (and others) to keep your blog brand strong.

Identifying Elements to Include

Because you probably don't have a marketing team, design team, PR team, and other sorts of teams at your disposal (well, I don't anyway), you can build your style guide to combine many sorts of things into one guide. The ideas I give you in this section include not only design-related pieces, but also things to include for content, linking, and post length.

This is your style guide, not mine or anyone else's. You can decide exactly what you find worth including and how much detail you want to provide. If you don't think you'll reference something, don't include it. This section merely seeks to give you lots of ideas.

Defining your blog's purpose, voice, and tone

Your blog's purpose provides the backbone for your blog design. Your blog's voice and tone bring that purpose to life.

You may know your blog's purpose by heart and be comfortable with your own voice and tone, but writing all this down serves as a gentle reminder of what you typically expect your blog to be. When you're deciding on blog changes or opportunities, referencing your blog's overall purpose, voice, and tone can bring clarity to making decisions that truly fit your blog.

If you end up creating personas, as I recommend in Chapter 3, you could include a short version of them in your style guide as well to remind you of the audiences you're trying to attract.

Formatting blog post titles

Your blog post titles not only need to grab attention due to their content, but they should also be consistent from post to post. Multiple blog post titles are often seen together on one page, such as when you have short teasers on your home page that lead to full posts. Plus, you have new readers who are soaking up post after post and regular readers who surely read every one of your posts. So, if there's one place to apply consistency, consider blog post titles one of the most important.

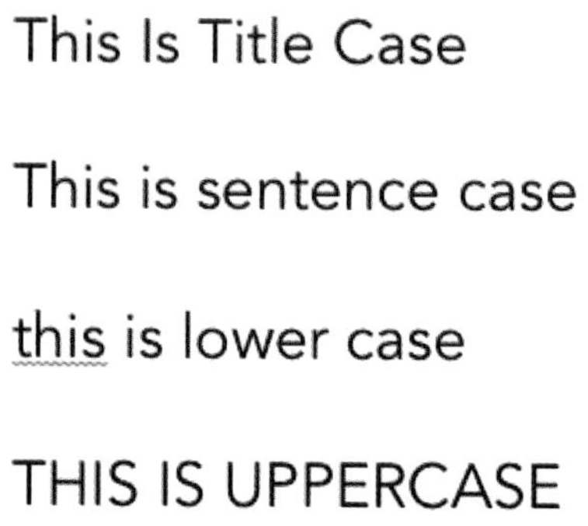

Here are a few things you may want to include in your style guide regarding post titles:

This Is Title Case

This is sentence case

this is lower case

THIS IS UPPERCASE

Figure 4-1: Choose from post title capitalization options.

- ✔ **Capitalization:** Do you write your post titles in title case, sentence case, lowercase, or uppercase (see Figure 4-1)? If you use Title Case, typical style does not capitalize articles (such as *a, an,* and *the*) or prepositions (like *on, from,* or *by*). You could keep a list in your style guide to remind you which words you don't capitalize.

- ✔ **Word or character count:** Do you want to stick to a certain number of words or characters so that your titles look uniform or so they take up only a certain number of lines?

- ✔ **Labels to special posts:** When you have a guest blogger, do a product review, or run a weekly series, do you include a specific label in the title? Here's an example: starting every review with `Review:`.

- ✔ **Special formatting:** Do you want to apply any other styles to your blog post titles? If you write a lot of news-related blog posts, perhaps you adapt that more journalistic style. For example, journalistic writing often eliminates articles in the beginning headlines (*a, an* and *the*) and uses a comma in place of *and*. As another example, maybe you want all blog post titles to end in punctuation like a period, question, or exclamation point.

Knowing how to structure a blog post

Applying certain guidelines to how you structure a blog post can help readers feel more comfortable with your writing and even reinforce your blog voice. When it comes to laying out your blog posts, here are some things to consider:

- ✔ **Post length:** You may want your posts to stick to a certain length either because of how your posts look visually or because you've determined that your readers prefer a shorter (or longer) post.

- ✔ **Paragraph length:** Long paragraphs hinder readability. You may limit paragraphs to a certain number of lines. Or you may style your posts so that each paragraph is just a few words or a short sentence.

✔ **Image placement:** If you wrap text around your images, your style guide can specify that and whether the image floats to the left or right side of the text. Or your style guide might specify that images are centered in the column above or below the text in a blog post. You can also clarify whether image placement changes depending on the type of post you write.

✔ **Headings:** Headings visually guide readers through your blog posts. HTML gives you up to six levels, with 1 being the most important heading. Within HTML, tags written as <h1>, <h2>, and so on indicate a heading's level. Blog post titles are <h1> headings; then, within your blog posts, you can use any level heading.

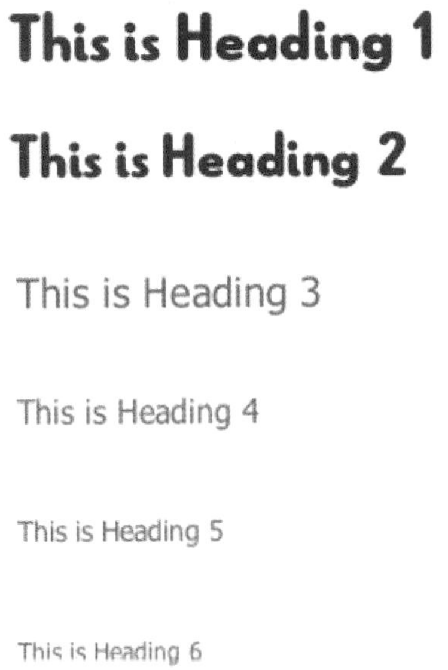

This is Heading 1

This is Heading 2

This is Heading 3

This is Heading 4

This is Heading 5

This is Heading 6

Figure 4-2: Use blog heading levels to guide your reader.

For your headings, you might choose to make them all one font, or maybe switch to another font when you get down to a certain level, like mine do (see Figure 4-2). Also, you may choose to write your blog post titles in Title Case but other headings lowercase. (Psst. You might notice that this book's style uses *Title Case* main headings and *Sentence case* subheadings.)

If a certain heading size looks too small, stick with certain levels for your blog posts — and denote that in your style guide.

Remembering your color palette

Because colors are one of your blog's most stand-out assets, you want to keep the shades you selected consistent. You'll find a reference of your blog's color palette to be an especially handy tool, and your style guide is the perfect place for this color reference.

When listing your colors in your style guide, I suggest you show the colors and list the technical specifications for each color you use.

✓ **Showing the colors:** Most word processors enable you to add a square shape and fill it with color. To get the exact colors, look for a Custom Colors option or something similar among the formatting options for a shape. I used the Colors dialog box in Microsoft Word for the Mac 2011 to add the color squares you see in Figure 4-3.

✓ **Listing the technical specs:** As I explain in Chapter 6, on the web, colors are specified using RGB values or hexadecimal codes. Include both the RGB and the hexadecimal value for each color.

For my style guide, I made simple squares in Microsoft Word so that my style guide includes a visual representation of each color, as shown in Figure 4-3. I then added a table to show all the color values.

COLORS:

Value	Light Blue	Dark Blue	Red	Pink	Brown
R	175	0	193	249	140
G	223	176	39	197	98
B	229	216	45	206	57
Hex	#AEDEE4	#00B0D8	#C1272D	#F9C5CE	#8C6239

Figure 4-3: My blog colors listed in my style guide.

Ensuring correct usage of fonts

Like colors, the fonts you use on your blog can make your blog design more memorable. (*Hint:* Chapter 6 is devoted to both fonts *and* colors.) You probably use more than one font on your blog, so for this part of your guide, display the fonts that you use for specific areas of your site.

Here are some places within your blog design where you might want to list what font or fonts you use and possibly their size:

✓ Blog header (blog name and tagline)

✓ Main blog post content

✒ Sidebar or footer content

✒ Special blog buttons

You can see how I did this for my style guide in Figure 4-4.

If you've played around with your fonts and know at what font size they look too gigantic, you may want to also note that in your guide. The same goes for the minimum size to use before your font becomes hard to read.

Applying consistent imagery

Images on your blog are so important to your blog design and your branding that I devote an entire chapter to them (see Chapter 15). Some things you might want to include in this section of your style guide are

✒ **Recommended width of images for your blog post:** I like to include widths for both horizontal and vertical images. Vertical images that run the width of my main column look gigantic, so I size them smaller than a horizontal image.

✒ **Sizes for design files:** In addition to images for your blog posts, you may end up creating designs for

- Your blog's Facebook page

- Your Twitter profile

- Your Google Plus page

- An e-mail newsletter

- Your sidebar

- Social media icons for your blog

- More places to extend your blog design that I cover in Chapter 17

FONTS:

1. MAIN FONT

Le Havre Rounded

Momcomm logo: all lowercase, 85 pt
Tagline: 18.5 pt
Sidebar graphics: no smaller than 24 pt
Footer images: 34 pt

2. BLOG CONTENT FONT

Tahoma
Only use for main blog content, not in design elements.

3. CONTENT BREW COURSE FONT

Only use for course-related graphics
For Content Brew logo: 95 pt (with customized "w")
For Content Brew handouts: 72 pt

4. PINTEREST IMAGE FONT OPTIONS
All of the above (minus Sherbet), plus:

Avenir (Mainly 35 Light and 95 Black)

BEBAS

Jigsaw (Mainly Medium and Bold)

Figure 4-4: Font guidelines for my blog.

Because you probably aren't updating most of these design files frequently, you save time by not having to search through old files for the right size. If you use a design program like Photoshop that saves a file that you can edit again, then you might not need to list file sizes. However, if you use a program like PicMonkey, then listing file sizes in your style guide comes in handy because you can't edit a file again once you leave the application.

Figure 4-5: A Pinterest-friendly image.

✔ **Pinterest-friendly image formatting:** As Pinterest (a social media site for bookmarking and sharing links via images) increases in popularity, many bloggers are creating images with text to grab someone's attention on Pinterest. See one that I did in Figure 4-5. For my Pinterest images, I often like to extend beyond my blog's colors and fonts and use colors or fonts that complement my branding. Write down things like the following:

- Colors

- Fonts

- Branding (Do you use your logo? URL? Watermark?)

Keeping within some parameters will keep you from spending too much time re-inventing the wheel every time you want to create a new Pinterest graphic. (Trust me — been there, done that.)

✔ **Images not to use:** Are there certain styles of images you don't want to use? For example, when using stock photography with models, you might decide that candid shots work better than models who are posed.

✔ **Preferred image sources:** If you find yourself using stock images or illustrations over and over from certain artists, include a list of favorite artists and links to their profiles on the places where you source their images.

Listing frequently used words

Every blogger has words or phrases that they use often, but perhaps you don't use them often enough to remember exactly how you write them.

Funny enough — I sell an e-book on my blog but often forget whether I typically use *e-book* or *eBook*.

You want to use words and phrases consistently from blog post to blog post. Although you might be tempted to not worry about how you've written that word in the past (or even in the same blog post), consistency makes your blog more professional — and, depending on the word, eliminates any potential confusion.

Of course, you don't need to worry about words that don't have potential for confusion, such as the town you live in. Include only those words that can be written numerous ways or that you have a hard time remembering how to write. Words with accents, hyphens, or specific capitalization are often words that you need help remembering.

You might wonder how most people determine how to write a specific word. You can often find the answer by doing a search for the word plus the phrase *AP Style* or *Chicago Manual of Style*. These are two stylebooks used by most publishers — and in some cases, the answer will be different between the two sources. For many words, there's no right or wrong way. Just pick a way and then stick with it.

Attribution of photos or quotes

When you use free photos within your blog post, the photographer often requires that you give him or her credit for the photo. To do so, you need to attribute that photo within the photo caption. To stay consistent, decide how you want to format the attribution and then add it to your style guide.

This also applies to attributing quotes on your blog. You can show how you attribute a quote or photo to someone, like this:

–Name (website name, if applicable)

Depending on the photo you're using, you may need to attribute a photo in a certain way. (For example, some photographers want you to use a copyright symbol; others request the wording *Courtesy of* . . . A free photo service may want you to include the service name as well as the photographer's name.) Be sure to check the licensing agreement.

Keeping handy your latest biography

If you're like me, you've probably been asked to provide someone with an author biography, and you go sifting through previous guest posts or old e-mails trying to find a bio you used at some point in the past. I quickly realized that wasn't too productive (no, really!) and decided to add my bios to my style sheet as well. True, a bio isn't really design related, but maintaining consistency is never a bad thing.

So, in my style sheet, I keep my main bio, a shortened version, and a first-person version. I also include word counts for each version because you might be asked to provide only a 100-word or 50-word biography.

Creating Your Style Guide

After you gather what goes into your style guide, now it's time to put your guide together. You could create something fancy, but I recommend building your style guide in a word processing document — like Microsoft Word — or within Google Docs. (And with Google Docs, you can access your style guide from anywhere with an Internet connection.)

My guide starts with my blog name and the date I last updated the guide. From there, I include my blog's voice and tone. After those core items, my best piece of advice is this: Keep your most referenced material at the top. You don't want to dig for the styles you continually need to reference. For me, that's my color breakdowns and frequently used words.

Just like your blog design, you want your style guide to have visual components to it. That way, you can easily scan your guide for the information you're looking for.

Here are a few ways to visually break up your style guide for easy scanning:

- ✓ **Headings for each section**
- ✓ **Screenshots for certain parts of your blog to illustrate a style in action**
- ✓ **Color key of colors used in your blog**
- ✓ **Font names you use shown in the actual fonts**
- ✓ **Simple tables**

Finally, build this document as you make decisions regarding your blog design instead of doing it all at once. If there are aspects of your current design that you plan to keep, put those in the document now.

You don't have to make your style guide overly complex. Even simply listing your color breakdowns or writing down the fonts you use works. The key is that you can reference the information easily when you need it.

Developing Guidelines for Blogs with Multiple Contributors

If you have more than one regular contributor on your blog, having a style guide becomes infinitely more important. You want your content to match your blog design, but keeping that consistency becomes harder when you're not the only person writing. When you have a style guide to share as a starting point for guest bloggers, you can bring new contributors up to speed faster.

In addition to the things I mention earlier in the chapter, here are some extra guidelines to consider including for a blog with multiple writers: Some of these guidelines might not relate directly to blog design, navigation, or formatting, but they all contribute to consistency — and, in some cases, the reputation of your blog's brand.

- **Title guidelines:** Outline the length of a blog post title or any special ways that contributors should write them. You may even provide suggestions and examples for writing a strong blog post title.

- **Limits to linking back to the contributor's own blog:** Guest bloggers benefit from writing as a contributor partly because they can add links to their own blogs within their guest posts. So that your contributors don't get carried away, though, you may want to impose limits to how many times in a blog post they can link back to their own blog (or at least mention to use good judgment).

- **Writing rules:** These rules aren't for you — you don't need to be reminded — but they are for your guest bloggers because not everyone writes the same way. When working with multiple contributors, your styles should be mentioned so no one has to spend time editing all blog posts to be the same. For example, people who learned to type on a typewriter will often use two spaces after a period instead of one, so you might need to remind writers to use only one space. Or, you might mention whether to use a comma after "and" in a serial list ("red, white, and blue" versus "red, white and blue").

- **Formatting tips for author bios:** If your contributors need to stick to a certain word count for layout purposes, remind them to include links to some of their social media platforms and any other tips you want to provide on how to structure their author bios.

- **Original content rules:** Tell your contributors whether you allow them to republish content already published on another blog or website.

- **Caution words:** Outline certain words or phrases that you don't want to be used on your blog. For example, you may not want bloggers to use profanity, or there may be expressions (or even entire topics) you don't want used on your blog.

✔ **Do Not Mentions:** Do Not Mentions are links that you don't want contributors to include in their blog posts. You may not want them to reference a business that you don't trust or a website that sells a product you wouldn't recommend.

✔ **Recommended Resources:** On the flipside of the Do Not Mentions, you can list trusted resources to link to or places to gather research. Having these resources handy might also encourage contributors to link to these sites.

Part II
Choosing the Visual Design Elements

Discover how to put the polishing touch on your blog design by adding a favicon at www.dummies.com/extras/blogdesign.

In this part. . .

- Kickstart the creative process by gathering design ideas, creating a mood board, and looking at your blog analytics.

- Find out how to select fonts that show your blog's personality, which fonts to avoid, and how to combine complementary fonts.

- Discover the color wheel and what colors mean and learn how to choose the right colors for your blog design.

- Learn about common layout types and explore what to look for in selecting a blog theme or framework.

- Dig into customizing your blog header, footer, and background with tips on what to include and what to avoid.

- Modify your design by learning the basics of HTML and CSS. Plus, learn to use a tool that teaches you more about the code behind your blog design.

5

Gathering Design Ideas

....

In This Chapter

▶ Finding design inspiration through mood boards

▶ Analyzing other blogs for design ideas

▶ Discovering how blog analytics can aid in design decision-making

▶ Hiring a designer, purchasing a predesigned template, or designing your blog yourself

....

Decisions, decisions. Blog design is full of decisions. When you think about all the possibilities out there, it's easy to overwhelm yourself with all the directions you could take. Ack!

Earlier chapters in this book give you a good grasp on some core design principles, helping you identify your audience (or who you want it to be) and establishing some concrete goals for your blog. With that knowledge tucked into your back pocket, it's time to take a deep breath and start narrowing down your focus.

Although you still have many more decisions to make (as explored in later chapters), this chapter gets you actively gathering design ideas that will form the foundation for your overall design. For this chapter, roll up your sleeves to put together a mood board and study other blog designs. Here, you can also read how to make navigation design decisions based on your own analytics. Finally, I guide you through one of the biggest decisions of all: whether to design your blog yourself, purchase a design template, or hire someone to design your blog for you.

Creating a Mood Board — And Why

Back in your school days, do you remember grabbing a giant white poster board and pasting it full of cutouts from magazines and newspapers? That collage you made was essentially a *mood board*.

Techniques for creating a collage of ideas have evolved (although I show you how to make one by hand, too), the purpose of creating a mood board remains the same: From fashion design to interior design to corporate design creation, people use mood boards as a way to explore creative inspiration and spark creative ideas.

A mood board conveys a design idea by mixing textures, words, images, colors, and more. You may think that making mood boards sounds like a waste of time — but don't underestimate them without giving it a shot. As a blogger, mood boards kick-start the creative process for designing your blog.

You don't have to know exactly what your blog design vision is at this point. That's what your mood board is for! Use it as a tool to explore and play with your ideas. Your board doesn't have to be logical nor does everything you add have to tie together. If something makes an impression on you, include it!

Regardless of who ends up actually developing the design, mood boards save time in the long run because through this exploration process, you can take those fuzzy ideas and begin creating a clearer vision of what you want to your blog design to be.

In Chapter 3, I talk about voice and tone. Using the words that describe your voice and the tone of your blog makes a good starting point for creating a design mood board. Start looking for images that represent those words.

Even if it takes you a while to create a mood board, consider it time well spent because you gain a better a sense of the look and feel you want to achieve in your blog design. And if you're turning over your design to a designer, a mood board can give the designer a better idea of the blog you envision.

Compiling ideas by hand

Creating a mood board by hand might be a little old-fashioned, but you'll find that doing something tactile can really spark ideas for your blog design. Plus, you can add certain elements to a mood board that you can't do with digital versions (unless you have certain tools like a scanner or pen tablet).

Start with a large surface on which to place your ideas (say, poster board, corkboard, or even some wall space), some pens and colored markers, paper, scissors, and tacks or glue. Find a space in your home where you can spread out and get to work.

Here are a few things you can add to a mood board created by hand:

- **Pictures:** Images from magazines or newspapers, personal photographs, printed screenshots
- **Words:** Words, samples of fonts, phrases, or quotes
- **Color:** Paint swatches, paper, paint, markers
- **Ephemera:** Trinkets, memorabilia, or other things that relate to your blog topic (like your first opera ticket that turned you into an opera fanatic)
- **Doodles:** Your own drawings or drawings from others

For the mood board you see in Figure 5-1, I compiled font ideas, quotes, images, and other elements that fit my style.

Figure 5-1: Start with a mood board, created by hand.

Brainstorming on Pinterest

Pinterest, one of the world's most popular social media platform, works like an online pin board. You create boards around a specific topic and then add pins from your own image library or other things you want to bookmark from around the web. Pinterest is all about visual appeal.

As a tool for creating mood boards, Pinterest gives you an easy way to showcase your ideas and things that inspire you. In Figure 5-2, you can see how a mood board can translate into design. Laura Mayes from Blog con Queso (http://thequeso.com) shared her Pinterest board with her designer, who then created a eye-catching design to reflect her love of color.

© Laura Mayes, Blog con Queso

Figure 5-2: See how a Pinterest board can translate into a blog design.

Pinterest has some advantages that make creating a mood board extra easy:

- **Secret Boards:** If you don't want your mood board to be seen by every-one, use *Secret Boards,* which stay private until you delete them or make them public. Visit your profile and scroll to the bottom of the page to click Create a Secret Board. You can also go on a pinning spree without overloading your followers' feeds with 20 pictures of fonts you like.

- **Multiple boards:** If you aren't sure of the design style you want for your blog, make multiple boards, each with its own unique look and feel. You can play around with different styles without lumping them into one board.

- **Contributor boards:** With Pinterest, you can invite other pinners to pin to your board. This comes in handy if your blog has multiple contribu-tors who may want to contribute ideas to the blog design. You can even ask your pinning-obsessed friends to contribute to your board if they come across anything that really fits your style or personality.

When searching for ideas on Pinterest itself, don't be surprised if your search query comes up short with results. Pinterest's search function isn't very helpful most of the time because it partly relies on pinners providing a helpful pin description. ***Remember:*** Search engines can't interpret images, so they rely on text. Try Google instead but add *Pinterest* to the end of your search query. You often get results for Pinterest boards or pins that you might not otherwise find through Pinterest.

Keeping track of ideas with Evernote

If a handmade board or one on Pinterest doesn't seem appealing, try Evernote to collect items for a blog design mood board. Evernote (`http://evernote.com`) is a program that makes it easy for you to store articles, images, and even your own audio recordings in one place. Evernote also has a robust app for smart phones and tablets that syncs with the desktop application.

You can use Evernote as a place to contain and organize anything related to your mood board. In Evernote, you organize Notes into Notebooks. Notes can be a saved article, a photo, an audio clip, or text that's typed directly into Evernote. I sometimes jot down ideas in a physical notebook and then take a picture from my Evernote phone app so I don't misplace them. Similar to a mood board done by hand, you could also doodle or sketch an idea and then photograph it for Evernote. The app even turns your handwriting and text from images into searchable content. In Figure 5-3, you can see a mood board Notebook that I created.

Figure 5-3: Create a mood board notebook in Evernote.

To save online inspiration — fonts, images, or even entire websites — install the Evernote Web Clipper, which allows you easily to clip articles from around the web.

When you're ready to start compiling your inspiration into a mood board, take screenshots from your notes then lay them out in a collage using a program like PicMonkey (`www.picmonkey.com`) or Photoshop. (I talk about PicMonkey collages in Chapter 15.) Or just keep your ideas in Evernote. Whatever works for you.

Studying Other Blogs

When you look at other blogs with an eye for design and navigation, you might be surprised by all the inspiration you gain. A single design element on someone's blog could give you an idea for a blog header. Or someone's main blog color may be the perfect shade to sprinkle through your design in much smaller doses.

Surveying the blogging landscape also helps you spot trends in blog design or discover new plug-ins or widgets you may want to use.

This section walks you through what to look for when it comes to another blog's design and navigation. I also challenge you to look at blogs focused on topics completely different from yours. Doing so can give you a fresh design perspective.

Imitation isn't the same as inspiration. If someone would look at your design and think (or say), "That looks just like so-and-so's blog!", then someone might say you copied a design. The more blogs that inspire you, the less your blog will look like someone else's.

Knowing what to look for

Surfing from blog to blog, looking at nice designs, is fun, but keep your jaunts productive, too. Keep a short list of things to look for on another person's blog. Then take notes about anything you like about someone's blog design. You can also keep track of things that inspire you by using some mood board ideas, as I describe in the previous section.

To kick-start your list, here are some things you can look at:

   ✒ **Overall branding:** Look at how the blog name, tagline, blog colors, fonts, and other design elements tie in to one another. How many fonts and colors are used? How did the blogger or designer create hierarchy with them?

✔ **General layout:** Are two columns or three used? Note any special galleries or rotating banners and the number of blog posts featured on the home page.

✔ **Sidebars:** See what key content is placed on the sidebar. Can you easily discern a hierarchy that signals to you what is most important?

✔ **Advertising:** Is the advertising overbearing to you as a blog visitor? Is advertising shown in unusual places? How many potential advertisers are allowed? Is there a special blog page created just for advertisers?

✔ **Navigation:** How is top content displayed? What about a search box? Where are categories listed?

✔ **Interaction:** Do readers leave lots of comments and share their posts on social media platforms? If so, look at how the blog's commenting system and social sharing buttons function.

✔ **Footer:** If the blog has a footer, what things are included? How does the footer design fit into the rest of the blog design?

Just because a certain design element works on one blog doesn't mean that it will work for you. Use other sites for inspiration but stay true to your own style and personality.

Looking outside your niche

By looking within just your own niche, you may inadvertently box yourself into a certain way of thinking. You might find yourself including something in your design because everyone else does, when it might not be the right choice for your blog. Looking outside your niche can help you bring a fresh approach to your own niche.

Look at blogs outside your niche and even corporate websites or company blogs.

However, in addition to looking at things that all blogs have (blog colors, a navigation menu, and so on), consider how you can apply part of a blog's design or navigation to your own blog. For example, if you write about travel, perhaps you notice how food bloggers often take close-up shots of their food. Maybe you get the idea to incorporate a close-up travel shot into your blog header versus a typical scenic landscape. Check out the many possibilities to take a fresh twist on your blog design!

Digging into Blog Analytics to Improve Navigation Design

Making your blog design easy to navigate means that visitors are more likely to return. Even if they never subscribe to your blog or follow you on a social network, effective navigation design means your visitors can find the content they need or explore your blog more easily.

In this section, I assume that you're using Google Analytics (www.google. com/analytics) to track your blog's statistics. Of course, you might be using another program like Clicky (http://clicky.com) or Statcounter (http://statcounter.com), and that's okay, too. You should be able to find similar data within these analytics programs even if the presentation of the data might vary.

If you're unfamiliar with analytics, you can find an overview of Google Analytics and Clicky at www.dummies.com. Although the process of setting up Google Analytics on your blog is beyond the scope of this book, know that you need to already have a blog.

In this section, I tackle a few areas where you can uncover navigation or functionality issues that may hinder a visitor's experience with your blog navigation design. Although you can surely go deeper into analytics, these next few sections give you a good grasp of how visitors use your site and what you can learn from that data.

Uncovering navigation issues by looking at bounce rate

A *bounce rate* is the percentage of visitors who leave your blog without visiting more than one page. If I land on your home page, read awhile, and then leave your blog, that counts as a bounce. If I follow a direct link to an older posts or a page of yours and then leave, that's a bounce, too. Any bounce rate less than 60% is typically considered decent — and rate less than 40% is pretty darn good.

This is why you want to track bounce rate: When you have a lower bounce rate, not only are you getting visitors to stay on your blog longer, but you're also helping them easily get the information they're looking for by guiding them with good navigation design.

People are naturally skimmers when it comes to online content. If you can make both your content and navigation design awesome, you'll keep people on your site longer.

To find the bounce rate for individual posts and pages, take the following steps.

1. **Visit your Google Analytics dashboard (**`https://www.google.com/analytics/web`**) and log in.**

   If you have more than one blog, select the blog you want to look at.

2. **From the left-side menu, choose Content⇨Site Content⇨All Pages.**

   This brings up data on all individual blog posts and pages, sorted by page views.

3. **Click the Performance button (see Figure 5-4).**

   Look for the third button on the far right; it looks like three stacked bars.

   By choosing to view the data using Performance, you can pull up two sets of data to compare.

Choose Bounces from this menu   Performance button

Page		Pageviews		Bounces
1. /2011/09/how-to-block-a-facebook-page-from-posting-on-your-facebook-page/		8,063		17.36%
2. /		5,431		1.04%
3. /2012/11/how-to-mrk-pinterest-like-a-pro/		4,335		15.87%
4. /2012/02/pinterest-search-why-it-sucks-and-how-you-can-improve-it/		4,236		4.20%
5. /blog-designers/		3,986		0.96%
6. /2012/11/ways-bloggers-can-use-pinterest-secret-boards/		3,126		11.95%
7. /2012/10/what-pr-friendly-means-to-pr-people/		2,744		7.11%
8. /2012/04/highlight-facebook-post/		2,452		1.98%
9. /2011/05/how-many-page-views-do-small-medium-and-big-blogs-get/		2,366		2.39%
10. /2012/02/how-to-see-if-your-content-is-pinned-on-pinterest/		2,093		0.91%

Figure 5-4: Look at page views to bounce rate.

4. **Choose Bounces from the right drop-down menu.**

   Because the left column already reads Pageviews, you can now see the bounce rate of your posts and pages with the highest number of page views. See Figure 5-4.

On your blog's home page (shown by a forward slash, /), a high bounce rate isn't necessarily a bad thing. If your blog layout has more than one full article on your page, visitors might read more than one post. They could even share your article via social media without affecting your bounce rate one way or the other. However, if your blog's home page design shows only partial blog posts with links to *Read more*, a high bounce rate could signify trouble.

Here are some reasons that prevent visitors from navigating to other parts of your blog:

- **Wrong keyword or phrase:** People find your blog post or page with keywords that aren't actually relevant to that page's content.

- **Outdated information:** Your blog post may contain content that needs to be updated. You could reference a product that's no longer available, your tutorial could refer to an old version of a product, and so on.

- **Visual appeal:** Does this blog post have an image? Is there enough contrast between your text and your background? Are your fonts hard to read? Any of these reasons could make a visitor click the Back button and leave your site.

- **Nowhere to go next:** Are you linking enough to other pages relevant to that topic? Often, I find that plug-ins that automatically pull related posts aren't enough to get people to click. Try including links to relevant posts within your text *(interlinking)* or adding a call to action at the end where you suggest what similar post to read next (which can lead a reader to take action by visiting another blog post).

- **Technical issues:** Does the page have random code showing? Is an image broken? Is something else not rendering properly? If a page looks awkward, a visitor may leave your site.

On the flip side of a high bounce rate, a really low bounce rate (like less than 10%) could potentially signify navigation design issues as well. If your blog has less than a 10% bounce rate, look closer at your overall navigation structure. Your navigation may confuse visitors or make visitors click through too many pages to find what they're looking for. Then again, it may just be a really great bounce rate!

Finding opportunities to highlight key content

You want visitors to notice your best content. Looking at your most viewed content in Google Analytics can help you undercover ways to bring that content to a new audience. To see the most viewed content on your blog, follow these instructions:

1. **Visit your Google Analytics dashboard (**`https://www.google.com/analytics/web`**) and log in.**

   If you have more than one blog, select the blog you want to look at.

2. **From the left-side menu, choose Content⟳Overview.**

   This brings up data on all individual blog posts and pages, sorted by highest number of page views.

3. **On the bottom right of the screen, select View Full Report.**

   You see your top ten pages and each page's page views, average time on page, bounce rate, new visitors, and more. See Figure 5-5.

	Page	Pageviews ↓	Unique Pageviews	Avg. Time on Page	Entrances	Bounce Rate	% Exit	Page Value
1.	/2011/09/how-to-block-a-facebook-page-from-posting-on-your-facebook-page/	8,063	4,163	00:00:16	4,159	15.20%	50.66%	$0.00
2.	/	5,431	2,297	00:00:50	1,710	2.22%	27.38%	$0.00
3.	/2012/11/how-to-rock-pinterest-like-a-pro/	4,335	2,245	00:04:04	2,182	26.49%	47.52%	$0.00
4.	/2012/02/pinterest-search-why-it-sucks-and-how-you-can-improve-it/	4,236	1,944	00:00:34	1,901	8.05%	42.04%	$0.00
5.	/blog-designers/	3,986	1,445	00:02:08	1,267	2.76%	31.01%	$0.00
6.	/2012/11/ways-bloggers-can-use-pinterest-secret-boards/	3,126	1,714	00:01:02	1,590	27.36%	48.02%	$0.00
7.	/2012/10/what-pr-friendly-means-to-pr-people/	2,744	1,363	00:02:28	1,215	21.32%	42.20%	$0.00
8.	/2012/04/highlight-facebook-post/	2,452	1,227	00:00:11	1,221	5.90%	49.14%	$0.00
9.	/2011/05/how-many-page-views-do-small-medium-and-big-blogs-get/	2,366	1,170	00:00:26	1,153	7.55%	45.69%	$0.00
10.	/2012/02/how-to-see-if-your-content-is-pinned-on-pinterest/	2,093	972	00:00:25	959	3.44%	44.77%	$0.00

Figure 5-5: Top content sorted by highest number of page views.

After you're able to dig in and see what content is the most and least popular, you might find that you can do the following in your blog design:

- **Highlight new visitor opportunities.** If certain pages get a high percentage of new visitors, make sure those visitors come back. You could create a custom welcome message on these pages that directs them to a Start Here page, to a newsletter subscription page, or to follow you on Twitter.

- **Showcase great but overlooked content.** As you look through this report, you may start to see that some of your great content isn't getting as many page views as you'd like. If this content really shouldn't be missed, you may decide to highlight it on your sidebar. You might also want to check that you properly categorized the post so readers can navigate to it more easily.

- **Build new targeted pages.** As you look through your top content, you may consider designing a new blog page that not only highlights a top post but also gives you an opportunity to showcase other similar posts.

Perhaps you ran a blog post series around a certain topic. You could create a page that highlights the entire series.

Or perhaps one of your top posts is part of a category that you want to highlight on your blog. You can create a page highlighting some posts from that category and add a link to see the rest of the posts in that category. You could even create a blog page like Reader Favorites or Best of the Year that highlight unrelated, yet popular, posts.

After you create a targeted page like one of these, you can build that page into your navigation menu design or add a graphic in your sidebar that directs people to the page.

I once ran a series on my blog about blogger business cards. Two of the posts had great traffic, but the other three did not. I created a new page that incorporated all five posts and linked to each separate post. To draw attention to this page, I created a banner on my sidebar, as shown in Figure 5-6.

the guide to blogger
BUSINESS CARDS

Figure 5-6: Banner in my sidebar.

Looking at referral traffic

Referral traffic is the traffic you receive that comes from sites other than search engines. You might receive traffic from social media sites like Facebook, Twitter, or StumbleUpon (www.stumbleupon.com). Or you might receive traffic from other blogs or websites that link to you.

By looking at the places where your traffic comes from (and doesn't come from), you can make navigation design decisions that help meet your goals. To take a peek at your referral traffic, follow these steps:

1. **Visit your Google Analytics dashboard (**https://www.google.com/analytics/web**) and log in.**

   If you have more than one blog, select the blog you want to look at.

2. **From the left-side menu, choose Traffic Sources⇨Sources⇨Referrals.**

   This brings up the top ten sites that bring traffic to you, as shown in Figure 5-7. At the bottom of the page, open the Show Rows drop-down menu and choose 50 to get a more complete picture.

3. **Go one level deeper by clicking the Performance button (refer to Figure 5-4) and choosing Bounces from the right column drop-down menu.**

   Now you can more easily spot problem areas in your blog's navigation design.

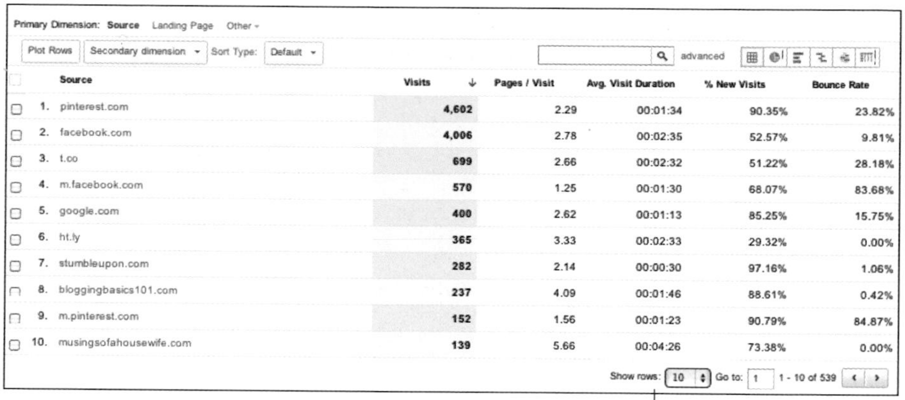

	Source	Visits	Pages / Visit	Avg. Visit Duration	% New Visits	Bounce Rate
1.	pinterest.com	4,602	2.29	00:01:34	90.35%	23.82%
2.	facebook.com	4,006	2.78	00:02:35	52.57%	9.81%
3.	t.co	699	2.66	00:02:32	51.22%	28.18%
4.	m.facebook.com	570	1.25	00:01:30	68.07%	83.68%
5.	google.com	400	2.62	00:01:13	85.25%	15.75%
6.	ht.ly	365	3.33	00:02:33	29.32%	0.00%
7.	stumbleupon.com	282	2.14	00:00:30	97.16%	1.06%
8.	bloggingbasics101.com	237	4.09	00:01:46	88.61%	0.42%
9.	m.pinterest.com	152	1.56	00:01:23	90.79%	84.87%
10.	musingsofahousewife.com	139	5.66	00:04:26	73.38%	0.00%

Show Rows drop-down menu

Figure 5-7: Referral traffic for this blog shows that Pinterest and Facebook dominate.

You can glean so much from this information! Here are some helpful things you can learn from your data:

- **Top social media sites for referral traffic:** For whichever sites bring you the most traffic, make sure you have those corresponding social media sharing buttons in a visible spot on your blog. (That is, the buttons that allow readers to share a blog post or page on a social media network.) You may even decide to add a widget to your sidebar or footer that showcases your content on one of those platforms (like how a Facebook widget allows visitors to Like your page without having to go to your actual business page).

  My analytics (see Figure 5-7) show that Pinterest generates some of the best traffic for my blog, so I might decide to a create special page that features my most pinnable blog posts. The page would enable visitors to pin my content to their Pinterest boards easily.

- **Areas to encourage navigation deeper into your site:** If you click any of the referral sites, you can often glean even more information. For example, view the most popular posts that attracted Twitter users to your site. Or see which pins from Pinterest brought you the most traffic. Although not all the referral data is that helpful, you can use this information to determine whether you should add custom messages to posts or add more links to other relevant posts.

- **Opportunities to grow your social media network:** If certain pages attract a high percentage of new visitors, they likely came from someone else sharing a blog post of yours. If these visitors are new to your blog, they probably aren't followers or fans . . . yet. You could add an additional message to these pages to capture them as new followers.

TIP

If you're trying to increase your presence on a social media platform but your efforts aren't generating much traffic yet, look at your blog design to see ways you can incorporate that platform more (sharing buttons, widgets, and so on).

Studying In-Page Analytics to see how users navigate

One of the coolest features of Google Analytics is the In-Page Analytics. This feature lays data over your actual blog design to give you a nice visual representation of where people click within your site.

To take a look at the In-Page Analytics, follow these steps:

1. **Visit your Google Analytics dashboard (**`https://www.google.com/analytics/web`**) and log in.**

   If you have more than one blog, select the blog you want to see.

2. **From the left-side menu, choose Content⇨In-Page Analytics.**

   This is where the magic happens! Your home page appears, as shown in Figure 5-8. The default view overlays your home page with bubbles containing percentages that note what percentage of visitors clicked on each element. Scroll down the page to see the clicks for your entire page.

Figure 5-8: In-Page Analytics overlays onto your blog.

3. **To see how many clicks a certain design element received, move your mouse over the bubble.**

   This shows you the actual number of clicks as well as the destination link.

4. **(Optional) Click the Show Color button to see the data represented in colors.**

   Unless you deselect Show Bubbles, you'll see both the percentages and the colors.

By looking at the In-Page Analytics, you see what's relevant to your current blog visitors and can look for missed opportunities. In-Page Analytics highlights opportunities to do the following:

✔ **Tweak your navigation menu.** Do you wish visitors were clicking certain tabs in your navigation menu more often? Perhaps a new page name or rearranging the order of your tabs would encourage more visitors to click the tab. If you have drop-down menus for some tabs, perhaps one of those pages should be featured more prominently in the navigation menu.

✔ **Rearrange elements in your layout.** Look at the items receiving the most and fewest clicks. Does that fit with what you were hoping? For example, if a button to your e-book receives fewer clicks than a less important button, you might decide to move your e-book button to another section of your sidebar. You may even decide the e-book button doesn't stand out enough, leading you to entirely redesign the button.

✔ **Highlight low-traffic but important pages.** If key pages aren't attracting the number of visitors that you hoped for, look for opportunities within the rest of your site to drive traffic to these key pages. For example, if you offer consulting services but your Services page doesn't receive many clicks, you might decide to add a button on your sidebar or link to the page from your About page.

Don't just stop at your home page! Your blog is completely clickable within In-Page Analytics. Click any element on your home page to visit that page on your blog to find similar opportunities for improving your design and navigation.

Deciding Who Designs Your Blog

By cracking open this book, you obviously have a little bit of the do-it-yourself spirit. When it comes to designing your blog, you may find that you can do lots of things yourself, like adding a plug-in to WordPress or a widget to Blogger. But when it comes to putting together a comprehensive blog design, do you want to take on a little, a lot, or nothing at all?

Luckily, there's more than one way to design your blog. In this section, I cover benefits and challenges for each option so you can make a choice that suits your needs.

Hiring a designer

If you don't have the time or inclination to design a blog yourself, hire someone to do the work for you! Hiring a designer costs money, but you can often find a designer whose rates are within your budget and who fits your style. Having a blog professionally designed can cost anywhere from a few hundred dollars to $5,000 or more. The range in cost is sort of like pricing a vacation. When you plan a vacation, your costs will depend on where you want to go, where you stay, and how much you want to do. Blog design can also range in price, depending on which blog platform you want, the designer's experience, and how comprehensive of a design you want.

Hiring a designer or design firm to create your blog designs has both its benefits and challenges.

Benefits of working with a blog designer

When you work with a blog designer, you

✓ **Get exactly what you want.** When you work with a good designer, you don't have to settle for blog design that's limited because you don't know how to do something technical. You get what you want without needing the knowledge to accomplish it.

✓ **Exercise creative power.** Good designers can translate your blog vision and your passions into a blog design that's just for you. They can also help you weed out the blog elements you don't really need or suggest creative ways to solve your design or layout challenges. For example, Catherine Horgan from Closet of Style (www.closetofstyle.com) loves layers. She loves to layer clothes and mood boards as well. After a design discovery meeting with designer Laurie Smithwick of LEAP Design, she ended up with a site that matches her passions, as shown in Figure 5-9.

✓ **Receive support.** A designer can also handle the really technical stuff, like making sure your blog looks the same in Internet Explorer as it does in Google Chrome. Plus, after your blog design is installed, a designer works with you to iron out any kinks or technical issues with your new design. If you need help troubleshooting or help with blog maintenance, many designers offer blog maintenance packages or charge by the hour. You always have someone to help you out of a bind.

© Mood board by Laurie Smithwick, LEAP Design, Closet of Style image
© Closet of Style, www.closetofstyle.com

Figure 5-9: Turning mood board inspiration into a blog design

Challenges of working with a blog designer

And here are the challenges:

✏ **Cost:** Yes, you have to fork over some dough to have someone design a custom blog for you. Although many designers offer special design packages, you may end up having to add on extra design elements to fit your needs.

Some designers offer premade designs, which are typically sold with just minimal change options, such as customizing the design with your blog name or choosing which social media buttons to include. Although you run a risk that others in your niche will have the same design, you can get a professional design for a lower cost.

- **Dependence on designer:** If you hire someone else to design your site, you won't learn as much about how to use your blog as you would designing it yourself.

- **Designer mismatch:** Perhaps the designer's style doesn't match yours, or the designer just isn't pleasant to work with. Depending on your contract, you may need to pay more creative fees for additional design options. See the sidebar "Questions to ask a blog designer" for some tips on selecting the right designer.

Questions to ask a blog designer

Not all designers are created equal. I asked Laurie Smithwick, founder of LEAP Design and co-founder of Kirtsy, to share a few questions to ask a blog designer or agency to ensure you hire someone right for you.

1. May I see some samples of your work?

You should never hire anyone whose work you haven't seen or whose work you don't love. Some designers will have an online portfolio, and others may send you a list of links. Either way is fine as long as there is enough work shown for you to develop a good sense of the designer's style and decide whether you like it. (Assume that the job the designer does for you will look very much like his or her previous work.) A designer's portfolio will also give you a sense of how long he or she has been in business. You don't want to be someone's first or second job — look for someone who's been designing websites for several years.

2. Will you provide me with references? Or, may I call some of your clients for a reference?

Be sure to speak with a few of the designer's past (or current) clients to see what working with the designer is like. Pay close attention to what these references say. You can assume that the way the designer treated other clients is how you'll be treated. You want to be sure that the designer you hire does everything he or she promises to do and follows the timeline you both agreed to. Ask references about the designer's attitude toward clients: Is it respectful and inclusive, or disparaging and defensive?

3. What content management system(s) do you use?

A content management system (CMS) helps an administrator (ideally, you) update and manage your site without having to write any code. This means you can easily make changes, or add images, pages, or posts to your site using a simple WYSIWYG dashboard. WordPress, Drupal, and Joomla! are three of the most commonly used CMSes. Do not hire a designer that wants you to use their custom-made CMS because you'll get locked into working exclusively with that designer. If you use a more mainstream CMS, you'll never have trouble finding someone who can work with what you already have — even if you stop working with the designer who built your site.

4. Who will own the images, content, and code when the job is done?

Ideally, you should seek to hire a designer who will design your site and deliver it to you as a complete package when the job is done. Stay away from designers and firms who want to lock you into an ongoing hosting account with them. You should own your domain name as well as your hosting account. You should also have access to the hosting account, the server, and the CMS administration. If you don't understand what any of these things mean, do a quick bit of research to develop a basic knowledge. Don't hire any designer who tells you that they own your code — you're *buying* a website design, not renting it.

5. How do you price your services?

Web design prices can vary wildly, depending on the size of your site, the amount of time involved in designing and building it, the level of experience of the designer or design firm, and other factors. Some designers may offer a flat rate, while others may price on more of an *à la carte* basis. Some bill by the project, and others charge by the hour. Make sure you know all the details of your designer's pricing structure so there are no surprises when it's time to pay the bill.

6. Can you develop a version of my site for mobile devices? Or, alternatively, will you be using a responsive design?

Mobile versions of sites are becoming *de rigueur* now because so many people access the web through their phones and tablets. Ask your designer whether a mobile site is part of the basic design package or costs extra. Alternatively, ask whether your designer is using *responsive design* — that your site automatically adjusts in size from a large monitor down to a standard phone screen.

7. What kind of tech support do you offer, and for how long?

Your designer should be willing to fix any coding or layout issues discovered within the first month or so without charge. (This does *not* include changes or additions to the original scope.) Find out what they offer in terms of maintenance and web development for the long term, after that initial grace period has ended. You want to know how to price these additional services, and also what turnaround time will be for individual maintenance requests. Ideally, you don't want to have to wait longer than two days for fixes.

Purchasing a predesigned theme or template

If you don't want to hire someone to design your blog but don't quite want to do it yourself either, a predesigned template might be the perfect middle road because you don't have to know a lot about the technical side of blog design. Predesigned templates widely vary from great designs to not-so-great ones. With the knowledge you can glean from this book, you can likely create a blog design that you're happy with.

Of course, purchasing a predesigned theme or template has both benefits and challenges.

When you opt for a predesigned theme or template, you benefit from the following:

✔ **Fast set-up:** With predesigned templates, you can get your new blog design up and running faster than having someone else do it for you (or doing it all yourself). The base design is already complete, ready for you to customize it.

✔ **Customization capabilities:** Just about every predesigned template allows you to tweak design elements, such as color, layout, and fonts. In Figure 5-10, the WordPress predesigned blog template from Templatic (`http://templatic.com`) is for someone who wants to highlight an e-book and blog about their topic. To make changes to the design and content, you simply add images and make content changes within your theme. In Figure 5-11, you can see that simply modifying this text will change the first feature box to your content.

✔ **Inexpensive yet still professional look and feel:** A predesigned theme or template still gives you a blog design that looks professional but at a lower cost (because it isn't customized by someone just for you).

Figure 5-10: Perhaps start with a predesigned template for WordPress.

The downsides of a predesigned theme or template include the following:

✔ **Not as unique:** Although you can indeed customize a predesigned template to an extent, your blog design won't be as unique as one that's made by you or a designer. Ensure upfront that you can tweak the design enough so that your blog won't look generic.

✔ **Limitations in customization:** Many templates do offer some flexibility in design, but you may be stuck with the general layout or the location of a certain design element. Some templates are more customizable than others, though, so check the features for the template before purchasing it.

Designing it yourself

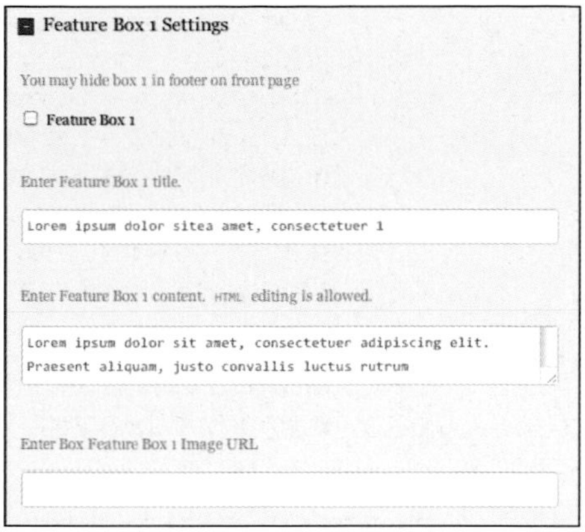

If you have a passion for learning new things and don't mind experimenting, try designing your blog yourself. Of course, your reasoning could be less adventurous — say, you might just not have the funds right now to pay someone else to design your blog. Regardless the reason, designing your own blog can be rewarding!

When you get stuck, my best tip is to research your way to the answer. You're definitely not the only one who's ever designed their own blog. The Internet is full of tutorials,

Figure 5-11: Use template customization options.

forums, and videos that can teach you how to do something. Between this book and the Internet, you could teach yourself many, many things about design. Bloggers who design their own blogs themselves typically work on blog frameworks like Genesis (which I go over in Chapter 7) or add customization to predesigned templates that offer a lot of flexibility.

Digging into designing your blog has some benefits and challenges.

Benefits of designing your own blog

Here's the good news if you go on your own:

- ✔ **Lower cost:** Creating your own blog design is budget friendly. You might spend some money on imagery, a special plug-in, or a theme to serve as the shell of your design, but those outlays are far less than what you'd pay to hire someone.

- ✔ **New skills:** Design programs, HTML, and CSS may be unfamiliar to you when you start, but as you work through your design, you learn new skills that allow you to make your own changes to your blog whenever you want. Blogger Laura Tremaine rolled up her sleeves to design her own blog, Hollywood Housewife (http://www.hollywoodhousewife.com), as shown in Figure 5-12.

- ✔ **Fits your style:** No one has a better sense of your tastes than you! You don't have to worry about finding the perfect premade theme or working with a designer who can't quite nail the look and feel you're after.

Figure 5-12: Blogger Laura Tremaine's DIY blog design.

Challenges of designing your own blog

On the other hand:

- **Takes time to learn:** Heading into unknown territory can be exciting, but you'll undoubtedly spend many, many hours designing your own blog. Something that takes a professional designer two minutes to complete may take you longer if you have to learn how to do it.

- **Lack of technical assistance:** Certain coding mistakes can cause other areas of your sites to not work — or worse, can crash your blog. In addition, small tweaks to your site can be time consuming.

- **May not get exactly what you want:** You may have a cool idea for your design but not know how to create it. While searching online for a tutorial can often work, you may find certain ideas just go beyond your current abilities.

If you design your own blog but get stuck with something, you can always hire someone just to create a single design element.

6

Selecting Fonts and Colors

*B*right shades, moody tones, punchy fonts — when it comes to designing your blog, selecting fonts and colors often becomes the most fun part of design. Different fonts have different personalities, and each shade of color can imply different things. This chapter guides you through making the best choices of fonts and color for your blog design.

If you already have a blog, you can read this chapter from the perspective of deciding whether to change your existing colors and fonts. If you're starting a new blog or completely redesigning your blog, this chapter can help you select colors and fonts that match your personality and blog content.

Colors and fonts communicate a lot about your blog's brand and make an impression on your readers, so you have to get these right.

So keep reading to see how to find the perfect fonts for your blog and select ones that don't clash. I also give you a crash course on the color wheel, what colors mean, and how to effectively use color throughout your blog design.

Choosing Fonts

Ah, fonts. They're swirly, scripty, scribbly, and full of personality. The fonts you use talk for you, becoming an extension of your brand and setting the tone for your words.

When you look at your overall blog design, you work with two different kinds of text:

- ✔ **Content text:** You can identify this text on a blog because it can be highlighted with your cursor. Think blog post titles, headings, and content as well as text in your navigation menu and elements such as bylines and blog post comments. You control the fonts for this text within your cascading style sheet (CSS), which I talk about in more detail in Chapter 9.

- ✔ **Graphical text:** This kind of text is a part of an image, such as a blog logo image, header, or other graphical element created in a photo-editing or graphics program (like Adobe Photoshop or Illustrator).

In these next few sections, I walk you through things to consider when selecting fonts for your blog design. Before we get to the details, though, you should understand the four common types of fonts, which I describe in Table 6-1.

Table 6-1	Common Font Types	
Font Type	*Definition*	*Typical Use*
Serif	Has lines or hooks (serifs) extending from parts of a letter.	Commonly used in print publications. Some serif fonts can be harder to read on-screen but can still be used effectively.
Sans serif	No lines or hooks.	Web content, especially paragraphs of text, is most readable in a sans serif font.
Decorative	Includes script, handwritten, or novelty type fonts.	Good option for graphical text within a blog design. Not a good choice for blog post content.
Monospace	All letters and numbers take up the same width (like typewriter keys being the same size).	Best for displaying computer programming code or to replicate typewritten text.

In Figure 6-1, you can see examples of these four font types. Check out the differences between serif and sans serif for the capital T or a lowercase *i*.

This is a serif font.

This is a sans serif font.

This is a decorative font.

`This is a monospace font.`

Figure 6-1: Examples of the four main types of fonts.

Exploring what fonts say about your blog

Just like people, every font has its own personality. Some fonts are serious, some are whimsical, and some just scream boldness. The ones you choose for your blog design should mirror your blog's own voice and personality. Allow your font to help set the mood for your blog's content. You have so many fonts to choose from that deciding which ones fit your blog design is no easy feat.

Just because you like a font doesn't mean it's the right font for your blog design. Text on your blog — say, your blog name or a sidebar heading — makes different impressions on your reader, depending on the font you use. For example, a travel blog that uses a more conservative font may appear to focus on upscale vacations — or, conversely, could use a casual, handwritten font to appear to be more about family-friendly travels.

When selecting a font, consider the topics you write about and the voice and tone in your writing. Say you blog about social media. Well, that alone doesn't help you when selecting a font. What voice do you write in? What angle do you take? Nuances like these can help you better choose a complementary font.

Or, say you blog about a serious topic with a serious tone. In that case, you don't want to choose a whimsical, swirly font. However, if your topic is a serious one but you take a different approach — such as an inspirational journey through a battle with illness — then perhaps a swirly font fits.

In Figure 6-2, check out the font choices of The Art of Manliness (`http://artofmanliness.com`) blog. The font choices have an old-timey, vintage feel that harkens back to a time long before computers. A modern font wouldn't have fit with the tagline (*Reviving the lost art of manliness*) or tone of this blog. (For more on taglines, see Chapter 8.)

© artofmanliness.com

Figure 6-2: The fonts used in this header tell you about the blog's personality.

If you're having a hard time figuring out which fonts fit your blog (or even if you just want more possibilities), try this: Write down some words that describe your blog as a whole. Then look at the font style categories on any of the font providers I discuss in the upcoming section, "Finding fonts," and match one of your words with one of the font style categories.

Also, look at all the characters and letters of a potential font. For example, if your blog name has an ampersand character (&), make sure you like that font's ampersand before you choose it. On my blog Adventuroo, I fell in love with the font Cocktail Shaker. I really love the font's lowercase letters but don't care for the uppercase, so I decided to use the font only in lowercase in my blog design.

Choosing web-safe fonts

When you flip through a magazine, those fonts have essentially become images printed onto a page. And on the web, text within graphical elements (like a logo) work the same way.

However, content text (which I define earlier under the section "Choosing Fonts") is different. Online, from one computer to the next, content text — blog post titles and paragraphs within your blog posts, for example — can display differently.

How's that again? Fonts don't necessarily look the same on all computers? What's with that? The reason is that my computer might not have the same fonts installed that your computer has. If you purchase and install a font that I don't have and then use that font in your blog design, your blog font may look great on your computer but be replaced with a monospace font on mine.

All computers come with a small selection of *web-safe fonts,* and these fonts are safe to use for your content text. If you don't want to explore font embedding (which I explain in a moment), then sticking with common web-safe fonts such as the following ones can ensure your blog looks consistent across computers and other devices:

- ✓ Arial
- ✓ Courier
- ✓ Georgia
- ✓ Times New Roman
- ✓ Trebuchet MS
- ✓ Verdana

Expanding your options with embedded fonts

At one point, live text was limited to using web-safe fonts. Luckily, you now have many more interesting choices regarding fonts, thanks to font-embedding technology, which enables you to embed a font into your blog's web pages. With an embedded font, visitors see the font you selected for your design, even if that font isn't web-safe.

So what's the catch? Embedded fonts can slow the download of your blog in a visitor's browser. Also, for embedded fonts to work, your visitors' web browsers must support font-embedding.

When it comes to fonts, a browser knows what font to display by the font name listed in your CSS (Cascading Style Sheet). With a web-safe font (Figure 6-3), a browser displays the font correctly by pulling that font's information from a computer's operating system. With an embedded font, a browser displays the font correctly because that website's CSS defines where a browser can find the font files it needs to display (since the font isn't on the website visitor's computer).

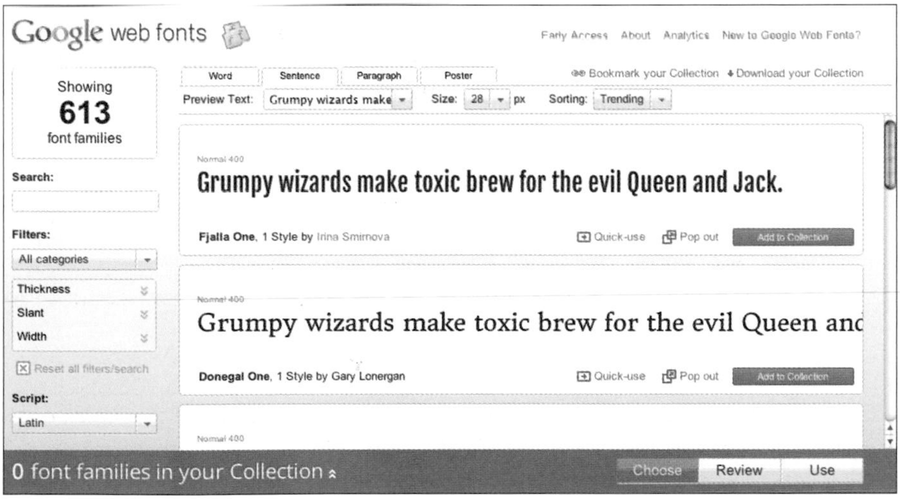

Figure 6-3: Web-safe fonts in Google.

Services like Adobe Typekit (`https://typekit.com`) and Google Web Fonts (`www.google.com/webfonts`) host the fonts for you. When someone visits your blog, your CSS knows to display an embedded font by pulling the font files from another location besides your computer.

To use embedded fonts with one of these services, they provide you with the code you need to make a font display on your blog. Nice! From there, you need to be able to add the code they provide to your blog's HTML document, usually in a file called `header.php` on WordPress or by editing your template file in Blogger. You also need to be able to alter your CSS in order to change from your current fonts to the names of the fonts you want to embed. I cover modifying CSS to change your fonts in Chapter 9.

A more advanced way to use embedded fonts is to use the `@font-face` property within your CSS. To do this, you need to be familiar enough with coding to either code it manually or use a service like FontSquirrel, which helps you generate the code and files needed to use the `@font-face` property. The font files can either be hosted on your own server or with a font service like FontSquirrel. For more about `@font-face`, start with this article about embedding fonts at Dummies.com: `www.dummies.com/how-to/content/enhance-your-site-with-custom-fonts.html`

Knowing which fonts to avoid

Just like anything creative, telling you which fonts to avoid is mainly a matter of opinion. After all, someone out there uses those fonts for a reason. So instead of telling you, "This font is bad, and that font is ugly," I want to share some reasons why you should avoid certain fonts or types of fonts:

⮑ **To begin, avoid opting for an overused font.** Comic Sans, Papyrus, and Brush Script are three culprits (and some of the most loathed fonts out there, too); see Figure 6-4. These fonts scream, "Amateur!" and do little to set your blog design apart from other blogs in your niche. I consider these the three fonts to avoid at all costs!

Comic Sans

Papyrus

Brush Script

Figure 6-4: Avoid using these fonts.

⮑ **Be wary of using fonts that are illegible.** Sure, that may sound funny — after all, you'd think that a font's purpose is to be easily readable. However, some fonts have so many flourishes or so much of a distortion effect that certain words become hard to read.

Finding fonts

With so many places on the web to find fonts, it can be hard to find the best sites. In addition to Google Web Fonts (`www.google.com/webfonts`), the following lists point you to some of my favorite places to look for fonts, free or for-fee.

As you go on your font-finding quest, you need to be familiar with font licenses. Font licenses dictate how you can and can't use a particular font. You'll commonly see fonts listed as personal use, commercial use, or both. Generally speaking, here's what these terms mean:

- *Personal use* refers to usage that isn't meant to make a profit, such as using a font on a personal blog (that doesn't generate income) or using a font to create an invitation for your child's birthday party.

- *Commercial use* refers to usage where a company or individual may profit either directly or indirectly from the font's usage. For example, a person who designs blogs for a living directly profits from a font that they use within a blog design they sell to a client. As an indirect example, because I earn money on my blog through advertising, online courses, and e-books, I am indirectly profiting from a font's usage on my blog. Therefore, I need a font with a commercial license.

While I provided a general overview in font licensing, each font website varies in how it categorizes fonts for use. Always read the font license before you download or purchase a font.

Free fonts

The following are my favorite resources that offer free fonts:

- **dafont.com:** (`www.dafont.com`) dafont is definitely one of the most popular free sites for fonts. At the top of the dafont home page, you can find many categories and subcategories of fonts to choose from — more than 18,000 fonts available for download as of this writing.

- **FontSpace:** (`www.fontspace.com`) Browse examples of the most popular fonts, new fonts, and new designers. Fonts are clearly marked for personal or commercial use, or both.

- **1001 Fonts:** (`www.1001fonts.com`) This website offers more than 3,500 fonts in a variety of categories.

- **Font Squirrel:** (`www.fontsquirrel.com`) All Font Squirrel fonts are free for commercial use, and Font Squirrel offers some of the best quality free fonts available. As you can see in Figure 6-5, the site is clean and easy to navigate.

Figure 6-5: Font Squirrel can help you turn any font into a web-safe font.

For-fee fonts

With so many free fonts available, you may wonder why you should ever pony up money for a font. Although you can't deny the attractiveness of "free," and although the web is full of places to get free fonts, here are some benefits to paying for a font that you really like:

- ✔ **Originality:** Many bloggers never pay for a font. So, purchasing a modestly priced font means that fewer designers will likely have it, and fewer readers will likely have seen it. That raises your professional and cool factors.

- ✔ **Full character set:** Free fonts come with all letters of the alphabet and all numbers, but don't always have additional characters you might need (such as accented letters) or punctuation (such as quotation marks). Check the character set in the font's profile before downloading or purchasing.

- ✔ **Well-kerned characters:** Without proper *kerning* (spacing between characters), some letters might look too far from another, like a capital W beside a capital A, or run together, such as "rn" looking like an *m*. Fonts that you purchase often have better kerning than a free font.

If you'd like to check out fonts available for a fee, I suggest you start your search at the following websites:

✔ **Typekit:** (`https://typekit.com`) Using one font can be free. Typekit, by Adobe, is a popular way to use great-looking web-safe fonts in your blog design.

✔ **Fontspring:** (`www.fontspring.com`) Fontspring makes it easy to find high-quality fonts, some of which are free. This site is a great resource if you're looking for fonts to use in both graphic text and content text on your blog.

✔ **MyFonts:** (`www.myfonts.com`) This site offers more than 100,000 fonts to choose from (not that you'd look at that many). MyFonts is also the home of the fun and helpful WhatTheFont, where you can upload an image or enter a URL, and the site tries to find the closest match in its database.

✔ **Fonts.com:** (`www.fonts.com`) Fonts.com has more than 150,000 fonts, which covers just about everything you can think of. The site highlights best-selling fonts and also offers a list of the top 100 fonts. Fonts.com also has a font-identifying tool that walks you through a series of questions when you need to find the name of a font.

✔ **Veer:** (`www.veer.com`) Veer offers a wide variety of fonts (and images too). Just be aware that the licenses for these fonts covers only graphical text, not content text.

At many of these sites, you can test how a font looks with your own words. In Figure 6-6, I'm testing how a blog name looks in a particular font with a particular color.

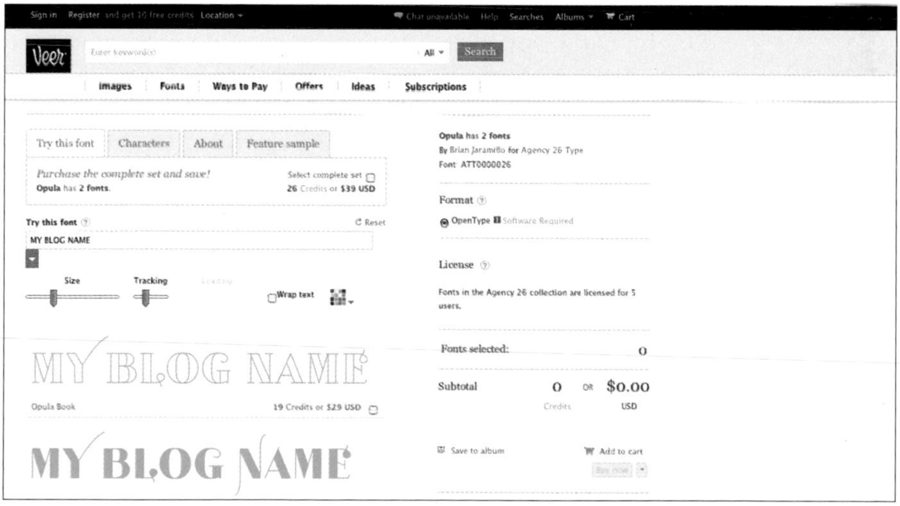

Figure 6-6: Test a font with your own words and custom color.

Of course, you can also find many high-quality, professionally designed fonts at the free sites I mention in this chapter, Google Web Fonts or Font Squirrel.

Some fonts can give you sticker shock because sites often show font packages, which include entire font families. A *font family* comprises various styles and weights, such as italics, condensed, bold, and semi-bold. If there's a font within a font family that you really like, you can often purchase a specific font versus the entire family to keep the cost lower.

Combining complementary fonts

A widely accepted design principle says that you shouldn't use more than three fonts on a layout such as a blog design. Anything more makes a design look messy and hinders concentration. If you've ever received a flyer or newsletter with seven or eight completely different fonts, you probably found the lack of unity in the design made it hard to distinguish what parts were most important. And it was probably just hard to read in general!

But as you may have already discovered, simply combining any two or three fonts doesn't always work because they can clash, look too similar, or just look "off." Other times, two fonts look great together, and you can't place just why.

An understanding of how fonts contrast and complement each other can help dispel some of the mystery and guide your font selection. Typically, you can combine fonts by choosing two to three complementary fonts that contrast one another. To start, consider how you can find contrast among your fonts:

✔ **Thickness:** Is your font skinny or fat? Thicker fonts often look nice paired with thinner fonts. Many font families come in different thicknesses, often classified with names such as Light, Medium, Book, Bold, or Heavy. Consider those options, too, when pairing fonts.

If you decide to use a very thin font, be sure to test the font's legibility within your blog design. A thin font for main headings may be overshadowed by using a thicker font as body text. On the flip side, a thin font used for body text may disappear into the background if the font size is too small.

✔ **Style:** Earlier in this chapter, I talk about the four common types of fonts (serif, sans serif, decorative, and monospace). Try combining a serif with a sans serif font, or a scripty font with a typewriter font. Aside from these types of fonts, there are also so many other classifications of fonts, from grunge to retro, handwriting to calligraphic. The ways to provide contrast based on styles are endless. See Figure 6-7 for an example of an all caps font paired with a wider, slimmer font.

MY AWESOME BLOG
A really great tagline right here

Figure 6-7: Try pairing a thicker, all caps font with a wider, slimmer font.

- **Height:** Just as fonts can be thin or thick, they can also be short or tall. Some fonts often appear taller because they are *condensed,* meaning that the kerning is tight, which also provides contrast. Note how the all caps font in Figure 6-7 is taller than the font that's mostly lowercase. Both the font sizes and the all caps versus mostly lowercase provide contrast in this font pairing.

In addition to looking at contrast, you can combine fonts that have something in common. For example, you might choose two fonts with tall letters but that are different styles. Or choose fonts within the same family, like pairing a bold and light version of the same font.

Fonts with too many similarities tend to conflict with one another, so be sure they don't have *too* many things in common. No matter how you decide to combine fonts, the fonts you choose should have complementing personalities.

Aside from looking at a font's style and personality, you can also get technical and look at the following:

- **Letterform:** *Letterform* is essentially a letter's shape. Two fonts with similar letterforms often look good when paired together. Compare the letters *a, g,* and *e* to get the best sense of a font's compatibility. For example, in Figure 6-7, the capital A in both fonts has the same letterform.

- **x-height:** *x-height* refers to the height from the baseline to the upper part of a lowercase character, such as an *x* (see Figure 6-8). Looking at x-height helps you determine fonts of similar proportions. Pairing fonts of similar proportions often look more uniform than fonts with different proportions. Plus, fonts with larger x-heights are typically easier to read so they are good for large blocks of text.

Figure 6-8: The font on the left has a larger x-height than the font on the right.

Assigning roles to fonts

When you assign roles to your fonts, you help keep your blog design looking professional. Keeping your font's purpose clear makes your blog navigation design more effective and your overall design easier on the eyes.

After you choose two or three complementary fonts that also have enough contrast to stand out from each other (see the preceding section), give the different fonts you choose specific roles in your design. To start, establish a visual hierarchy for the fonts. Think about the text elements you have within your blog design, such as the following:

- Blog name
- Tagline
- Navigation menu
- Blog post title
- Subheadings
- Blog post and page content
- Sidebar titles
- Footer headings

Each element should have a consistent look yet appear cohesive when looking at your entire blog design. By giving each text element a specific look, you create a hierarchy that helps the reader scan your page and digest your content. With the two or three fonts you choose for your blog design, you can establish hierarchy in these text elements by using the following:

- **Color:** Color naturally attracts the eye, so colored text elements catch the most attention. For example, using a black blog post title with green text beneath would feel a little off because a reader's eyes might pull to the green text, completely bypassing your post's title.

  Save bolder colors for more important text elements to attract the most attention.

- **Size:** Larger font sizes denote more importance than smaller ones. This means your blog post titles need to be larger than your blog post content. On that same line of thought, subheadings with your blog posts should be smaller than your blog post titles but larger than your blog post content.

- **Weight:** Use weights — for example, light, bold, and italics — to create hierarchy without adding more fonts to your design. More heavily weighted text elements carry more importance than lighter design elements, so keep this in mind, especially when considering your blog post titles and blog post content text.

In the example shown in Figure 6-9, I chose three fonts. Here's how I chose to apply each font in the design and how I created a hierarchy within each font grouping as well:

GRAPHIC TEXT:

Blog Name

Sidebar titles

CONTENT TEXT (EMBEDDED FONT):

Blog post titles   Subheadings
Footer headings   Tagline
Navigation menu

CONTENT TEXT (WEB-SAFE FONT):

blog post and page content

Figure 6-9: Organize the two or three fonts in your design so that similar items are grouped together. Within each group, use size and color to create a hierarchy.

- The graphic text is an unusual font that appears only on a few elements that remain pretty static within a blog's design. (Use graphic text sparingly because search engines can't read it and creating graphic text is more work than content text.) For the blog name, I used both size and color to emphasize the blog name's importance in the design. I chose the same font for sidebar titles, to carry the font into other parts of the design, but the cool color and smaller size of the sidebar title font clarifies its relationship to the blog name.

- For the navigation and blog post titles in particular, I needed a font that could display as content text but wanted the font and color to make these elements stand out in the design. To accomplish this, I used an embedded font and grouped all the heading-type elements together with this font, but created a hierarchy of relative importance among the headings by applying different sizes and colors. This embedded font still complements the graphical text in that they use the same letterform, as illustrated in the lowercase *a*.

- For the blog post and page content font, note that the font selection is much plainer than the blog name and heading fonts so that the main text is easy to read in large bodies of text. This font is also web-safe. With a similar x-height to the other two fonts, this font rounds out the font choices nicely.

 You don't have to use all these formatting and design options. Just consider them as ways to give each text element a specific role within your blog design.

Choosing Colors

Colors matter, but don't take my word for it. According to The Institute for Color Research, between 62 and 90 percent of a person's assessment of an environment is based on color alone. Color can also improve readership by 40 percent. I don't know about you, but those stats got my attention.

So what colors jump to mind when you think about certain brands? How about UPS? Brown, of course. What about Coke? Red. Although you don't have to employ a strong color association, colors can help you define your overall brand.

Colors can also help establish a tone, or mood, with your readers. If your writing style is punchy and humorous, then bright, vivid colors would work better with your blog design than somber colors like industrial gray or a pale blue. See the section "Exploring what colors mean" to learn how different colors evoke certain emotions.

These next sections give you a better understanding of colors and how to combine them on your blog design. I also share a way to determine which colors work best for your blog and then list some inspirational places to find colors galore. To change the color for different elements of your blog design, refer to Chapter 9 where I go over how to accomplish this by modifying your CSS.

Getting to know the color wheel

Ah, our old friend, the *color wheel,* which is simply a circular diagram that shows relationships between colors and serves as a tool to help you understand why certain colors work better together than others. See Figure 6-10.

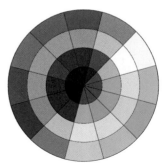

A standard color wheel shows primary, secondary, and tertiary *hues,* which are the purest form of a color:

Figure 6-10: A typical color wheel showing hues, tints, shades, and tones.

- **Primary colors:** You probably already know that red, yellow, and blue make up the three primary colors. All other colors stem from these three biggies. If you're wondering why all the talk about RGB (red, green, blue) and not RYB in image editing and web design, see the next section.

- **Secondary colors:** These colors are combined by mixing primary colors: orange (red+yellow), green (yellow+blue), and purple or violet (red+blue).

- **Tertiary colors:** This third level of colors are created by mixing a primary color with a secondary color: red-orange, red-violet, yellow-orange, yellow-green, blue-violet, and blue-green.

If you were to go a deeper into a color wheel (or play with a color picker online or in an image-editing program), you would see these variations of each hue:

- **Tint:** A hue made lighter by adding white
- **Shade:** A hue made darker by adding black
- **Tone:** A hue mixed with gray

Defining RGB and hex codes

If all colors come from red, yellow, and blue, you might be wondering why we often look at onscreen colors in terms of RGB and hex (short for *hexadecimal*) colors.

RGB is a three-color additive color model used for light-based devices, such as TVs, computer screens, and digital cameras. Pixels on backlit screens are dark until you add various levels of red, green, and blue light, which create an array of colors.

Hexadecimal numbers represent the red, green, and blue values with a six-digit code that begins with a hash (#) symbol. The six-digit code is essentially broken down into three, two-digit values that use a mix of numbers and letters. The lowest value given is 00 (meaning no light), and the highest is FF (meaning the highest amount of light). This makes sense when you think of two common hex codes you might see: #000000 (black) and #ffffff (white).

So, when designing blogs, you use hexadecimal numbers (hex codes) to give certain design elements color values. I talk about changing colors of certain design elements in Chapter 9, but know that you can create more than 16 million colors using hex codes! That means you definitely have lots of choices when it comes to colors for your blog design!

If you visit a website and love the colors, you can find out exactly what colors they are with ColorZilla (www.colorzilla.com), a free browser add-on for Chrome and Firefox.

Creating color harmony

Just as certain fonts go well together, so do certain colors. I'm sure you've seen a color scheme before and said, "Oh, that clashes!" And finding color harmony can be as simple as understanding one tool: the color wheel. After you understand how to create color harmony using the color wheel, creating color schemes for your blog design is much less of a mystery.

Here are the basic schemes created using the color wheel as a tool (as shown in Figure 6-11):

- ✔ **Analogous color scheme:** Uses three or more colors that sit next to each other on the color wheel.

- ✔ **Monochromatic color scheme:** Uses tints, tones, and values within the same family.

- ✔ **Triadic color scheme:** Uses three colors that are evenly spaced around the color wheel.

- ✔ **Square color scheme:** Uses four colors evenly spaced around the color wheel.

- ✔ **Complementary color scheme:** Uses colors opposite of one another on the color wheel.

- ✔ **Split complementary color scheme:** Uses one color paired with two colors on both sides of that color's direct complementary color.

- ✔ **Tetrad (or rectangular) color scheme:** Uses four colors arranged by two complementary pairs.

- ✔ **Diad color scheme:** Uses two colors that are two colors apart on the color wheel, with one color skipped in between.

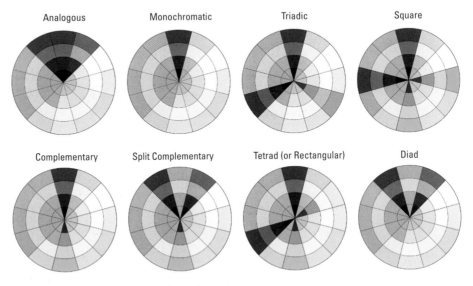

Figure 6-11: Different methods of creating color schemes.

In the everyday world, we may not talk about tetrad or diad color schemes, but most folks can relate to warm and cool colors. Looking at the color wheel again, you can see how the colors are divided into warm and cool (refer to Figure 6-10):

- ✔ **Warm:** Red, orange, yellow, and variations of those colors
- ✔ **Cool:** Green, blue, purple, and variations of those colors

And not to complicate life, but you can also have "cooler" oranges or "warmer" purples. For example, a cool color can have red, orange, or yellow undertones, and a warm color can have green, blue, or purple undertones.

 And here is why color choice matters: Both warm and cool colors can evoke both positive or negative emotions. Warmer colors can evoke a sense of anything from coziness and happiness (sunny yellow) to anger and aggression (blood red). Cooler colors can bring a sense of calmness and relaxation (sky blue) or can feel indifferent or subdued (steel gray).

Finding color inspiration

Colors, colors everywhere! With the color wheel as your foundation and guide, peruse the web for color inspiration. Many places offer colors and color schemes that you can use as-is or let them serve as a jumping point into creating your own color combinations.

- ✔ **Kuler:** (https://kuler.adobe.com) Kuler, shown in Figure 6-12, has long been one of my favorite sites for color combo inspirations. Create your own color swatch or choose one submitted by the community. The site showcases five-swatch color palettes that you can search by keyword, such as "nature" or "bold." You can even download these color palettes and open them up in Adobe programs like Photoshop and Illustrator. It's magical.

- ✔ **COLOURlovers:** (www.colourlovers.com) This community-based site allows users to create and share color palettes from all over the world. Here, you can also find paid color tools (such as ColorSchemer) to build color schemes, or you can design a seamless pattern (for free using Seamless Lite, or the paid version Seamless Studio).

- ✔ **Design Seeds:** (www.design-seeds.com) Jessica from Design Seeds has many years of experience as a color specialist, and it shows. She starts with a photograph and then creates a custom color palette based on the photo (without using an eyedropper tool that merely pulls a color from a photo). Her talent is impressive, and this site is serious eye candy. Each palette includes the hex codes so you can use a palette in your own blog design.

Figure 6-12: At Kuler, explore color swatches or build your own.

✔ **Pantone:** (www.pantone.com) Pantone is the authority on color. Sift through their top colors, the color of the year, and seasonal colors to find some cool ones that fit your blog.

✔ **ColorCombos:** (www.colorcombos.com) The ColorCombos site provides articles on color, color combination palettes, and tools like the Color Tester tool, which lets you play around with color combinations.

You can find color inspiration from everyday things all around you: nature, products or displays in a store, photos, everyday household items, food, paint swatches, and more.

And if you have an iPhone or iPad, give the Palettes app a whirl (http://itunes.apple.com/us/app/palettes). Create color schemes by pulling colors from a website or picture or add colors using one of five color models. Palettes comes in three offerings: Free, Basic, and Pro.

Exploring what colors mean

Colors evoke emotion. Colors have meanings that vary between cultures and even personal preference. Of course, the shade of a color can change the meaning, too. For example, yellow might be cheerful, but a darker yellow might be considered dingy. An olive green can feel earthy, while a forest green can symbolize affluence.

However, speaking in generalities, Table 6-2 gives you a sense of what some basic colors typically mean to Westerners.

Table 6-2	Color Meanings
Color	*Various Meanings*
Red	Passion, love, energy, danger, strength, importance, powerful
Orange	Heat, endurance, vitality, health, inviting
Yellow	Happy, courage, energizing, pleasant, cheerful
Green	Safety, wealth, nature, freshness, calming, renewing
Blue	Loyalty, calming, truth, tranquility, responsibility
White	Innocence, purity, clean, sterile, light
Black	Elegance, power, death, grief, formal, authority
Brown	Earthliness, warm, dependability, wistful, woodsy

When selecting colors for your blog, take a pre-emptive stance and research the color's meaning for any negative connotations that might relate to your topic. For example, if you have a food blog, steer clear of using a lot of blue. Some say that the color blue suppresses the appetite.

Deciding on colors to match your brand

The colors that visitors see when they land on your blog make a psychological impact within seconds. Not only do humans unconsciously attach meaning to certain colors, but visitors will also form instant impressions about your blog based on color.

This association happens so instantly you probably don't realize it — but, colors can make or break your blog design. I'm sure you've been to a blog or website that immediately felt welcoming and cozy. Or perhaps you've been to a website with colors so loud and mismatched that you assumed the blog's content would be horrible.

Colors also convey emotion and visually set the tone for your blog. In fact, your colors should help reinforce what your blog is about. For example, if you blog about a serious subject, you probably don't want to use loud, fluorescent colors. If your writing is hysterically funny, you don't want subdued, muted colors.

In Figure 6-13, notice how the blog Intimate Weddings (www.intimate weddings.com) uses light colors to create an intimate setting. The blog wouldn't give off the same vibe with a turquoise rather than a pale blue, or a bright orange rather than a softer, lighter orange.

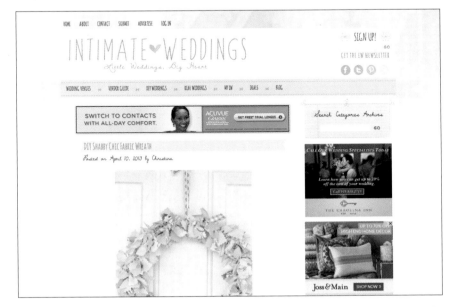

© Layout and design by Christina Friedrichsen and Carolynn Giordano (Two Brunettes); Web programming Example 7

Figure 6-13: The color choices for the Intimate Weddings blog complement the site's content.

Deciding on the exact colors can seem like a fun yet overwhelming process. Start by looking at some of the places that I mention in the earlier section, "Finding color inspiration." If you want to try creating a color scheme yourself, follow these basic steps:

1. **Start with a basic color that inspires you.**

   It's your blog, so you should like the colors, but also consider your audience. If you love hot pink but your blog is geared toward financial advisors, you may want to start with another color that you love.

2. **Jot down the topic you write about and a few words that describe your blog's voice and tone.**

   If you write about many topics, try to think as broadly as possible. See Chapter 3 if you need help defining voice and tone. Bringing these tidbits of information top-of-mind gets those creative juices flowing so you can choose a color that really fits your blog.

3. **Select a more specific color based on Steps 1 and 2 to narrow down your basic color to a hue, tint, shade, or tone that will be the most fitting.**

   Do bright colors fit your blog the best? Are pastels the way to go? Earthy?, rich?, warm?, cool?, and so on. Also remember to consider what certain colors mean.

4. **Finish your blog design's color scheme by adding more colors.**

   See the earlier section, "Creating color harmony" for help with creating colors that look good together.

If you aren't sure which color to start with, try this exercise a few times with a different starting color. You can then have a few color schemes to choose from.

Determining how many colors to use

You don't just need to choose colors for your blog design: You also need to consider how many colors and how much of each color will appear in your design. You really don't have to abide by any set rule for this, but the following guidelines offer a good starting point:

- **Start with three colors.** White and black typically don't count toward your three-color palette. What I'm talking about here are the splashes of color that call attention to different parts of your blog to add visual appeal. Again, three isn't a rule but a nice starting point. Many blogs (including my own) use five or six colors, and some use just one or two.

  If you decide to add colors beyond your initial three, combining them effectively becomes trickier. To use more color while still maintaining coherence among the colors in your design, try using tints, shades, and tones from one color.

- **Apply colors using the 60-30-10 rule to create a harmonious design.** The 60-30-10 rule stems from interior design but is often used by web designers to create a nice balance of color. Typically, the 60-30-10 rule means:

  - A *primary color* covers 60 percent of your design.

  - A *secondary color* covers 30 percent.

  - An *accent color* finishes the remaining 10 percent of your design.

  You don't have to follow the 60-30-10 rule exactly. In fact, many bloggers modify this rule a bit, because their blog's purpose is showcasing photography. (Food bloggers, travel bloggers, and of course photography bloggers all come to mind.) On these blogs, the design is mostly white so that photos stand out and "design" colors don't interfere with how the color photos are perceived. If your blog uses lots of photos or you simply want a white, airy design, you can still maintain the 60-30-10 proportions among the colored elements.

A great example is the blog Oh My Veggies (`http://ohmyveggies.com`), shown in Figure 6-14. Kiersten's blog uses a colorful palette of yellow, green, and orange without detracting from her mouth-watering food photos. The blog design still gives off a vibrant feel without being too heavy with color. Moreover, notice how the blog uses the three colors in different proportions, using mostly yellow, then green, and then just a few splashes of orange.

The upshot: Vary the degree to which you use each color in your design. You don't want all the colors to have equal weight.

Figure 6-14: This blog uses bright colors that don't overtake the food photos.

7

Developing Your Overall Blog Layout

In This Chapter

▶ Exploring a variety of layout types

▶ Choosing a blog theme or framework

▶ Looking at options for laying out your home page's main content

▶ Changing full posts to excerpts

▶ Including advertising that doesn't scare away your readers

*E*very blog starts with a skeleton. In fact, one of the greatest things about using a blog platform is that you don't have to build a site completely from scratch. Whether you're designing your blog for the first time or going through a redesign, creating your overall blog layout is like forming the skeleton that you then flesh out with your design and content.

This chapter walks you through building that skeleton and then some. In this chapter, I talk about blog layout types as well as choosing a theme or framework that becomes the foundation for your blog design. I also discuss options for featuring content on your home page and show you ways to create blog post excerpts. In looking at your blog design as a whole, you need to consider how advertising affects your entire design, so I cover that, too.

Getting Familiar with Common Layout Types

Figuring out how to lay out your blog isn't a cut-and-dried decision. Design is subjective. You might choose a blog design layout based on its functionality or just because you like how the layout looks. Deciding on a layout type makes choosing a blog theme or framework easier because you can immediately narrow down the theme choice (of course, you can change your mind). And although the layout types in this section are by no means a comprehensive list, they do give you a sense of the possibilities for your own blog design.

Two-column right sidebar

Your standard, run-of-the-mill blog design displays your main content on the left side with a sidebar that goes along the right side of your blog. But blogs designed using this layout can be anything but run-of-the-mill. In Figure 7-1, The Nailasaurus uses a two-column layout, drawing attention to the main post with a large photo that you see before you scroll down further into the blog post. The font in the navigation menu also exists in the sidebar, and the clever social media nail icons reinforce what this blog is about. Together, these design elements unify the blog header, sidebar, and main column.

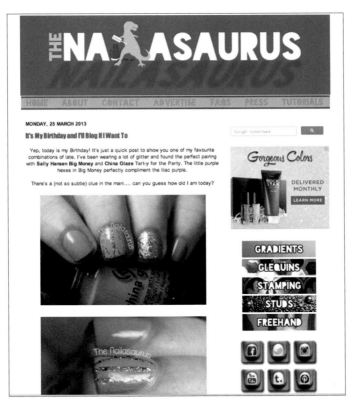

© Samantha Tremlin, www.thenailasaurus.com

Figure 7-1: This blog uses a two-column layout.

Here is why this layout works well for blog design:

✔ **We read from left to right.** Because English and most other languages move from left to right, this layout style makes your most important content (blog posts) the first thing someone sees to read. In fact, a study from the Nielsen Norman Group (www.nngroup.com) concluded that web users spend 69 percent of their time viewing the left side of the page.

✔ **This layout is familiar to blog readers.** Because this layout type is so popular, readers who frequently visit blogs are familiar with where to look for the blog post content and sidebar information.

Of course, using a blog layout that so many others choose can also make your blog harder to stand out in a sea of blogs. In addition, while using only one sidebar usually makes a blog design less cluttered, you have to be more selective as to what content to feature.

Split sections of your single sidebar into two parts if you need more space but don't want to commit to two full sidebars.

Two-column left sidebar

The mirror image of the previous layout, this two-column blog design showcases your main blog content on the right side with a sidebar on the left. Opting for a sidebar on the right is definitely the more common choice in blogland, but using a left sidebar can still make an impact. In Figure 7-2, you see the blog The Two in Love (www.thetwoinlove.com) uses this layout style beautifully. This blog design starts off with a large blog name and photo that pull you down towards the navigation menu and social media buttons.

© Becky Hankla at TheTwoinLove.com, Blog Design by Bri Lamkin at TheSecretLifeofBee.com

Figure 7-2: This layout features main content on the right side, drawing attention with large graphics like this gallery of images.

Because we read left to right, content placed in a left sidebar often takes more prominence than content in a right sidebar. This makes a left sidebar a good place to have advertising or something important you want the reader to know or do. In addition, you want your main column to be especially attractive in order to draw the reader's eye over to read a post. You can achieve this with good imagery and a blog post title style that uses a special font or color.

A blog design that uses a left sidebar does have some disadvantages. First, this layout type can negatively affect search engine optimization (SEO). Search engines scan content from left to right (just like how most humans do) and place more importance at what they scan first. You want search engines to read your main content first rather than something like navigational links or an advertisement.

You can get around the search engine disadvantage by ensuring that the HTML structure of your site places your main content first instead of after the left sidebar content. The good news is that many themes do this for you; otherwise, you have to adjust your CSS to implement this, which may not always be easy to implement. For an introduction to CSS, see Chapter 9.

Three-column right sidebars

Another common blog design layout type features a main column on the left with two sidebars on the right side. The blog grain edit (`http://grainedit.com`), shown in Figure 7-3, uses images to highlight featured posts and a gray box to draw attention to subscription options and social media links.

Many bloggers like having two right sidebars because more key sidebar content can appear toward the top of the page. However, with two sidebars, you can easily get carried away with heavy advertising, buttons, or widgets, making your design look junky and cluttered.

If you'd like the extra sidebar space that two sidebars offers, create a hierarchy to avoid a cluttered design. Some bloggers merge the two columns at the top of the blog layout and separate the columns further down the page. In addition, group similar items within the same column. For example, don't place some social media buttons in one column and a few more in the other. Place all the social media buttons together in the same column.

If you decide to go for a three-column layout with right sidebars, keep your sidebars a reasonable width so they don't make your main column too narrow.

Figure 7-3: This blog keeps the sidebars uncluttered and balanced.

Three-column with split sidebars

This layout also uses two sidebars, but the sidebars appear on either side of your main content area. Symmetrical design can sometimes come off as too static, but it can also provide balance and order to your blog layout. Figure 7-4 shows the blog Olivine's Charm School (`http://olivinecharmschool.com`), which features a beautiful three-column layout with split sidebars.

With sidebar content separated by a main column, one of the best ways to decide what content goes in which sidebar is to place key sidebar content in the left column, where your readers will look first. Olivine's Charm School uses the left sidebar for navigation, instead of displaying the navigation across the top — a great example of keeping a three-column layout looking clean and organized, with important content in the left sidebar.

When working with a layout that splits up your sidebars, avoid making your sidebars so large that your main content feels squeezed in the middle. A narrow column for your main blog content hinders readability.

© Olivine, Design by Freckled Nest

Figure 7-4: This design points you to the left column, which houses the navigation menu.

Magazine style

Magazine-style blog designs have two distinct calling cards: they rely on imagery and serve as a portal to your content.

This layout type often features small teasers of text with images. Sometimes, though, bloggers use only images with very little text. In Figure 7-5, you can see how the Parent Pretty blog (http://parentpretty.com) features a larger image as the star of the page and blog post teasers. After you click an image or blog post title, the full blog post opens.

For blogs that write about highly visual topics like fashion or travel, this layout type can work great. However, magazine styles also work well for bloggers who write about many different topics. Typical blog layouts put the most recent content at the top of the page, but magazine-style layouts give readers to a chance to see blog post excerpts from different categories all at one time. When a reader clicks to read more, they are directed to a full blog post. When done well, this layout style helps readers easily scan a home page to find the topics they're most interested in. The layout then directs readers to individual posts around those topics.

Magazine-style blogs also give bloggers a chance to break away from the typical left-column, right sidebar look on their home page. A magazine style layout can help a blog appear more like a large online publication (similar to a professional magazine) rather than a blog.

So what's are the downsides of magazine-style blog layouts?

© ParentPretty.com, blog design by PurrDesign.com

Figure 7-5: This design focuses on imagery to entice readers to click over from the magazine-style home page.

✒ They can easily become cluttered and overwhelming. To avoid this, consider the hierarchy and organization of your home page content. For example, Dear Crissy's blog includes a post excerpt with a large photo to showcase the most current post. A comparatively large image tells visitors where to look first. Underneath this most recent post, other blog posts are organized by category to help readers navigate to the content that interests them most.

✒ If you feature four topics on your home page yet write about only one of those topics every six months, your home page can look outdated, which looks especially awkward if that post was time sensitive.

✒ This layout asks readers to click to reach your a full blog post, versus having at least one full post on the home page.

Adaptable layouts for different devices

When working on your blog design, you might wonder what layout width your blog design should be. Lucky for you, blog theme developers handle that for you. Most blog themes adjust your blog layout to work with your visitors' screen sizes by using either a fluid or responsive layout.

A *fluid layout* is based on proportions so that blog elements take up the same percentage of space from one screen size to another. In essence, fluid layouts shrink or enlarge a layout design proportionally.

A website with *responsive design* takes fluid layouts a step further by using queries that determine what device type the visitor is using. The website then presents a different layout based on that device. For example, a layout could be three columns on a computer screen but only two columns on a tablet. I cover responsive design a little more in Chapter 10.

Many developers create blog themes that fit the 960 Grid System, This grid system uses 960 pixels as a maximum width with portions of a design divided into 12 or 16 columns. With this grid system, your blog's main content would fit within this width and then your background image or color would fill the sides to fit the width of the visitor's screen resolution. You can learn more about how the grid system works at 960 Grid System (`http://960.gs`).

To see what your design looks like at different resolutions and even on different devices, give Screenfly (`http://quirktools.com/screenfly`) a try.

Selecting a Blog Theme

One of the biggest decisions you make about your blog design is deciding which blog theme to choose. A *blog theme* is a collection of files — such as `functions.php` and `style.css` files — that work together to produce the functionality and design of your blog. Some themes adhere to a certain layout type, and others give you the flexibility to adjust the theme layout to reflect your preferences.

Overall, you choose a theme based on your blogging platform. (Your platform is the service or software that transforms the content you input into the blog format that your visitors see and use online.) Popular platforms range from free services that host your blog for you (such as WordPress.com, Blogger, and Tumblr) to more advanced options such as WordPress.org (which requires web development skills to set up and host yourself). The free options are easier to use but less flexible. The advanced options are more flexible but require web development skills. Regardless of your platform, your blog's theme must work that platform and all the popular blogging platform's offer a variety of themes you can choose from.

These next few sections get you familiar with things to look at when picking out a theme, whether you should invest in a premium theme, and places to find themes.

Considering a theme's flexibility

Not all blog themes are created equal. Some give you more design flexibility than others. Here are some things to consider when selecting a theme for your blog design:

- **Overall design:** Of course, how a blog theme looks should play a role in your decision. Thinking about the things you decide about your blog (see Chapter 3), ask yourself how well the design — before any customizations — fits with your brand.

- **Customization:** Some themes enable you to make a lot of customizations in your design and functionality whereas others don't. When deciding on a theme, understand what design changes (like a color scheme) you can make from the theme's options. Also, pay extra attention to how much you can customize a header because this becomes the first part of your design a visitor sees.

  In Figure 7-6, you can see customization options (color scheme, link color, layout) for the WordPress theme Twenty Eleven, which is quite basic compared with some other themes.

- **Layout options:** In the beginning of this chapter, I share some common layout options. Some themes provide layout options, while others might keep to one style (like solely a magazine layout).

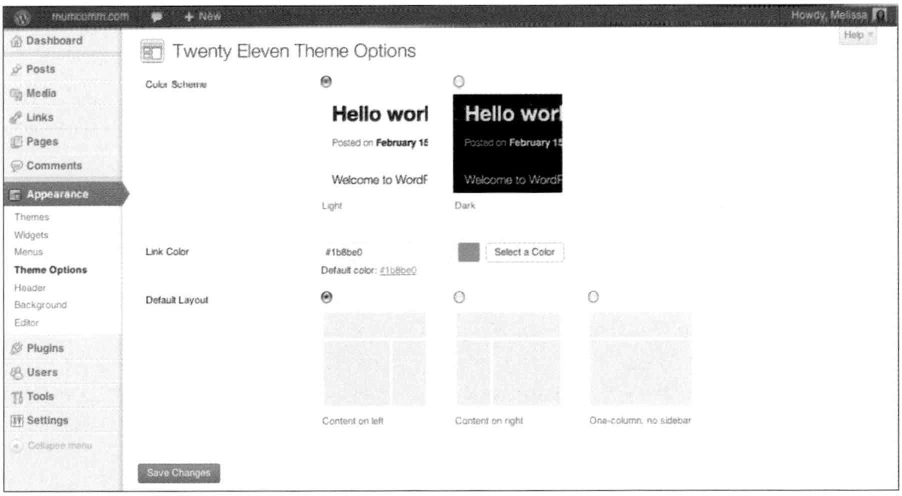

Figure 7-6: Some themes offer minimal choices.

✔ **Widget-ready:** Widgets enable you to easily add content and features to your blog design, such as a category list and search box for readers to search your content. Nearly all themes allow you to use widgets (if a theme doesn't, don't use it), but some also offer custom widgets, like one that shows Recent Posts or an image gallery.

✔ **Page templates:** Some themes include multiple page templates that make it easy for you to create a full-size page with no sidebar or a page that showcases your images in a predesigned gallery.

✔ **Cross-browser tested:** Many themes are tested to ensure they work on all major browsers.

✔ **Search engine optimization:** Some themes are developed to make it easier for search engines to index your site. Also, some themes are built with a structure to ensure that important content precedes less important content so search engines read your blog post content first. I cover search engine optimization more in Chapter 12.

✔ **Date last updated:** Before deciding on a theme, check to see the last time it was updated. Themes should stay current with the latest platform releases.

✔ **Responsive design:** Responsive designs ensures your blog design looks great on all devices, whether someone is viewing your blog on their desktop, a tablet, or a mobile phone. Read more about responsive design in Chapter 10.

If you're unsure about downloading or purchasing a particular theme, try doing an online search for "Theme Name + Review" to see whether anyone has written about their experiences with that theme.

Choosing between a free or premium theme

With blogs being so popular, blog themes have sprung up all over the web. Literally thousands of themes are available that might work for your blog design. Aside from a theme's flexibility, one of the main factors in choosing a blog theme is, of course, the cost.

You can find many, many free and premium themes. Of course, a free theme is, well, free!, and you aren't out any cash if you decide months down the road that you don't like your theme. In addition, if you're just starting out as a blogger and unsure whether blogging is for you in the long run, a free theme is probably the best solution for you.

Premium themes can range in price but offer many advantages:

✔ **More customization options:** Premium themes typically have more ways that you can customize your theme. You can often make changes without doing any coding by using the option panels shown in your dashboard. As I mention in the previous section, some themes include custom widgets and page templates, too, like the Raffinade theme on Themeforest (see Figure 7-7) which costs about $35. The search box is customized to match the design and this theme also.

✔ **Well-coded:** Premium themes are more likely to have cleaner code under the hood of the design. A poorly coded theme can slow down your blog's loading time and make it more difficult to interpret the code if you need to modify it. Sure, a free theme can most definitely be well coded, but developers of premium themes have more at stake because a poor-quality theme can hurt their reputation and affect sales.

Sometimes a poorly coded free theme is a result of inexperience, but occasionally, a free theme has malicious code that can harm your blog. If you stick with the reputable theme sources I discuss in this chapter, you're not likely to run into this problem. If you find a theme by doing a basic Google search, research the provider first to make sure others have worked with this provider for some time and its themes are worthwhile.

Figure 7-7: For a fee, premium themes offer a robust list of features.

✔ **Support:** Nearly all premium themes offer some type of support for implementation or customization issues with a theme. Larger theme developers or framework creators such as Thesis (`http://diythemes.com`) even have robust support forums where you can learn and get support from peers and moderators.

✔ **Security:** Premium themes are more likely to be updated along with the blog platform's updates. Many blog platform updates are to fix security issues or potential issues so a free theme that hasn't been updated can leave your blog vulnerable.

You can definitely find great, high-quality free themes that you'll be happy with. If you consider using a free theme, just stick with reputable sites to ensure the quality.

Finding sources for themes

Finding the perfect theme can sometimes feel like trying to find a needle in a haystack. The following list doesn't cover every great site out there, but it should give you plenty of themes to choose from should you decide to use a theme.

WordPress.org

WordPress.org (`http://www.wordpress.org`) is flexible platform for new and experienced bloggers. You install and host this platform from your own server. Most bloggers pay companies like Hostgator a fee to host their blogs versus needing to own their own server. For more about self-hosting, refer to Chapter 1.

✔ **WordPress:** free; `http://wordpress.org/extend/themes`

✔ **WordPress:** premium; `http://wordpress.org/extend/themes/commercial`

✔ **WPExplorer:** free and premium; `www.wpexplorer.com`

✔ **WooThemes:** free and premium; `www.woothemes.com/product-category/themes`

✔ **ElegantThemes:** premium; `www.elegantthemes.com` (see Figure 7-8)

✔ **Themeforest:** premium; `http://themeforest.net`

✔ **The Theme Foundry:** premium; `http://thethemefoundry.com`

✔ **Templatic:** premium; `http://templatic.com`

Figure 7-8: ElegantThemes offers clean, professional theme designs.

Blogger

Blogger (www.blogger.com) is a popular hosted blog platform from Google. Instead of handling the blog hosting yourself, Google hosts the blog for you (for free).

- **BTemplates:** free; http://btemplates.com
- **Blogger Templates Hub:** free; http://bloggertemplateshub.com/blog
- **Splashy Templates:** free; www.splashytemplates.com

Both WordPress.org and Blogger

These two sites are good places to find themes for both WordPress.org and Blogger:

- **Deluxe Templates:** premium; www.deluxetemplates.net
- **Etsy:** premium; www.etsy.com (search for "WordPress theme" or "Blogger theme")

WordPress.com

WordPress.com (www.wordpress.com) is a free hosted blogging platform option for WordPress. One of the biggest differences between WordPress.com and WordPress.org is that you can't upload plug-ins or install a custom theme with a WordPress.com blog. However, you can customize the more than 200 themes that are provided. You can find these themes at WordPress. com (`http://theme.wordpress.com`).

Tumblr

Tumblr (`www.tumblr.com`) is a free, easy-to-use hosted blogging service. Tumblr is a considered a *microblogging*, platform, meaning that the platform is geared towards publishing short posts of text, images, and videos.

- ✔ **Tumblr:** `www.tumblr.com/themes`
- ✔ **Themeforest:** `http://themeforest.net/category/blogging/tumblr`

Gaining more flexibility with a WordPress framework

If you're looking for the most flexibility to build whatever your heart desires, I suggest you look into WordPress frameworks as the basis for your blogging platform. A WordPress framework is basically a very plain structure that supports a custom WordPress.org theme (known as a *child theme* because, in the hierarchy of files that create the blog, the framework is the parent and the theme is the child). You can purchase a child theme to layer on top of your framework (then customize it) or build your own child theme, using the framework as your base.

With so much flexibility, give yourself time for the learning curve until you get the hang of how that framework operates. *WordPress Web Design For Dummies* by Lisa Sabin-Wilson can help you learn the technical skills you need to get started.

Note that you can't just put a regular WordPress. org theme over a framework. You have to use a child theme.

You can find free and premium WordPress frameworks that might suit you. Some frameworks offer more drag-and-drop functionality, and others provide extensive menus with ways

to customize your design. Here are some popular WordPress frameworks:

- ✔ **Genesis:** $59.95; `http://my.studiopress.com/themes/genesis`
- ✔ **Thesis:** starting at $87; `http://diythemes.com`
- ✔ **Headway:** starting at $87; `http://headwaythemes.com`
- ✔ **Canvas:** starting at $70; `www.woothemes.com/products/canvas`
- ✔ **PageLines:** starting at $97; `www.pagelines.com`
- ✔ **Hybrid:** free; `http://themehybrid.com/hybrid-core`
- ✔ **Thematic:** free; `http://wordpress.org/extend/themes/thematic`
- ✔ **Atahualpa:** free; `http://wordpress.org/extend/themes/atahualpa`
- ✔ **WP Framework:** free; `http://wordpress.org/extend/themes/wp-framework`

Exploring Ways to Showcase Blog Posts on Your Home Page

Regardless of the type of blog layout you want (see earlier sections on your choices), you still need to consider how to display blog posts on your home page. Some bloggers feature full blog posts, some just use excerpts, and others use a mix of both.

Although your layout type may dictate the need for only excerpts — say, a magazine-style layout — you still need to consider how many posts you display on your home page.

Your main goal here is to attract, not distract. A nice balance of blog posts pulls readers into your content rather than distracting them with too many choices.

Showing full blog posts or excerpts

Unless you decide on a layout type that calls for just excerpts or images (like magazine-style layouts), you have decisions to make regarding how content displays on the home page.

Using *full blog posts* means that if someone visits your home page, they see your latest blog post displayed in its entirety. Some bloggers show just one full post; other bloggers show a few.

When you show full blog posts, your visitors don't have to click a link to finish reading an entire post. Visitors can fully concentrate on reading through your entire post without having to break and wait for a new page to load.

On the downside, full blog posts can slow your home page's download time, especially if your home page includes a lot of full posts or if your posts have many images. In addition, full posts can limit a visitor's ability to see the breadth of your content, because you can fit only so many posts on your home page. Using a sidebar that effectively shows a wider array of posts gives readers a chance to see more without using post excerpts.

Of course, you can make some posts on your home page excerpts and still show full posts. See the section, "Creating blog post excerpts" for some ways on how to use excerpts.

Using *excerpts* mean that you show snippets or teasers of multiple blog posts on your home page. To read the full post, a visitor clicks a link: something like Read More.

Using only excerpts on your home page has benefits as well. With excerpts, you fit more content in the same space, meaning you can show visitors more of what you offer within the main content area. With more to see in one location, visitors can easily scan multiple blog post titles and determine which posts they want to read.

Figure 7-9 shows a good use of post excerpts. With excerpts, Mom Spark (`http://momspark.net`) highlights the blog's diverse topics. A hero image (a large, attention-grabbing image at the top of a page) above the home page's main column signifies the most important post, and other excerpts nicely highlight other posts worth reading.

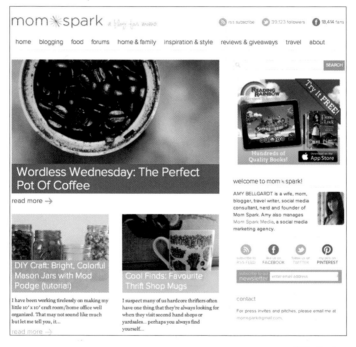

© MomSpark.net

Figure 7-9: This design highlights each excerpt with an image and a different color over the blog post name.

Because a visitor has to click to view a full post, using excerpts also encourages comments because the comment field is on the page with the full post. If you have full posts on the home page, visitors have to load a separate page after they read the post to comment. You also see an increase in page views due to visitors having to click (although better traffic should never ever be the main factor in the decision).

The downside of using excerpts is that not everyone will take the action to click a link to finish reading a blog post, especially if the excerpt content doesn't entice the reader enough. Instead, that visitor may read a little bit of each post excerpt and then move on. Also, if you already show full blog posts but then change to using excerpts, some readers may resist the change.

When making a decision between full posts and excerpts, consider your blog's topics as well as how long your posts typically are. If you write about a lot of different topics, using post excerpts makes that fact more apparent to your readers because they see snippets of different blog posts rather than scrolling through entire posts.

If your posts are shorter in length, using full blog posts might make more sense. A reader might be annoyed to click Read More and see only one more paragraph of content. Shorter, full posts can allow you to show more on the home page without using any Read More links.

Not all visitors start at your home page. Many people click a link from a social media site or a search engine that goes directly to an article. The decision for using full posts or excerpts affects just those who land directly on your home page, who often aren't familiar with your blog.

Deciding how many posts to put on your home page

Whether your home page displays full blog posts or excerpts, you need to decide how many posts should appear in your home page's main content section. If you want full posts on your home page, the number of posts to use mainly depends on two things:

- **Length of posts:** If your blog posts are long — text, images, or both — you probably want to include only one full post on your home page. If your posts are shorter, maybe you could use as many as three.

- **Sidebar length:** Some bloggers have a lot of sidebar content, and others keep it to a minimum. You don't want so many blog posts in your main column that visitors have to scroll way past your sidebar content. That leaves your content with empty space beside it. On the flip side, you don't want your main column to end and still have a never-ending flow of sidebar content, either.

When considering how many excerpts to include, some of that decision may be dictated by the blog layout or theme you use. In addition, consider the following:

- **Length of excerpts:** If your excerpts are on the longer side, you may want to use fewer of them. If you go for shorter excerpts, make them long enough to entice the reader to actually click through to the rest of the post.

- **Categories to highlight:** One of the great things about using excerpts is that you can show a better variety of your content in your home page's main column. That being said, if you show excerpts by categories and have 12 categories, posting 12 excerpts may look too confusing to a visitor. Instead, choose your most popular ones to showcase.

After you decide how many posts you think work for your blog and make the adjustments on your site, be sure to check that your home page looks great visually with a good use of color, images, and overall appeal.

Creating blog post excerpts

So you want to use some blog post excerpts on your home page. Great! This section shows you a few common ways to do this in WordPress.org.

The most obvious way is to select a theme or framework that either uses excerpts automatically or makes it easy for you to add them. For example, a magazine style theme uses excerpts by default. Also, WordPress.org frameworks like Thesis and Genesis make changing your posts to automatic excerpts (sometimes called *teasers*) really easy to do.

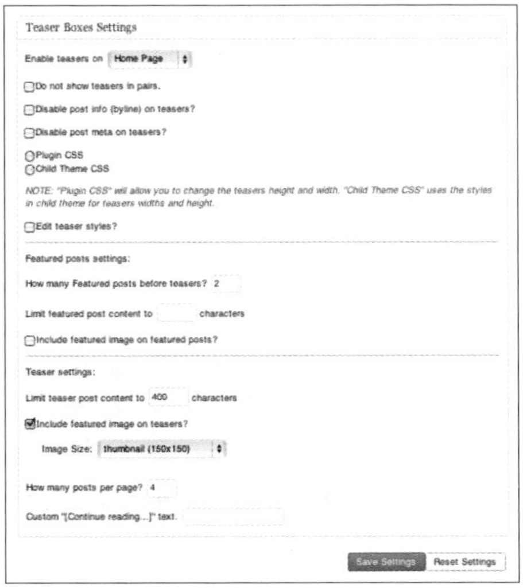

In Figure 7-10, take a look at the teaser options for the Genesis framework. The featured post settings (middle section) let you place more prominence on your most recent posts by making them different than the other teasers. To make featured posts display as full posts, just leave the field blank for the Limit Featured Post Content to *xx* Characters. In the Teaser Settings section, you have options for teasers that display in pairs underneath the optional featured posts. Finally, you can select the number of posts and customize the "Continue reading" text.

Figure 7-10: Teaser options depend upon framework settings.

If your blog theme doesn't have teaser-creation options in your dashboard settings, you can do it yourself within the WordPress.org theme.

To make every post on your home page an excerpt that offers a teaser of your blog post, follow these steps from your WordPress Admin area:

1. **Log into your WordPress.org dashboard.**

2. **Go to Appearance⇨Editor.**

   This brings up all your template files, the files that control how your site displays on the web. On the right side, you see a list of your template files while one file loads in the main window.

3. **Click your `index.php` file to open the template in the main window.**

4. **Find code that starts with `<?php the_content`.**

   The exact location of this code varies by theme. If you don't see it in `index.php`, look for templates called `content.php` or `loop.php`.

   For example, in the Twenty Eleven theme, this code can be found in the `content.php` file. The entire snippet looks like this:

   ```
   <?php the_content( __( 'Continue reading <span class
           ="meta-nav">&rarr;</span>', 'twentyeleven' ) ); ?>
   ```

5. **Change `the_content` to `the_excerpt`.**

   This makes your blog posts always display on your home page as excerpts instead of full posts.

   You can also customize the excerpt link from `Continue reading` to something else.

6. **Submit your changes by clicking Update File.**

As an alternative, you can also create a simple post excerpt for individual posts, rather than modifying a PHP file to automatically do this for every new post. Here's how to do this in WordPress. (In Blogger, look for the Jump Break tool in your Post Editor.)

1. **Log into your WordPress dashboard.**

2. **From your menu, choose Posts⇨Add New.**

3. **Type your post and then decide where you want to end the excerpt, putting your cursor there.**

4. **Click the Insert More Tab button from the Visual Editor (it looks like two boxes stacked on top of each other, separated by a dashed line).**

   This places a faint line with a More tab to mark the place where your excerpt ends, as shown in Figure 7-11. If you click the Text tab, you see this button added the code `<!--more-->` to the HTML. Note that previewing this shows a full post because a preview shows your actual post URL — a *permalink* — not your home page.

5. **Click the Publish button to make your post live.**

   Visit your home page to see how your post excerpt appears. You can see in Figure 7-12 that on the home page, the post ends with a Continue Reading link to lead to the full post.

To change Continue Reading to something a little more exciting, click the Text tab (refer to Step 4 of the preceding list) and then add your custom content to read something like `<!--more See How the Story Ends-->`. This changes the message for that particular post only, but have fun with it!

Insert More Tab button   Click the Visual tab to use the Visual Editor

Marks where excerpt ends   Click Publish to make post live

Figure 7-11: The More tab within your blog post marks the end of your excerpt.

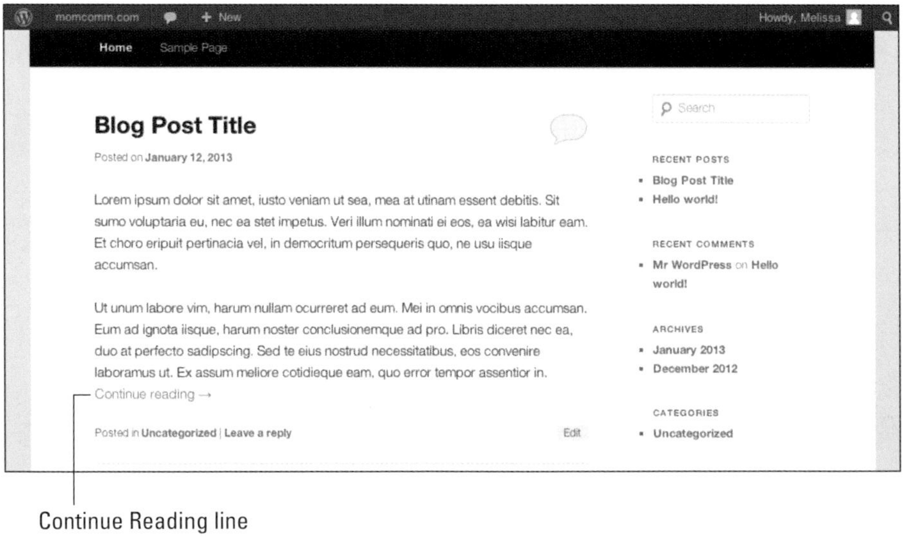

Continue Reading line

Figure 7-12: A Continue Reading link appears at the bottom of this post excerpt.

One final option for using excerpts is using a featured post carousel or gallery that rotates a large image and sometimes a teaser for a selected number of blog posts. Jump to Chapter 15 for some gallery plug-in options.

Deciding Where to Place Advertising

Some bloggers get into blogging primarily to make money, so they advertise on their blog from the get-go. Some bloggers start writing and later decide to try advertising. And of course, some bloggers want to keep their site free from advertising. (If that's you, just skip this section.)

Advertising plays a crucial role in the impression your overall blog design makes on the reader. How do you use advertising in a way that actually makes you money but keeps your users from thinking you're greedy? These next sections highlight some things to keep in mind so your readers don't go running.

Putting your visitors first

Although your readers probably don't mind you wanting to earn revenue from your blog, they don't want to be bombarded with ads. Whether you use a design network or sell your own ads directly, good blog design puts your readers first while still making the advertising beneficial for you.

Advertising can be located in just about any place within your blog design. Common advertising areas include the top banner (also called a leader board), anywhere within the sidebar, and within the actual blog post content (see Figure 7-13). You sometimes even see advertising replace a blogger's entire background.

Figure 7-13: Here are common places for bloggers to place advertising.

When deciding where to place your advertising, consider whether your advertising hinders the usability of your blog. Ads should never make your blog harder to use or confusing to the reader.

Here are some common culprits of not-optimal advertising:

- **In-text ads:** These are contextual ads that hyperlink words in your content to ads. When you hover over those words, they pop up with an advertisement. They tend to look unprofessional and spammy, especially when a lot of words within a blog post are linked. Also, in-text ads sometimes apply links to words completely out of context. For example, I've seen an in-text ad of a city name link to a travel site when the name was actually the name of the blogger's child.

- **Autoplaying ads:** Avoid any advertising that automatically plays videos (with sound) or music. These types of ads interrupt the visitor from exploring your site or reading your content.

- **Intrusive ads:** This type of ad can include anything from pop-overs and pop-unders (ads that display in a new browser window underneath the current browser window) to those ads that sweep over your blog when someone hovers over them.

  Be wary of using ads that do this because they interfere with your content being read. Most browsers have pop-up blockers so pop-up ads may not be displayed, anyway.

- **Oddly placed ads within blog posts:** Oftentimes, bloggers place text or banner ads within their blog post. This is fine when done well, but make sure that the size or the location of the ad doesn't affect the ability to actually read the post. In addition, a very large ad at the bottom of your post content could separate your content too far from your comment section, making it less easy for visitors to comment. Also, check your text-based ads to ensure they don't look too much like the blog post. Otherwise, you might frustrate or confuse the reader.

Avoiding advertising overload

You've probably been to a website where you felt like you just got smacked with a wall of advertising. Maybe on your blog, you've added advertising piece by piece — an ad network here and a row of ad banners there — but never stopped to look at your blog design as a whole.

So, if you have an existing blog, take a step back and take a look at your blog design's overall look and feel. Does an ad interfere with your overall blog design? Is advertising making it hard to concentrate on your content?

Too many ads in a sidebar, for example, become such a big jumble that you're essentially reducing the effectiveness of those ads. There are just too many things to look at in one view! In addition, a lot of bold, flashy graphics detract from your message and leave your visitor feeling overloaded with ads.

Good advertising placement should catch attention of visitors (after all, you want them to click) but never at the detriment of your overall design. Your blog content should always be easy to spot right away.

If you run ads with an ad network like Google AdSense — a program that allows you to display targeted Google ads on your blog — you don't always have control over the exact ads that run although you can sometimes make exclusions, depending on the network. Look at your ads from time to time to ensure nothing surprising sneaks past you.

One blog that does advertising right is the popular Young House Love (www. younghouselove.com). John and Sherry earn the majority of their income through advertising, but their blog doesn't feel overrun with ads. They organize the advertising in their sidebars into a few sections. One main advertiser appears above the fold. Two sections for sponsors are separated by ad size, with one size taking up wider with than the other (Figure 7-14). The blog features a We're Digging section for affiliate products, too. The result is a lot of advertising without feeling overwhelming or interfering with content.

Taking care of your current advertisers

Not only do your readers matter, but so do your current advertisers. If you sell advertising space on your blog, you have a direct relationship with your advertisers. You gotta treat them right!

Have you ever been to a blog whose advertising section looks like the image in Figure 7-15? Surrounded by vacant advertising space, the one ad completely gets overtaken by Advertise Here buttons. Not only is this a disservice to the advertiser, but too many blank ad spaces can also deter potential advertisers. The blank spaces give the impression that your site isn't attracting enough visitors.

So what do you do? Try not to have more than one Advertise Here blank at any given time. (If you have eight spots or more, you can possibly get away with two blanks.) Then fill the rest in with affiliate marketing buttons. Also, consider adding a link like "Interested in advertising with me? Contact me." underneath the ads and link to your contact info.

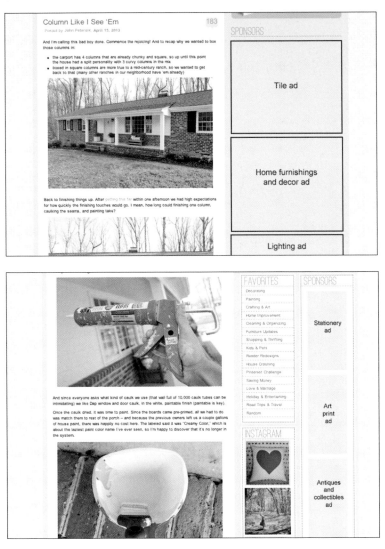

Figure 7-14: This design showcases advertising.

Figure 7-15: Don't fall victim to blank ad spaces.

8

Customizing Your Header, Footer, and Background

....

In This Chapter

▶ Making a first impression with a blog header

▶ Determining whether to use a tagline

▶ Creating a blog header that gets visitors clicking

▶ Building a footer than gets noticed

▶ Adding a background to your blog design

....

Colors, fonts, and graphic elements all play into your blog design. Separately, they each communicate just a bit about your blog's content. When you put them together, the magic really starts to work.

This chapter tackles three components of your blog design: your blog header, footer, and background design. When you look at these three parts as a whole, you see a mix of content, fonts, and graphic elements brought to life in a cohesive blog design.

A blog header, footer, and background all play an important role in your overall blog design, yet they do so in very different ways. In this chapter, I describe each element's role in your overall blog design. You see how a blog header sets the tone for your blog, whether you need a tagline, how to size a header, and even how to create a simple header. In addition, I explain how a footer can get readers to take action and show you ideas that you can build into your footer. I also walk you through creating a custom background pattern and how to decide whether a solid color or pattern works best.

Expressing Visual Identity with a Strong Blog Header

Your blog's visual identity speaks volumes about its content, tone, and credibility.

Your blog header becomes the first opportunity to present your blog. I'm not exaggerating when I say that without a well-designed blog header, you potentially shoo away new visitors because either your blog header doesn't look professional (which diminishes your credibility) or doesn't sync with the voice and tone of your content (which confuses new visitors).

Making a great first impression

I imagine you've purchased a car at some point in your life. What made you choose the cars that you test drove? Maybe a friend recommended a certain model, or you researched a car with great safety ratings. Even with those suggestions, you probably didn't peek in the window to see the interior unless you liked the look of the car's exterior at first glance.

Only after you notice the car's exterior do you peek into that window and even open the door for a test drive. Like a car's exterior, your header attracts a visitor's eye and creates a new visitor's first impression of your blog.

To make a first impression, one study shows that you have less than two-tenths of a second. The study also states that it takes about 2.6 seconds for your visitors' eyes to spot the area of a website that most influences their first impression. So, when you design your blog header, ask yourself, "Does my blog header communicate enough of what my blog is about?"

That doesn't mean your blog header design needs to literally say what you write about. Focus on the impression the header leaves in a reader's mind.

In Figure 8-1, the blog Momma's Gone City (www.mommasgonecity.com) leaves a positive impression with a header that uses just one image along with the blog name. Jessica writes about parenting, fashion, and adjusting to city life — and the image subtly conveys that. Even the movement of her traveling into the subway helps pull the reader down into her blog.

© Jessica Shyba, Momma's Gone City

Figure 8-1: The header for this blog fits perfectly with its topics.

When designing your own blog header, ensure that your header communicates what you blog about by incorporating the following characteristics:

- **Professional:** You don't need to hire someone to design your blog, but successfully applying the tips and ideas you can glean from this book give your blog a professional feel, making visitors place more trust in you and your content.

- **Memorable:** From the colors to the fonts to the words, your blog header design should showcase what makes your blog memorable. If you're a humor blogger, your blog header better have an element of humor to it, whether it's a funny photo or laugh-out-loud tagline. (More on taglines in just a bit.)

- **Attractive to your target audience:** Your blog header design should at least partly align with what attracts your target audience. If you blog about children's crafts, readers don't expect your header design to be stark, muted colors. On the opposite end, that doesn't mean you have to use a childlike font with every letter a different color, either.

If you don't have a solid grasp of your audience or how your blog stands out, see Chapter 3 to get to know your blog a little better.

Deciding whether you need a tagline

You already know a new visitor forms an impression about your blog based on your header design, but design alone doesn't explain what your blog is about. Blog names can often be descriptive enough, but not all blog names stand on their own. If you didn't already know about Amazon.com, would you know that it's an e-commerce site just based on its name? Nope.

For that, you need a *tagline,* which supports your blog name and design by summing up your blog's key message in just a few words. Standing alone, taglines range from seemingly random to very descriptive. However, after you pair your blog name and header design, a tagline complements your branding and gives you the opportunity to tell your story so that the reader doesn't have to guess what you're all about. Consider how movie studios often give movies a memorable tagline to drive interest in a movie. For example, *Jaws* had the tagline "Don't Go in the Water." Combined with the movie name (and that famous image of a shark with its sharp-toothed mouth wide open), the tagline creates a more powerful emotion of fear than the name alone. With a great tagline for your blog, you put readers in the right frame of mind for reading your content.

Hmm. If you study other blogs, though, you'll notice that not every blog has a tagline. So, do you really need one? Try this test to decide. Spend about three seconds looking at your blog design through the eyes of a new visitor.

(Remember: That's about as long as it takes to make an impression — a very short 2.6 seconds to be exact.) Then ask yourself: *If someone were visiting for the first time, would they know what my blog is about in those few seconds?*

If your blog name and header design describe your blog's content well enough, then you could do without a tagline. However, a good tagline serves to reinforce the message your blog name and header design send to the reader.

Here's an example. Say your blog is named something like The Smith Family News. A generic name like that does nothing to tell new visitors what your blog is about. Adding a tagline within your blog header design gives those visitors more insight as to why your blog is unique. What about your family? Why should people care? What's interesting about your blog? Maybe it's *Tales about life with all boys* or *Inspiration from a family healing after tragedy.*

Just like blog header designs, taglines don't have to be literal. Johnny B. Truant (`http://johnnybtruant.com`) uses his online pseudonym as his blog name. As you can see in Figure 8-2, his tagline *The Internet Made Awesome* gives you the sense that he blogs about web-related topics, while the tone gives you the impression his blog will be punchy and helpful all at the same time.

Website © 2013 by Johnny B Truant, Website Theme Design © 2011 by Logan Zanelli and GenesisThemeDesign.com, Illustration © 2009 by N.C. Winters

Figure 8-2: This tagline is clear and catchy.

Choosing an effective header size

When designing your blog header, you have to decide how large or small to make it without compromising that all-important first impression. When thinking about header size, consider what shows up *above the fold,* which is the part of your blog a reader sees before they have to scroll further down the page. A great header design entices a visitor enough to read a blog post, click a link in the navigation menu, or explore your blog in some other way.

The best size for your blog header width will vary depending on your blog theme. Within your blog's dashboard, on the tab where you upload your header, your theme or framework may suggest an optimal size based on your layout. If you're unsure what width to make your header, see Chapter 9 for an explanation of using Firebug to determine the sizes of blog elements.

As far as height goes, many designers will tell you not to exceed 200 to 300 pixels high for a blog design. In general, a header larger than this pushes all your content and menus below the fold (the area that a user has to scroll down to see, although this area varies slightly depending on your screen size). Having said that, using a large header isn't a bad thing when done effectively.

If you're considering using a blog header design that goes way under or way over those 200 to 300 pixels, then consider these points:

✓ **Small header height**

> *Pro:* A small, well-designed header not only communicates what your blog is about, but it also leaves a lot of space above the fold to show a visitor other things that might interest them. In Figure 8-3, notice that Chris Garrett's blog header (www.chrisg.com) doesn't take up much space. At first glance, you see not only the header, but also a navigation menu, two headlines from recent posts, a little blurb about Chris in the sidebar, and a graphic encouraging visitors to sign up for his e-mail list.

> *Con:* A small header design may not have enough visual oomph to draw in a reader. Picture a generic header design that includes just a blog name in a standard font. Although that doesn't take up a lot of space on your overall layout, that type of header lacks the ability to visually showcase anything about your blog to a new visitor.

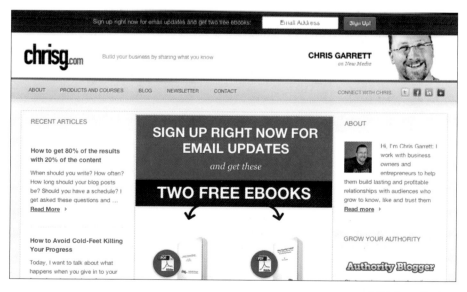

© Chris Garrett, ChrisG.com

Figure 8-3: This blog uses a small header size that still gets noticed.

✔ **Large header height**

Pro: A large header can be done right and really pack some punch. If you want a larger header, be sure that at least some important component of your blog design — such as your menu navigation — shows above the fold. In Figure 8-4, you see that the header on Mama's Losin' It (www.mamakatslosinit.com) takes up a lot of space, yet you can still see a top navigation menu and the section showing her latest blog post.

Con: Large headers take up a lot of real estate in your overall blog design. When done ineffectively, a large header covers all the space above the fold, leaving no room for a navigation menu, blog post title, sidebar, or anything else before your reader has to scroll down. That means you lose the opportunity to show more of your blog and must rely on your reader's desire to scroll down to see more.

© www.mamakatslosinit.com, Site Design: Jamie Varon, www.shatterboxx.com

Figure 8-4: This large blog header grabs attention.

Always test your header in different screen resolutions to see how it looks. The worst thing that can happen is your header is so large that readers have to scroll from one side to another to see it. Not only will this cut off your design, but as Internet users, we rarely scroll from side to side because that movement feels awkward. See Chapter 7 for more information about page width.

Designing a simple header

Don't be intimidated designing a header just because you can take the design in so many directions. With the content presented in this book, you can give it a good shot.

To get your creative juices flowing, I want to show you how to create a really simple header design. I'm using Photoshop, which is available for both Macs and PCs — and, unlike some web-based editing programs (like PicMonkey), you can use your own fonts. (Read how to get your own fonts in Chapter 6.) Photoshop is a pricey investment, but luckily you can create everything you'd need for a blog design with Photoshop Elements, which costs less than Photoshop. (Read more about Photoshop, Photoshop Elements, and other editing programs in Chapter 15.)

To create a simple image-based header in Photoshop, follow these steps (for Photoshop Elements, the steps are similar but not exactly the same):

1. **Open Photoshop.**

2. **Choose File⇨New.**

   A window pops up, asking for you to title your file and input dimensions. For this header, I set the dimensions to 1000 x 288 pixels.

3. **Create a new layer by pressing Ctrl+Shift+N (PC) or ⌘+Shift+N (Mac).**

   This layer is where you create a rectangle that constrains your image to a certain size without needing to crop it. This is a *mask*.

4. **Give your layer a title and then click OK.**

   I called mine Image Mask.

5. **Within this layer, you then create the rectangle that you use to mask your image.**

   a. *Select the Rectangle tool from the Tools panel.*

   b. *From the Control Panel menu at the top, click the Geometry Options drop-down arrow (see Figure 8-5).*

   This opens the Rectangle Options dialog box.

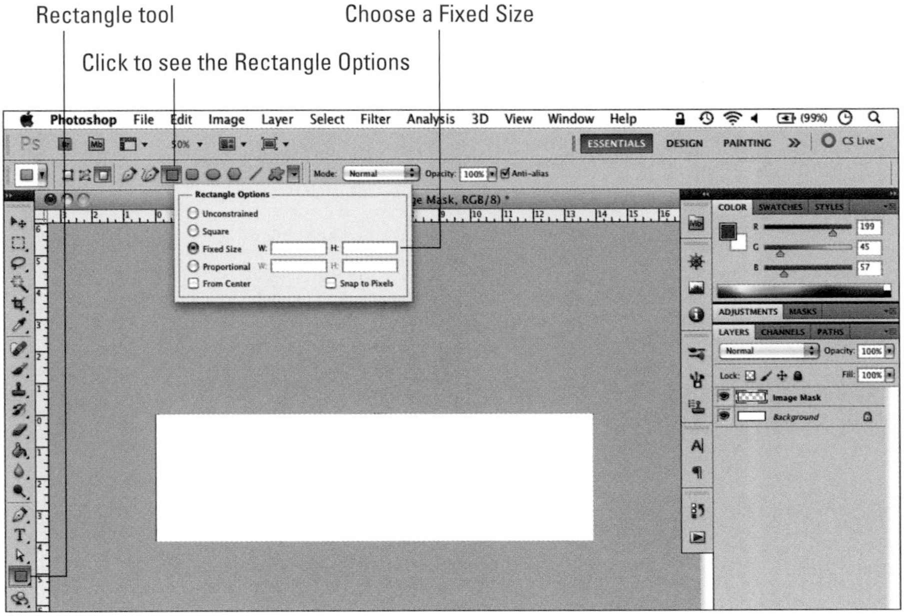

Rectangle tool

Choose a Fixed Size

Click to see the Rectangle Options

Figure 8-5: In the Control Panel, you can set a shape to be a specific size.

> c. *Enter dimensions into the W (width) and H (height) text boxes.*
>
>   I input 1000 and 200 pixels so I can fill the entire width of my blog design but have room for my blog name at the top. Note that Fixed Size is selected by default.
>
> d. *Move your cursor into your canvas.*
>
>   A plus sign appears.
>
> e. *Click to drop a rectangle onto your canvas.*
>
> f. *Move the rectangle into position by clicking the Move tool from the top of your Tools panel. Then click and drag your cursor on the rectangle to move it into desired position.*

6. Place your photo into the file.

> a. *Open the desired photo in a separate file.*
>
> b. *Using the Move tool, click and drag that image into your header image file.*

Don't worry about exactly where you place it.

7. Mask the image.

Remember that a mask hides the parts of your image that don't show through the rectangle shape you created. Using a mask prevents you from having to crop the image to the exact proportion you want for your design.

a. *Place your cursor on the line between the photo layer and the Image Mask layer in the Layers palette.*

b. *Hold down the Alt key (Option on Mac).*

The cursor symbol becomes two overlapping circles.

c. *Click to create the mask.*

With the mask now created, you can move the mask up and down so that the area of your photo you'd like to display is visible. In Figure 8-6, the black line indicates my image's actual dimensions; only a portion of the image shows up in the rectangle.

Figure 8-6: This image of peaches constrains to fit within the mask.

8. **Add and format the blog name.**

   a. *Click the Type tool from the Tools panel.*

   b. *Click the cursor anywhere on the canvas to start typing (and type the name).*

   c. *Use the Control Panel at the top to control the font, size, and other type-formatting settings.*

   To adjust the color, select the color square within the Control Panel. You can either enter color values or use the Eyedropper by clicking a part in your photo to pull color from there. (See Chapter 6 for details about color in your overall blog design.)

9. **When you're done adjusting the font, select the Move tool from the Tools panel to move the blog name into the desired location.**

   I like the look of the blog name sitting atop the photo. You can see my final blog header design in Figure 8-7.

10. **Save the Photoshop file by choosing File⇨Save.**

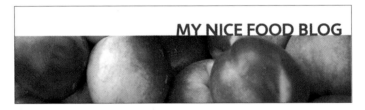

Figure 8-7: Finished blog header. Nice!

Because blogs can't read Photoshop files, now you need to make the photo web-friendly. Starting with the Photoshop file already open, you can do this in a few easy steps:

1. **Choose File⇨Save for Web & Devices.**

   A Preview window opens, showing your image.

2. **Click the 2-Up tab at the top left of the window.**

   This shows you two versions of your file: the original and the one you are saving from the original.

3. **Try an image format from the Presets menu options, using the JPG or PNG options.**

JPG files are a better choice if your blog header is heavy on photographs. PNG files are better for illustrations (like graphs or icons) and text-heavy images.

As you select a Preset, the preview image updates, showing you any changes in quality.

4. **Select Save to save the file onto your computer.**

You can then add the file to your blog, using whatever tools and methods your blog software makes available.

Photoshop and Photoshop Elements enable you to create fairly complex graphics using layers, masks, and more. If you invest in one of the these programs, check out *Photoshop For Dummies* by Peter Bauer or *Photoshop Elements For Dummies* by Barbara Obermeier and Ted Padova for help getting the most out of either of these powerful programs.

Enhancing Navigation with a Blog Footer

Oh, the footer: blog design's underdog. As bloggers, we get so wrapped up with all that stuff above the fold — like the header and top of the sidebar — and sometimes forget to make an impression in the last place a visitor often sees: the blog footer.

Sometimes people just think of blog footers as a place to put the boring stuff, such as privacy policy links or copyright information, but footers can be much more than that. This section shows how a blog footer can provide visitors with helpful navigation paths so your footer becomes less of an afterthought and more of a way to fuel your blog goals.

Creating a useful footer

Before you get into actually creating a blog footer, you should know what role a footer plays in relation to your entire blog design. A blog visitor doesn't scroll straight to the bottom of your page to see your footer (unless they're looking something specific). Instead, the majority of your blog visitors sort of stumble onto it. They read a great blog post, maybe take a look at your sidebar, and then mosey their way down to the bottom of your page until there is nowhere left to scroll.

When visitors get to the bottom of your page, what they want to know is, "What do I do now?" With that in mind, think about how the things you add in the footer fuel your blog goals.

A great footer example is from The Everywhereist (www.everywhereist.com). As you can see in Figure 8-8, a bold line lets you know that you're in footer territory. Geraldine's blog footer highlights everything from social media links to her e-mail list to her Flickr feed. Underneath the more visual elements, you have the copyright, a privacy policy link, and other footer-like content, followed by a subtle yet impactful strip that mimics her blog header.

Figure 8-8: This blog footer provides options for places to visit next while maintaining a clean design.

Determining elements to include

Keeping the reader's question in mind — *What do I do now?* — start by listing the things you want to include in your footer. I want to give you a lot of ideas to choose from, but remember not to cram in everything. Make choices that go back to the goals for your blog design. (For help on that, see Chapter 3.)

Some blog footers simply show a row of links. Some have three or four columns of content. And some include both, like Dear Crissy's footer shown in Figure 8-9.

Figure 8-9: This footer features links and other content.

As for what type of a links to include, a blog footer often includes links, such as

- ✔ **Copyright information:** Although you don't need copyright info to protect your content and blog design, having the copyright symbol on your page can deter potential infringers. Using something like © *2013 Momcomm – All Rights Reserved* prevents someone from saying they didn't know your content was copyrighted. Make this a must-add to your blog footer.

- ✔ **Back to Top link:** After a reader scrolls all the way to the bottom of your page, it's nice to easily get back to the top of your page with the click of a button.

- ✔ **Privacy policy:** A privacy policy lays out your blog's policies regarding how you gather, use, disclose or manage someone's personal data. For bloggers, this often covers things like advertising, affiliate links, and sponsored content as well as whether your blog uses cookies.

- ✔ **FAQ:** Some bloggers may want a frequently asked questions page, which works well in a navigation menu, too.

- ✔ **Advertise:** Blogs sometimes include a link to an advertising page.

- ✔ **Blog designer:** If you hire professionals to design part or all of your blog design, they may want you to put a link to their website in your footer. Grant this wish — they are awesome!

- ✔ **Archives:** Footers sometimes have a link to an archives page of all your posts arranged by date. Instead of a link to a separate page, some blogs include an abbreviated archives in the footer.

- ✔ **Sitemap:** A link to a blog's sitemap can help visitors with a mission find what they're looking for by getting a high-level view of your content. See Chapter 10 for more about sitemaps.

Just because I consider each of the preceding items "standard" doesn't mean that you should include them all. Choose the ones that are important to your blog, and then run with it.

Now, consider all the potential ways you can add other content to your footer. When you want your footer to have more oomph, consider the following additions to your footer:

- ✔ **Social media buttons:** If your social media buttons are at the top of your blog (like they should be), readers no longer see them at the bottom of your blog. Placing these buttons also in your footer subtly reminds readers to subscribe, friend, or follow.

- ✔ **About you or your blog:** You can add a little blurb about you or your blog and then link to a fuller About page for all the details.

✔ **Facebook widget:** This widget makes it easy for readers to like your blog's Facebook page, because they don't even have to leave your blog to do so. I talk more about this widget in Chapter 11.

✔ **Latest tweets:** Give readers a glimpse of the things you tweet by showing a few of your most current tweets.

✔ **As seen on:** Have you been featured or interviewed by a high-profile show or publication? Show off your credibility by highlighting any publicity you or your blog have received.

✔ **Widget for visual social media platforms:** Showcase your awesome shots from Instagram, Flickr, and Pinterest.

✔ **E-mail sign up:** Give users another opportunity to subscribe to your e-mail list by making the sign-up form conveniently displayed again at the bottom of your blog.

✔ **Recent posts or comments:** Highlight the latest posts you've written or comments others have left. *Note:* Try not to use them both because they can clutter your footer with too much text.

✔ **Link to other sites you own or contribute to:** Give readers an opportunity to enjoy other places you write by including them here.

When deciding what awesomeness to put into your footer, picture a blog reader making their way to the end of your blog and wondering what to do next.

In Figure 8-9, you see a footer that shows both links and visual elements as well. Crissy has a large Twitter following, so having her latest tweet and a button to follow her makes it easy to grow that audience even further. In addition, she's growing her e-mail list with a simple e-mail subscription form.

Incorporating a footer into your design

Unlike a blog header design, creating a footer for your blog design can't be done in a photo-editing program. A footer is a live, clickable part of your site, not a static image.

How you actually add a footer on your own blog really depends on the platform and theme that you use. Many WordPress themes and Blogger templates include a "widgetized" footer, which lets you add items to your footer through widgets just as you would do on a sidebar.

As you can see in Figure 8-10, the WordPress Twenty Eleven theme lets you drag widgets (such as Recent Posts or Search) to the footer and then customize from there.

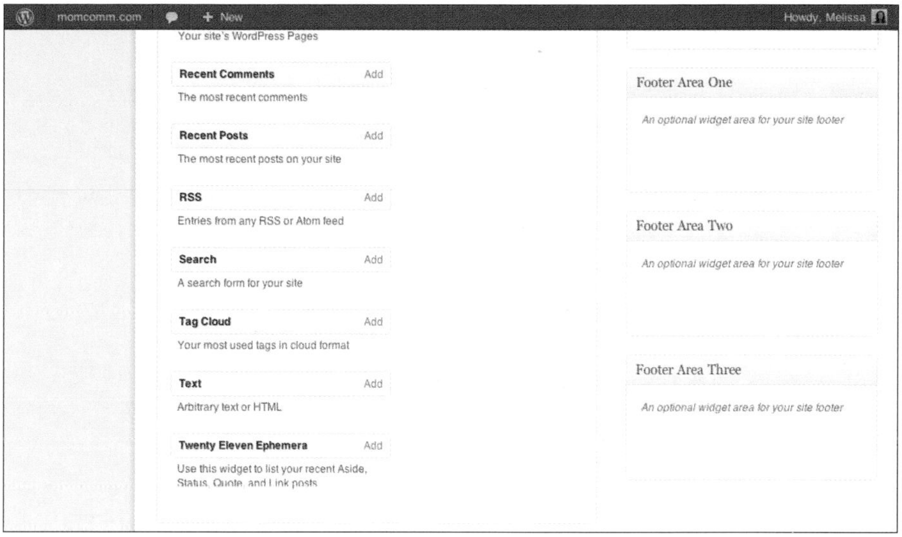

Figure 8-10: In WordPress, go to Widgets from your dashboard to see these widgetized footer boxes.

Some WordPress themes offer a widgetized footer as a plug-in add-on, such as the Genesis Widgetized Footer plug-in:

```
http://wordpress.org/extend/plugins/genesis-widgetized-
            footer
```

Both options make it easy to create a footer without getting into coding your site.

Polishing Your Design with a Blog Background

A blog background provides an important supporting role to your overall blog design. A good background design complements your content rather than overtaking it. Your background should be consistent with the overall branding of your blog design and help set the tone for your site.

In this section, I talk about ways to create a background that gives your overall blog design a polished finishing touch.

Deciding on a solid or graphical background

While your background design plays a supporting role to your overall blog design, you still have choices to make. You can go with a solid colored background for a simple look or go a little (or a lot) more complex with a graphical background. The decision rests partly in your header design. Is your header full of design elements or colorful photographs? Then try a solid colored background. Is your header design clean and simple? Then a graphical background can add some pop to your blog design.

Regardless of which one you choose, you don't want to make the fatal mistake of distracting from the star of your blog: your content. Strive for a background design that provides balance in the overall look and feel of your blog design.

For a solid background color, try pulling a color from your blog's color palette or use a neutral color, such as white or gray. To go one step beyond a solid color, use a gradient background that subtly blends two colors.

Many blog platforms or themes default to having white behind the main content and sidebars, leaving the sides of your blog design for the actual background color or pattern. If that's not the case and your background color shows up directly behind your content, be careful not to use a really dark color behind your main content. Most users find this design choice extremely hard to read, even if the text is white. Use white text on a dark background only in small doses, not for your main content.

With a graphical background, you add complexity to your blog design. Here are some popular ways to use a graphical background:

- ✔ **Textures:** Cross-patterns, lines, linen, or other textures add subtle visual interest to your background design. Single colors or colors within the same color range make nice low-contrast textures. In Figure 8-11, Erin of Design for MiniKind (http://designforminikind.com) uses a subtle gray texture for her blog background.

- ✔ **Illustrations:** If you're feeling artsy, you can use a graphics program to create a visually engaging background design that incorporates design elements that you downloaded or created yourself.

- ✔ **Large image:** Using large images that cover your entire background can really create a cool effect. When done right, they make a big impact without pulling readers away from your content.

- ✔ **Tiled patterns:** A common background tiles a pattern across the width of your blog, forming a seamless design. In the upcoming section, "Creating your own background pattern," I show you how to create a simple background pattern.

With graphical backgrounds, you might find it harder for your background not to overwhelm your blog design. I give you some great choices in the next section.

Figure 8-11: This blog background adds interest but doesn't overwhelm the overall blog design.

Finding background patterns

You might luck out and find a pattern that fits perfectly with how you envision your blog design, but here are some places you can peruse to find patterns.

- ✒ **PatternCooler:** (`www.patterncooler.com`) This website should be your first stop if you want to use an existing pattern versus designing your own. From subtle to not-so-subtle, you can find just about anything you can think of: stripes, flowers, dots, teardrops, and so on. For extra awesomeness, you use the Editor here (`www.patterncooler.com/editor`) to customize the colors of any pattern.

- ✒ **COLOURlovers:** (`www.colourlovers.com/patterns`) I mention this site in Chapter 6 as a great source of color inspiration. It's also a great site for patterns. The website features patterns created (and rated) by the COLOURlovers community. You can customize any pattern's colors by clicking `Color This Pattern` underneath the pattern image.

- ✒ **Subtle Patterns:** (`http://subtlepatterns.com`) So many background sites have overly complex, sometimes garish background patterns. Subtle Patterns, shown in Figure 8-12, is a breath of fresh air. The textures on this site mainly consist of whites, blacks, or grays. However, you can change the color of the patterns with some photo-editing software, such as Adobe Photoshop.

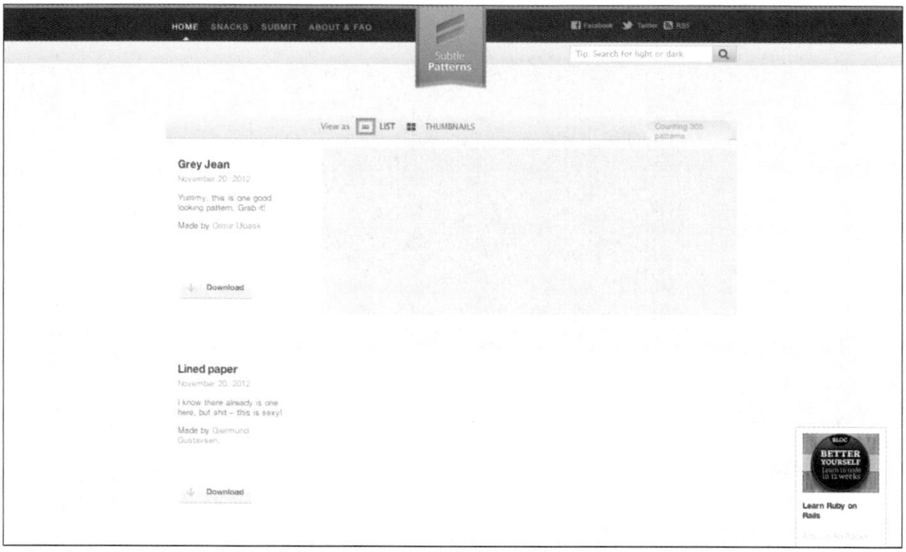

Figure 8-12: Don't overlook a subtle pattern that won't overtake your design.

- ✔ **Texturevault:** (www.texturevault.net) Texturevault offers professional textures and background patterns with lots of categories. This is the only site I mention that charges for textures; however, prices start at just $2. This site's tutorials explain ways to use textures in design.

- ✔ **Background Labs:** (www.backgroundlabs.com) You can download each background image as a GIF file or Photoshop pattern. All the patterns on the site are illustrations. You can also find backgrounds for your Twitter page and PowerPoint presentations here.

- ✔ **Texture King:** (www.textureking.com) For industrial or earthy textures, try this site. Categories like grunge, rust, metals, glass, and plaster give you plenty of options for a rugged or an earthy look. All the textures are photo-based, not illustrations.

Creating your own background pattern

Does something about your blog design or your creative instincts inspire you to create your own pattern? Sure, creating patterns can get complex, but it doesn't have to be. You can create your own seamless pattern with the user-friendly COLOURlovers Seamless Lite app.

First, you need to create a COLOURlovers account (don't worry — it's free!):

1. **Go to the COLOURlovers homepage (**www.colourlovers.com**).**

2. **Click Sign Up in the upper-right corner.**

    This directs you to the registration form.

3. **Fill out the form by entering a username, password, e-mail, and the security code you seen on-screen.**

4. **Click Create Account.**

    You are taken to a confirmation page. From here you can start using Seamless Lite by following the steps below.

To create a custom background pattern using Seamless Lite, follow these steps:

1. **Go to the Seamless Lite application (**www.colourlovers.com/seamless**).**

    You see a main window with a light gray square in the middle. This serves as the canvas for your pattern. What you design in this space will repeat itself to create a pattern. Shapes and layers to build your pattern are on the left side of the page. Click the slider on the upper right of the page to zoom into the canvas. You can see this interface in Figure 8-13.

2. **To begin a pattern, select a shape from any of the categories and drag the shape onto your canvas.**

    The shape automatically repeats in the darker gray space outside your canvas. This lets you see how your design would look when replicated into a pattern.

3. **Adjust the shape's size by clicking any of the points that frame the shape.**

    Hold down the Shift key to maintain the shape's proportions.

4. **(Optional) To rotate the shape, click the point above the shape. When the rotation arrow appears, rotate as you wish.**

5. **Add more shapes to build your pattern.**

    You can take your design in any direction you like. To continue using the exact same shape you created using Steps 2 and 3, use the Clone button under the Layers palette. As you can see in Figure 8-13, I cloned a hexagon three times, moving each hexagon into place after cloning it.

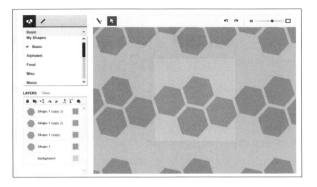

Figure 8-13: Repeat a base shape to form a larger pattern.

6. **When you're satisfied with your pattern design, click the Save button at the bottom of your page.**

   Sign in to your COLOURlovers account, or select *Click here to register* if you aren't already a member. After that's complete, fill out the required information and save your pattern template.

7. **Select colors for your pattern.**

   a. *Underneath your pattern, shaded gray squares denote the different shades of your pattern. Click a gray square to add color.*

   As you can see in Figure 8-14, a window appears for you to choose a color.

   b. *Pick your color by using the color picker or by inputting a hex code or RGB values.*

   Read more about hex codes and RGB values in Chapter 6.

   If you created a color not yet used by another COLOURlovers member, you are asked to name the color. Get creative!

8. **Enter your pattern name in the required field and then click Create Pattern to finish your pattern.**

   This brings up your pattern profile page with details that show your pattern's colors, ways to download the pattern, and other details.

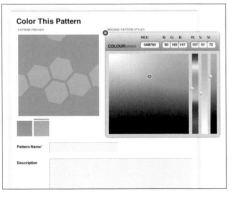

Figure 8-14: Use the color picker to select awesome colors for your pattern design.

9. **To save your pattern as a tile for your background, click the Preview link on the right sidebar, as shown in Figure 8-15.**

   This opens the tile in a new browser window.

10. **Right-click the tile, choose Save Image As from the menu that appears, and then save it to your computer.**

SHARE THIS PATTERN

SHARE ON 🅿 t f SU

GRAB THIS BADGE CODE

`<a href="http://www.colourlovers.com/pattern/3231773/t`

GET THIS PATTERN IMAGE

Your Screen [1280x800] // Preview // iPhone

390x300 // 800x600 // 1024x768 // 1200x800 // 1600x1200

Figure 8-15: Clicking Preview loads your tile pattern in a new browser tab.

When you use Seamless Lite, your pattern uploads to be viewed publicly by the COLOURlovers community. That's just how it is. However, you can download your final file and then delete it afterward. Or, in the right column, you can set the pattern's Creative Commons license so you don't grant rights to use your pattern.

If you want to keep your patterns private (and you plan on doing this more than once), try the desktop app Seamless Studio (www.colourlovers.com/seamless-studio). You can try it for free for 15 days and then purchase it for $49 ($29 if you become a COLOURlovers member for free).

Adding a background to your blog

After you have a background that you're ready to use in your blog design, it's time to add it to your blog. This section shows you how to create a solid background and a tiled background using the Twenty Eleven theme on WordPress.org.

Create a solid background

To add a solid-colored background, follow these steps:

1. **Choose Appearance⇨Background.**

   The Custom Background page appears. By default, the background color is white.

2. **To change the background to a solid color, you have two options:**

   - Enter the hexadecimal color code in the Background Color text box.
   - Click the Select a Color link and then use the color wheel shown in Figure 8-16 to choose a color.

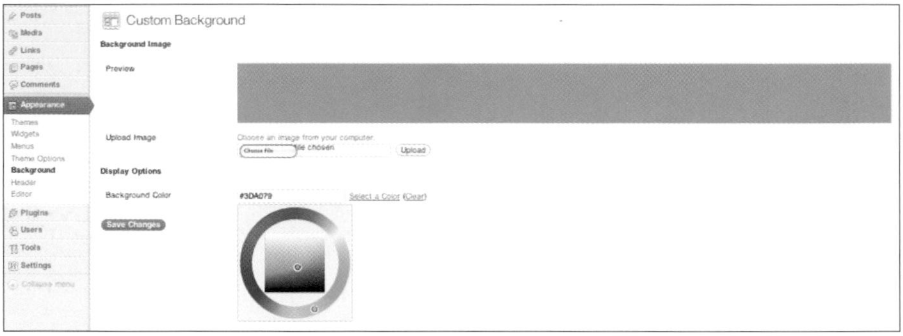

Figure 8-16: Use the color picker on the WordPress Custom Background page.

3. Click the Save Changes button.

Be sure to click this button, or your settings won't change.

Display a patterned background

If you have a pattern that you want to tile across your blog's background, follow these steps.

1. Choose Appearance⇨Background.

The Custom Background page appears. By default, the background color is white.

2. Upload an image from your computer by clicking the Choose File button in the Select Image section.

This opens a window and lets you select the image on your computer.

3. Click the Upload button.

After the image finishes uploading, it automatically shows up in the Preview window as a tiled image. Display Options also appear underneath the Upload Image feature, as shown in Figure 8-17.

4. (Optional) If needed, change the settings of your background image:

- *Position:* Use the Left, Center, or Right options to set the screen position of the background image on your blog design.

- *Repeat:* Use the No Repeat, Tile, Tile Horizontally, or Tile Vertically options to set whether or how the background image tiles within a browser window.

- *Attachment:* Use the Scroll option to let your background image scroll down the page. Use the Fixed option to set the background image so it doesn't scroll down the page.

5. **Click the Save Changes button.**

   Be sure to click this button, or your settings won't take effect.

Some WordPress themes don't let you display a patterned background. Also, other platforms like Blogger and Typepad have different methods for changing your background. Despite the platform or theme, you can always change your background by modifying your CSS, which I cover in Chapter 9.

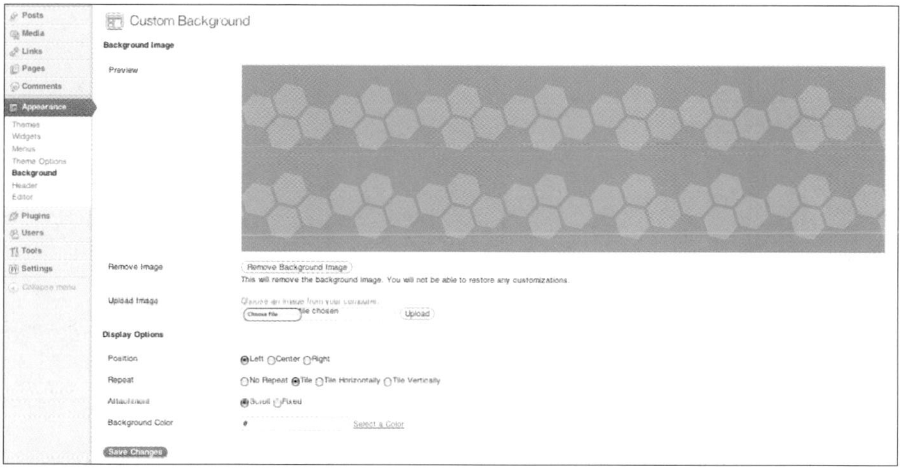

Figure 8-17: Display Options for a WordPress Custom Background page.

9

Customizing the Design with Coding Basics

1 was once asked whether I thought a blogger had to know code to be successful. One of the great things about blogging is that just about anyone with a computer and an Internet connection can set up a blog and publish a post.

However, bloggers like to tweak things. Adjust a color here, change a font there. Whether or not you design your entire blog, at some point you'll want to make at least minor changes yourself. That's when you could use some basic HTML and CSS knowledge. And where this chapter is your friend.

This chapter won't make you a coding expert. What it will do, though, is give you a greater understanding of HTML and CSS so you can make simple tweaks to your blog's content and design. I also give you one killer tool for learning more about how code works on your blog (and for making tweaks without messing anything up).

 Although this book doesn't get into detail about PHP, you should know what it is. In essence, PHP performs the functions of your blog. And because PHP makes your blog do stuff, if you mess up the code in your PHP file, your blog may not work properly or may crash altogether. There are some sections of this book where you need to alter your PHP, but for the most part, I stick to CSS and HTML. If you're interested in learning more about how website code works, check out *PHP, MySQL, JavaScript, & HTML5 All-in-One For Dummies* by Steve Suehring and Janet Valade.

One last word before you start: Always back up your blog before digging into code! Most hosted blogging platforms perform backups for you, but you can manually back up too (typically from an Export function within your dashboard). For WordPress.org, either back up through your host's control panel or by using a backup plugin like WP-DB-Backup (`http://wordpress.org/extend/plugins/wp-db-backup`) or WP Online Backup (`http://wordpress.org/extend/plugins/wponlinebackup`).

Seeing How HTML and CSS Work Together

To understand how HTML and CSS work together, you need to know what they are.

HTML stands for HyperText Markup Language. By "marking up" content within an HTML document, you instruct a web browser to display that content on a website in a certain way. This could be anything from turning text into a hyperlink to displaying an image.

To mark up your HTML document, you use *tags.* Tags contain an HTML element between less-than (<) and greater-than (>) symbols. These tags identify where your command begins and ends. For example, this snippet

```
<p>This is my wonderful paragraph.</p>
```

commands that everything between the opening <p> and the closing </p> is to display as a paragraph. Notice that the closing tag uses a / to mark it as ending the command.

CSS stands for cascading style sheet. CSS comprises a set of commands that can customize the look and feel of your blog design by styling the display of various elements on your blog, from the font color to a space around an image.

CSS rules include two basic parts:

- **A selector** (so called because it selects the HTML to which the CSS instructions apply)
- **At least one declaration** (which declares what the CSS should do)

  Then, each declaration has two parts:

  - **A property** (that is, what property the CSS changes)
  - **A value** (how that property changes)

For example, this CSS rule makes paragraph text gray:

```
p {color: #808080;}
```

And here is how:

- ✔ p is the selector, which selects the text in any pair of <p> tags in your HTML file.
- ✔ {color: #808080;} is the declaration.
- ✔ color is the property of the declaration.
- ✔ #808080 is the value of the property, or the hexadecimal code for the color gray.

Putting the HTML and CSS together, think of creating your blog design like building a house. HTML is the structure of your house; CSS is the paint and décor. CSS is useless without a structure to apply it to, just like paint does no good without walls to put it on.

Basic HTML Every Blogger Should Know

At some point in your blogging existence, you have to use some HTML. Even though you probably write your blog posts using a visual editor that lets you just click a button to, say, add a link or bold a word, you may have used HTML in other areas of your blog, such as to add an image to your sidebar. Of course, knowing some HTML doesn't hurt when you have to troubleshoot content that's not displaying properly.

These next few sections show you how to make some simple edits in your text formatting and blog design using HTML.

If you run into any issues with your code not working, make sure you use a closing tag (like </p>).

Inserting hyperlinks

As an Internet user, you know that hyperlinks are links that take you to another location or file by clicking a word or group of words. In HTML, hyperlinks look like the bold text in the following example:

```
<p>This is a <a href="http://www.momcomm.com">great blog
          post</a>.</p>
```

When you break down the HTML for the link, you notice the following elements:

- ✔ <a: This is a *start tag*. Hyperlinks start with an anchor tag, denoted by the a.
- ✔ href=: This is an *attribute,* which provides additional information about the HTML element and is always noted in the start tag.

✔ `"http://www.momcomm.com"`: The URL is the `href` attribute's *value,* which is the page, document, or file that you want the text anchored to. The value appears within the double quote marks. Here, you insert the web address where your visitors will go if they click the link. For the link to work, you need to include the full web address, which includes the `http://` (or whatever protocol your destination site uses, such as `https://`, `ftp://`, and so on).

✔ `>`: This closes the start tag.

✔ `great blog post`: This text displays on your blog and is clickable by your visitors. Figure 9-1 shows how the linked text displays in a blog.

This is a great blog post.

Figure 9-1: Blue text signals hyperlinked words.

✔ `</a>`: This is your *closing tag,* marking that the hyperlink is closed.

Formatting words

Adding simple formatting to words is, well, simple. Use an opening tag, followed by the text you want to format, and then finish with a closing tag. You can format words, sentences, or even entire paragraphs.

Here's what the code looks like:

✔ **Bold:** `<strong>This is bold text.</strong>`

✔ **Italics:** `<em>This is italics or emphasized text.</em>`

✔ **Strikethrough:** `<del>This is strikethrough or deleted text.</del>`

You can see each of these formatting options in action in Figure 9-2.

 Using strikethrough formatting doesn't delete any text. Bloggers often use strikethrough text to acknowledge an error, to cross out outdated information within a post, or to show humor or irony.

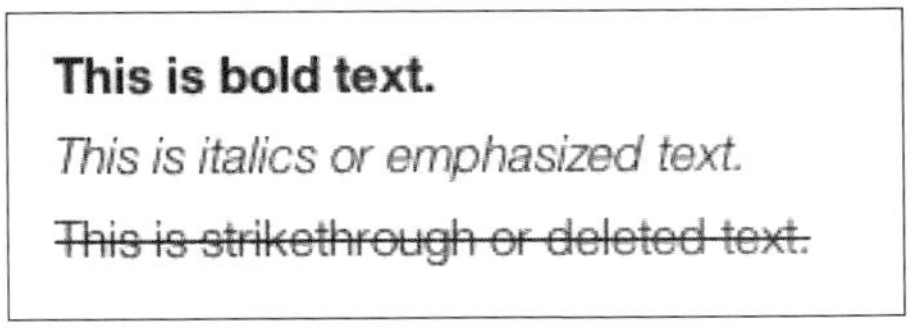

This is bold text.

This is italics or emphasized text.

~~This is strikethrough or deleted text.~~

Figure 9-2: Different types of text formatted with HTML.

Avoid applying underline to words on the Internet. Users assume that underlined words are hyperlinks, which may be confusing even if your hyperlinks are a different color and not even underlined.

Making lists

Lists take the form of numbered or bulleted lists. However, HTML doesn't think in terms of numbered or bulleted; instead, it thinks in terms of ordered and unordered lists:

- ✔ **Ordered list:** Numbered items
- ✔ **Unordered list:** Bulleted items

Makes sense, right?

When making a list, you use two types of tags to create a list: a starting and closing pair that begins and ends the list and denotes the list type (ordered or unordered). Within the list, subordinate tags denote the listed items.

For ordered lists, you use the main <ol> and </ol> (ordered list) tags with <li> (list item) tags inside. For unordered lists, you use <ul> and </ul> (unordered list) and <li> (list item) tags. As you can see in the following examples, you use a <li> and a </li> tag to denote each listed item, regardless of the type of list.

```
<ol>
    <li>I came.</li>
    <li>I saw.</li>
    <li>I conquered (this book).</li>
</ol>
```

```
<ul>
    <li>I came.</li>
    <li>I saw.</li>
    <li>I conquered (this book).</li>
</ul>
```

In Figure 9-3, you see that just the difference between an o and a u changes the list from a numbered to a bulleted list.

Don't forget to use closing tags with your lists. If you forget to close the list with an </ol> or </ul>, a web browser assumes that all the content underneath the opening tag is part of the list.

1. I came.

2. I saw.

3. I conquered (this book).

- I came.

- I saw.

- I conquered (this book).

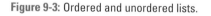

Figure 9-3: Ordered and unordered lists.

Inserting images

Great blog designs have one thing in common: They use images. Placing images into a blog post, sidebar, or other place just takes a little bit of HTML.

To display your image online, your image must be hosted on a server. For example, if you're working in WordPress.org, your image is uploaded to your server, and from there you can display the image by pointing to the image file, including your blog address and the subfolder (if applicable) where images are stored. To display images, HTML uses an `<img>` tag with an `src` attribute (`src` as in the image source, which in this case means the image's address online), like this:

```
<img src="http://www.blogname.com/location-of-image/
          imagefilename.jpg"/>
```

With proper permission, you can also source images that aren't your own. For example, an advertiser running a banner ad on your blog might want to host that ad on its website. Because you're sourcing the image from that site, the advertiser could update the banner ad, which then automatically updates on your blog (provided the ad provider didn't change the location of the image on its server).

To turn the image into a link so that clicking it takes a visitor to a URL, place the `<img>` tag inside a hyperlink tag, like so:

```
<a href="http://www.destinationURL.com">
    <img src="http://www.blogname.com/subfolder/
              imagefilename.jpg"/>
</a>
```

Making images clickable comes in especially handy when you want to connect a social media icon (which is typically an image file) to a social media profile page.

Finally, adding an `alt` tag description to your image code gives search engines a way to know what the image contains. The `alt` description also makes your web page accessible to people who use special devices (which read the text in the `alt` description aloud) because they have a disability, such as limited vision or blindness. To use an `alt` tag with your image, use `alt="Image File Description"` like this:

```
<img src="http://www.blogname.com/subfolder/
          imagefilename.jpg" alt="Image File Description" />
```

I talk more about the benefits of using `alt` tags in Chapter 10.

To put this all together, if you'd like to display a Facebook icon (stored within a subfolder on your server) whose filename is fbicon.png and have the icon linked to your Facebook page (http://www.facebook.com/mypage), your link and <img> tag look like this:

```
<a href="http://www.facebook.com/mypage">
    <img src="http://www.momcomm.com/images/fgicon.png" />
</a>
```

Basic CSS Every Blogger Should Know

Most bloggers have touched HTML at some point, but CSS remains a little more mysterious to someone just getting familiar with code. Your CSS lives within a file called a *style sheet,* usually named style.css. Some blogs may have more than one CSS file.

The following sections help you get some basic CSS under your belt so you can change the style of some blog design elements yourself.

If you have trouble finding the code for any of these, try Firebug, which I explain how to use later in this chapter.

Changing background color

One of the simplest changes to make in your CSS is changing the background color. In Chapter 8, I mention that themes let you change your overall background color in the theme settings. Easy!

If you don't have that option, it's time to dig into your CSS file. Not only can you change your overall background color, but you can also change the background of other elements in your blog design, such as the space behind your text.

To change your main background color, look for this code:

```
body {
    background: #FFFFFF;
}
```

Using the hex code #FFFFFF makes the background white. Just update the hex code to change the color. (See Chapter 6 for more about hex codes and how they work.)

Adjusting other colors

Just like the background color, you can also adjust any color by finding the corresponding CSS code and then changing the hex code color. For example, to change the color of your main headings (like your blog post titles), look for the `h1` selector, which applies formatting to the largest heading on your blog. Then simply adjust the hex color code (currently `#0000FF`) to whatever you want:

```
h1 {
    font-size: 18px;
    color: #0000FF;
    font-weight: bold;
}
```

In looking through code, you sometimes might see hex colors written as a three-digit code. Because hex (hexadecimal) codes are a set of three, two-digit sets, when the two characters in each set are the same, you can shorten the hex code by removing the duplicate character. In the preceding example, the blue color `#0000FF` can also be written as `#00F`.

Changing font properties

When you work on a blog post and want to format certain smallish things — say, apply bold to a word — you do this within your text editor or by using HTML. But if you want broader changes — say, change the font size for all your blog posts, or make every blog post title bold — you make blanket changes to the font in a particular page element by using CSS. Table 9-1 lays out some frequently used font properties and their values.

Table 9-1	Font Properties in CSS
Property	**Common Values**
`font-family`	`verdana, serif`
`font-size`	`em, px, %`
	(**Note:** In the context of sizing fonts, *em* is a measurement relative to the current font size. So, 2em is twice the size of the current font size.)
`font-style`	`normal, italic`
`font-weight`	`normal, bold, bolder, lighter`

Here's an example of how you would use these properties together to change a particular font:

```
font-family: trebuchet MS;
font-size: 16px;
font-style: normal;
font-weight: bold;
```

`font-style` and `font-weight` are self-explanatory. However `font-family` and `font-size` (such as using the Trebuchet MS font with a size of 16 pixels, as shown in the preceding code) need a little more explanation.

Font-family

As I explain in Chapter 6, only certain fonts work on the web. So, when listing the font family you want to use, always include fallback options, separated by a comma. That way, if your first choice doesn't render correctly for a visitor, that browser tries the next font you've specified (assuming that you did — and you should!). Ending with a generic font (`serif`, `sans-serif`, `monospace`) ensures that the browser will select a similar font if the font families preceding it fail.

Here's an example:

```
font-family: Georgia, "Times New Roman", serif;
```

In the preceding example, the browser will first try the font Georgia. If that fails, then it tries Times New Roman. If that fails too, then the browser will use any font that's a serif font.

Always use quotation marks to list a font family with more than one word, like what I did for Times New Roman in the preceding example.

Font-size

The `font-size` property sets the text size. If not specified, the default text size in browsers is 16px. The size of the text can be listed in one of four ways:

- ✔ **px:** px is a measurement in pixels (dots on a computer screen), with larger numbers representing larger text sizes and smaller numbers displaying smaller text.

- ✔ **em:** em is a unit of measurement equal to a specified font size. If the element you want to change is set at 16 px, then 1 em = 16 px. So, if you want to make the text bigger, a text size of `2.5em` would make it 40 px.

✔ **%:** Like using em, using a percentage (%) is also based off the <body> size. With the <body> size listed at 100%, a heading might be 120%, and a smaller bit of text might be 75%.

✔ **pt:** A point (pt) is ½ of an inch and is typically used for print typography. If you defined a font size for a website using points, a 14-pt font size might look larger or smaller than you intended because an inch is an inch is an inch.

Avoid using point sizes in your blog design.

Aligning text

Online text can be aligned to the left or the right, centered, justified, or inherited (taking the same value of the element's parent). Within your CSS, you can apply this alignment to any text element from a heading tag (like <h1>) to your paragraphs. The following CSS rules show you the ways you can align a paragraph:

```
p {text-align: center;}
```

```
p {text-align: left;}
```

```
p {text-align: right;}
```

```
p {text-align: justify;}
```

```
p {text-align: inherit;}
```

Adjusting margins and padding

Before I get to the nitty-gritty about margins and padding, you should understand a little about how they fit into the bigger picture. In HTML, each blog design element is considered a box. Each box includes a content area (such as a blog post title or a blog graphic) surrounded by optional margins, borders, and padding. Each of those form a box around the element. In CSS, the *box model* refers to those boxes generated by the optional margins, borders, and padding.

In this section, I want to talk only about margins and padding because bloggers often confuse the two. (At first, I did, too.) Here's the easiest way to explain the difference:

✔ **Margin:** The outer space of an element

✔ **Padding:** The inner space of an element

To put that into visual terms, take a look at Figure 9-4. Notice how the padding adds space around the content area but stays within the border as part of the element. Margins create whitespace outside the content.

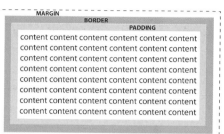

Margins and padding can be adjusted to the top, bottom, right, and left of an image. Because padding adds space *within* the element, note that it increases that element's size as well. So, an element that's 200px wide with 10px of padding on both the right and left sides will become 220 pixels.

Figure 9-4: A design or text element can be surrounded by padding, a border, and margins.

Sometimes you see padding or margins written in shorthand so the coding doesn't get too lengthy. For example, this code

```
padding: 10px 20px 30px 40px;
```

and this code

```
padding-top: 10px;
padding-right: 20px;
padding-bottom: 30px;
padding-left: 40px;
```

mean the same thing. If you notice, listing margins and padding go in a clockwise order starting with 12 o'clock.

Code can even become shorter. For example, this code

```
margin: 10px 20px;
```

means the top and bottom are 10px, and the right and left are 20px.

Styling links

In the earlier section, "Inserting hyperlinks," I show you how to use HTML to link text to a location or file. CSS lets you style that text depending on the state the link is in.

Links typically use these four selector options:

- ✔ a:link selects a link that hasn't been visited.
- ✔ a:visited selects a link that the user has visited.

   ✔ `a:hover` selects the link state when the user runs a cursor over it.

   ✔ `a:active` selects a link that becomes active the moment it's clicked.

The order of these link state selectors is important for the code to work. The `a:hover` selector must come after `a:link` and `a:visited`. The `a:active` selective must come after `a:hover`.

Hyperlinks often use underlines, but you can remove the underline in various states by using `text-decoration: none`. Here's an example of how to code a not-underlined link that's been visited so that the link turns purple with no underline:

```
a:visited {color: #800080; text-decoration: none;}
```

Accessing the CSS in Your Blogging Platform

As for exactly how to access your blog's CSS, it really depends on the blog platform you use. Here's how to access your CSS file or CSS options in a few of the most popular blogging platforms:

   ✔ **Blogger:** To modify your CSS in Blogger, you really don't have to touch too much code. Blogger actually gives you customization options such as changing fonts and colors of various blog elements. To access these options, open your Blogger Dashboard and go to Template➪Customize➪Advanced. If you can't do exactly what you want from the existing options, then you can add CSS by selecting Add CSS from the Advanced menu options.

   ✔ **Tumblr:** Tumblr allows you to add to the existing CSS. Click Customize in the top right of your screen. Then, in a customization toolbar, click Advanced to add CSS in the Add Custom CSS field.

   The Firebug tool really comes in handy for blog platforms where you can't modify the code but only add new code that overrides the code that already exists. You find out how to use this tool later in this chapter.

   ✔ **Wordpress.com:** Because Wordpress.com hosts your blog for you, you have to purchase its Custom Design upgrade to modify the CSS. (Chapter 1 explains the difference between hosted and self-hosted blogs.) You can find more information about upgrading at the following web address: `http://en.support.wordpress.com/custom-design/editing-css`

   ✔ **Wordpress.org:** To modify CSS on a Wordpress.org blog, you need to access your themes `style.css` file. From your Dashboard, go to Appearance➪Editor. You can find the `style.css` file under your theme's templates on the right side. You can also edit your CSS from your host's control panel or via FTP (File Transfer Protocol).

When using WordPress frameworks (like those I cover in Chapter 7), do not modify the CSS of the framework. Instead, modify the `style.css` file for your child theme. Most frameworks warn you within the framework's `style.css` file, but it's worth mentioning here too.

Inspecting Your Blog with Firebug

Ever since a friend introduced me to the wonders of Firebug, it's been one of my favorite tools. Firebug (http://getfirebug.com) is a free web-development tool that integrates with the Firefox browser. Firebug lets you look at your blog design and your code at the same time. Think of it as having X-ray vision! However, the coolest part is that you can make changes to your design in real time, yet the changes don't affect your live blog. That means you can play, learn, tweak, and code without worrying about a thing!

To set up Firebug, you need to use the Mozilla Firefox browser. There are a few ways to install Firebug but here's the most straightforward way.

1. **Visit the Firebug page on the Mozilla Add-Ons site**: http://addons. mozilla.org/en-US/firefox/addon/fircbug

2. **Click the Add to Firefox button.**

   A popup displays telling you to install add-ons only from authors whom you trust.

3. **Click Install Now from the popup window.**

   A message displays saying Firebug is now installed. The installation also adds a Firebug symbol onto your browser toolbar (Figure 9-5).

   To start using Firebug, click the Firebug icon or press F12.

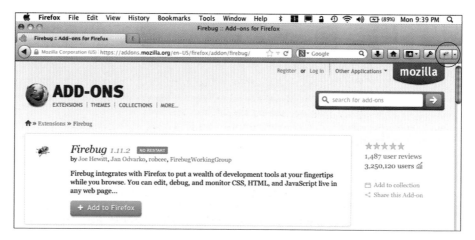

Figure 9-5: Firebug icon appears on your Firefox toolbar.

Firebug can do a host of awesome things, but I like to use the tool for three purposes:

✔ **Find what code affects which part of your design or content.** Firebug lets you inspect your blog's HTML and CSS. If you want to find out how to change a particular element's color but don't know which code to modify, click the rectangle-with-a-cursor-arrow icon beside the bug to inspect any element on your page. In Figure 9-6, I hovered over my blog header image, and Firebug tells me details about the HTML and the style (or CSS) of the element. I can see where my header image is sourced from, and under the Style tab, I see that my image has no border. The tool even tells me which line of the CSS I need to modify if I really want to make changes on my blog.

✔ **See how changes look (without really making them).** Firebug makes your blog a coding playground. Change colors, play with sizes, and adjust margins all you want. Nothing is altered in your live blog because you're not actually changing an actual HTML document or a CSS file. In Figure 9-7, I played with the CSS by changing the hex code color of my comment bubble from gray to green, just to see how it looks. (Read more about hex codes in Chapter 6.)

✔ **Find out the size of various blog elements.** If you're unsure of a blog design element's size, use the inspector tool and then click Layout in the right window. For example, I click the sidebar column in the visual pane at the top and then click the Layout tab in the lower right pane of the Firebug window. On the Layout tab, Firebug tells me my sidebar is currently 188 pixels (px) wide and 532 px high.

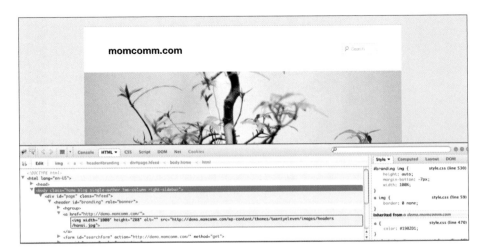

Figure 9-6: Use Firebug to see the code of an element.

Figure 9-7: Play with color changes in Firebug.

Firebug doesn't actually save any changes to your actual code. If you're exploring several tweaks to your code with Firebug, make notes of your modifications so you can then make them within your actual live code.

Part III
Designing for Easy Navigation and Interactivity

© grain edit, http://grainedit.com

Explore creative ways to welcome new blog visitors through navigation design at www.dummies.com/extras/blogdesign.

In this part. . .

✔ Incorporate effective navigation into your blog design and use SEO-optimized blog components.

✔ Discover ways to make your blog design mobile-friendly.

✔ Learn what to include in your navigation menu and how to give your menu some creative flair.

✔ Gain ideas for building a sidebar that benefits your blog visitors and learn what sidebar elements distract your readers.

✔ Explore ways to make your blog content easy to find by learning how to ensure old blog content gets found, to organize with categories and tags, and to put the spotlight on your blog posts.

✔ Find out how to make your content easy to share and learn to manage your comments without alienating readers.

10

Navigation and SEO Basics

In This Chapter

▶ Knowing why good navigation design matters
▶ Incorporating SEO to improve navigation
▶ Making your site look good on mobile devices

*N*o matter how awesomely designed a blog looks, visitors won't stick around if a blog is hard to navigate. A blog should be easy for visitors to move through, whether they just want to explore your blog or need to find something specific.

The next few chapters cover various aspects of making your blog easy to navigate, and this chapter first gives you a foundation of good navigation design by explaining how both you and your readers benefit. In addition, I cover ways to optimize your blog to bring in new readers from search engines. Finally, I cover a few ways to ensure that your blog is easy to navigate on mobile devices.

Discovering the Mission of Good Navigation

You may write wonderfully thought-provoking blog posts, but all the best writing in the world does you little good if your readers have to think too hard when it comes to moving around your blog. Good navigation as part of your blog design means that visitors can move through your site intuitively. They don't need help figuring it out because the navigation all makes sense.

I have to break something to you, though. Good navigation design means rolling up your sleeves and putting in some extra work. You may have to spend time trimming your blog categories (see Chapter 12) or making your site mobile-friendly, but the benefits are well worth the digital elbow grease.

Staying focused on your readers

Making decisions about how to best lay out your navigation design boils down to simply putting yourself in readers' shoes. Focus on the readers' experience by thinking of scenarios where a reader may end up navigating to or through your blog. Here are a few typical examples:

- ✔ A visitor performs a search on a search engine that leads to your blog.

- ✔ A visitor navigates directly to your blog and wants to read multiple posts from a particular category.

- ✔ A visitor clicks a link on someone else's blog that leads to a post or page within your blog.

- ✔ After exploring your blog a bit, a visitor wants to return to a page he or she already visited on your blog.

Good navigation allows blog visitors to get around your site easily, whether they're looking for something specific or just exploring.

When it comes to a visitor finding content or information, keep this simple rule in mind: People shouldn't have to click more than three times to find what they're looking for. While an old but well-known study from Joshua Porter ("Testing the Three-Click Rule," User Interface Engineering, originally published April 16, 2003, http://www.uie.com/articles/three_click_rule/) showed that people don't necessarily give up after three magical clicks, the point remains — the reader shouldn't have to click too many times to get to a destination.

Staying focused on readers also means encouraging them to read more than one blog post. You can drive readers to other posts through related post links, a popular post section, and more. I cover these techniques in the next few chapters.

In Chapter 3, I talk about knowing the types of users who visit your blog. Put yourself into the shoes of each of your reader types and decide how you can get them to the content you think they care about. You could even ask some friends or blog readers to serve as "beta testers" to see how intuitive (or not) the navigation is on your blog.

Limiting choice to drive action

As a blogger, you want to make your readers happy. In that quest, sometimes bloggers (and businesses, for that matter) try to be helpful by giving readers a lot of choices — subscription options, menu options, sharing options — hoping that they can cater to as many readers as possible. If you're a blogger who does this, you may want to reconsider how many choices you give your readers because giving people too many choices can backfire.

Sheena Iyengar and Mark Lepper published an often-cited study that makes this point ("When Choice Is Demotivating: Can One Desire Too Much of a Good Thing?" *Journal of Personality and Social Psychology* 49, no. 6 [2000]). The researchers and their assistants set up a table in a gourmet market and offered samples of different types of jam to passersby. Every few hours, the research team switched from offering 24 samples of jams to just 6 samples. Customers tried two jams on average, regardless of how many jams presented to them. Each person who sampled a jam received a coupon good for $1 off one jam.

Now here's where the number of jams comes into play. More people (60 percent) stopped by the assortment of 24 jams, yet just 40 percent were drawn in to a display of just six jams. However, 30 percent of those who sampled from the small assortment purchased the jam, whereas a mere 3 percent of those presented with 24 jams purchased a jar! When presented with fewer choices, people were more likely to buy.

The same principle goes beyond jam. When you offer fewer choices on your blog, readers are more likely to take action. This means instead of showing readers 10 or 15 social media platforms you belong to, just show the ones that matter the most to you — and that your readers use most.

Offering choice is a matter of keeping things organized and not overwhelming. Think about what you really, really need before you add more choices to your blog. Throughout the next few chapters, I talk about some ways to limit choice and clutter so readers can more easily use and navigate your site.

Easing Navigation with SEO-optimized Blog Components

Search engine optimization (SEO) essentially describes the process of increasing a website's visibility in a search engine's unpaid search results. SEO can help bring your blog to the attention of people using a search engine to find specific information. Say you write a post about how to plan a superhero birthday party. You surely hope that later, when someone types "superhero birthday party" into a search engine, your post shows up on the first page of results. This can bring you a lot of traffic, which any blogger would love.

Optimizing your blog doesn't mean that you'll rise to the top of the rankings. There are no guarantees in the world of SEO! But doing some basic SEO can make your site easier to get to from search engines than doing no SEO at all. The better you optimize your blog, the more likely you can bring people to your site via search engines.

SEO isn't about tricking search engines or writing keyword-stuffed blog posts. Instead, making simple adjustments to a few parts of your blog can optimize your content and attract new readers.

This section won't make you an SEO ninja, maven, or any other overused word. What it will do is teach you a few basic tricks to improve your blog's search engine visibility.

Building a sitemap

Websites often have two types of sitemaps — one mainly for search engines and one mainly for blog visitors.

An *XML sitemap* is a directory of pages that you want search engines to find. Think of it as a file that helps search engines learn about your entire blog. Without an XML sitemap, search engines will still most likely find your blog. Using the sitemap just supplements that.

One of the easiest ways to do this is through a WordPress.org plug-in. After you find and install an XML sitemap plug-in, the plug-in actually does most of the work for you.

To create a sitemap, install the Google XML Sitemaps plug-in:

```
http://wordpress.org/extend/plugins/google-sitemap-
            generator
```

Then follow these steps:

1. **Go to Settings⇨XML-Dashboard.**

   Leave the options selected as they are.

2. **Generate your sitemap for the first time by clicking the Click Here to Build It for the First Time link (at the top).**

3. **To see your finished sitemap, click the Sitemap link in the first sentence at the top of the page.**

   You can see an example of an XML sitemap in Figure 10-1.

If you use an SEO plug-in like I cover in the upcoming section, "Getting specific with a meta description," check whether the plug-in includes an XML sitemap as a feature.

As you can see in Figure 10-1, an XML sitemap may be search engine–friendly, but it's not user-friendly. For your blog visitors, you want to create an HTML sitemap or an archive page. Because most bloggers have archive pages rather than HTML sitemaps, I talk more about making archive pages in Chapter 12.

XML Sitemap

This is a XML Sitemap which is supposed to be processed by search engines like Google, MSN Search and YAHOO.

It was generated using the Blogging-Software WordPress and the Google Sitemap Generator Plugin by Arne Brachhold.

You can find more information about XML sitemaps on sitemaps.org and Google's list of sitemap programs.

URL	Priority	Change Frequency	LastChange (GMT)
http://demo.momcomm.com/	100%	Daily	2013-01-27 22:41
http://demo.momcomm.com/sitemap/	60%	Weekly	2013-01-27 22:41
http://demo.momcomm.com/about-me/	60%	Weekly	2013-01-27 22:36
http://demo.momcomm.com/blog-post-title-2/	20%	Monthly	2013-01-21 06:22
http://demo.momcomm.com/blog-post-title/	20%	Monthly	2013-01-20 05:21
http://demo.momcomm.com/sample-page/	60%	Weekly	2012-12-30 15:14
http://demo.momcomm.com/hello-world/	100%	Monthly	2012-12-30 15:14

Generated with Google Sitemap Generator Plugin for WordPress by Arne Brachhold. This XSLT template is released under GPL.

Figure 10-1: An XML sitemap in WordPress.

Creating proper headings

Headings help your blog readers digest content. As I mention in Chapter 4, within your blog's HTML, your headers are defined from h1 (the largest heading size) to h6 (the smallest heading size). As you can guess, larger headers signify more important content.

From a navigation design perspective, headings give your reader — as well as search engines — clues as to what's important on the page. Search engines weight the words in header tags as more important than the smaller words of your main content.

On a blog post, your headers for a blog post typically go like this:

✒ h1: Blog post title

✒ h2: Subheadings

✒ h3: Deeper subheadings to support h2 subheadings

Bloggers don't need to use h4, h5, or h6 too often, if at all. Ideally, don't skip headings levels — like going from h1 to h3 on a blog post — and use relevant keywords in your headings to help search engines know what the post is about.

To add a heading level to your blog post, go to your Visual Editor. In WordPress, the place to change the heading level looks like what I show in Figure 10-2. If you don't see the menu that lets you select a heading, click the Show/Hide Kitchen Sink icon (it looks like two stacked boxes containing dots and dashes).

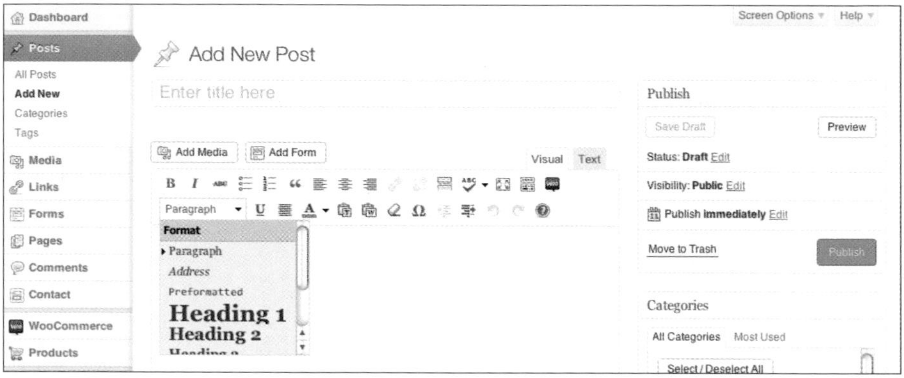

Figure 10-2: In WordPress, select heading levels here.

Using headings also helps with blog post readability, which I talk more about in Chapter 16.

Using an effective title tag

Your blog's *title tag* gives the search engine (and a reader visiting a search engine) a description about your blog. When someone lands on your blog, a visitor sees the contents of the title tag in the title bar and/or tab at the top of their browser windows, as shown in Figure 10-3. Technically, the title tag is an actual HTML tag that tells your browser what text to display in the browser window's title bar and tab. However, you probably filled out the contents of this tag via a visual interface in your blogging platform.

Figure 10-3: A home page's title tag uses keywords to describe a blog.

Good navigation within your blog design means fine-tuning areas that may at first look like small details, like title tags. When you look at where the title tag displays in a search engine, you can see how important it really is. Figure 10-4 shows you how a title tag looks when your blog comes up in a search. The title tag is the text after the blog name Momcomm.

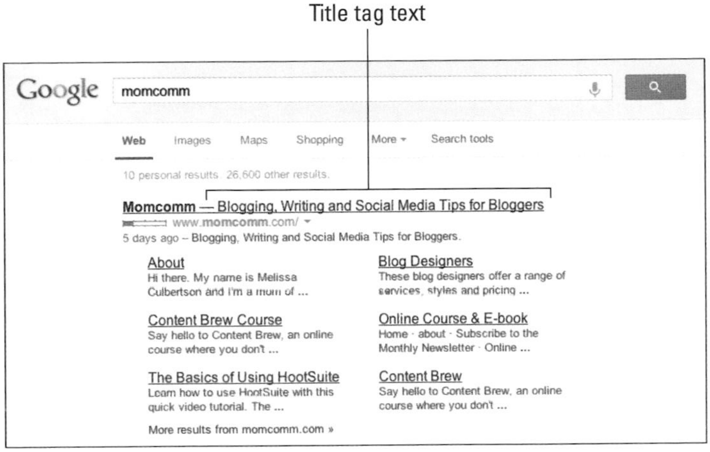

Title tag text

Figure 10-4: How a title tag looks in a search engine.

Unless you edit your code, the location to add your blog's title tag varies by blog platform. In WordPress, you can find the field under Settings⇨General⇨Tagline.

To see how the title tag looks in a WordPress dashboard, see Figure 10-5. Notice there's no section called "title tag." The title tag is the Tagline field. Many WordPress themes fill in the field with something generic like "Just Another WordPress Blog."

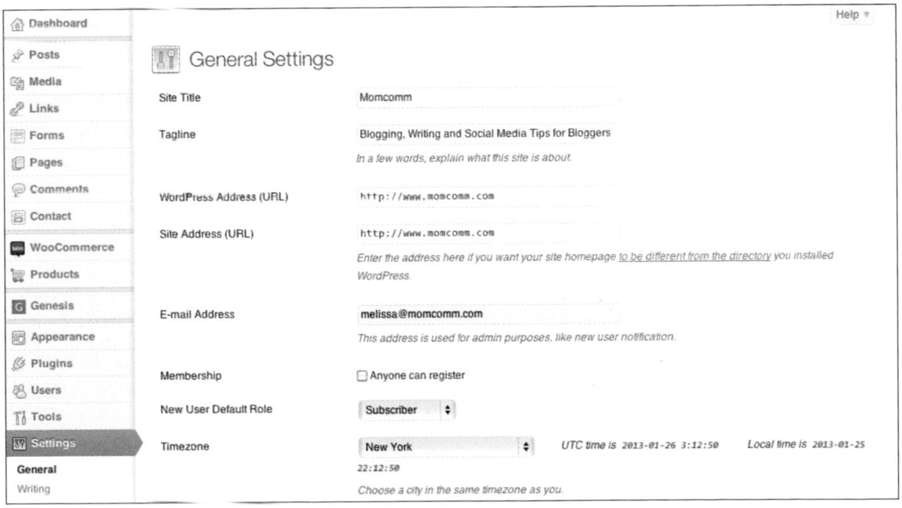

Figure 10-5: In WordPress, the text you enter in the Tagline field appears in the HTML title tag.

Trying to write something for the Tagline field can be tricky because you have to squeeze everything about your blog into a short statement. This field doesn't necessarily have to use your blog's actual tagline. (Read more about taglines in Chapter 8.) If your tagline is cute or clever but doesn't include relevant keywords, your title tag won't help with SEO. Instead, stick with these two simple guidelines:

- ✔ **Use a phrase that best describes your blog.** Search engines likely place greater weight on words at the beginning than at the end, so put the more important keywords closer to the beginning of the sentence.

- ✔ **Keep it short so search engines don't cut off words.** Using about 70 characters or fewer works best.

If you don't really have a niche, you might be thinking how you can sum up your entire blog into a short title. As a workaround, you could include a location ("blogging mom from Raleigh") or title ("freelance writer").

Title tags for your home page also go beyond your blog's home page. Effective SEO means ensuring search engine–worthy blog posts and pages have their own title tags. Blogging platforms automatically make a blog post or page's title its title tag (although you might customize it at times).

Getting specific with a meta description

Meta, whata? A *meta description* is a short paragraph that search engines use to describe your entire blog, a page, or a blog post.

One important component of search engine optimization is letting readers know where they're going. Although search engines don't use meta descriptions to determine your rankings, a proper meta description reassures search engine users that they are indeed headed to a page that has what they're searching for.

In Figure 10-6, you can see a search result for Twitter Name Change Checklist. Since I added a meta description to my blog post (I explain how to do so later in this section), that description displays in black text after the date the post was published. The meta description for my blog post on this topic reinforces to the visitors searching that the post is relevant to them.

Without a meta description for your blog posts or pages, search engines pull the first sentences from your post or page. Without a meta description for your overall site,

Twitter Name Change Checklist
www.momcomm.com/2012/01/twitter-name-change-checklist/
Jan 16, 2012 – If you're **changing** your **Twitter name**, grab a downloadable **checklist** so you don't miss all the places your **Twitter** handle may be listed.

Figure 10-6: How a meta description appears in Google.

search engines pull the first sentences from your most recent blog post, which may not be relevant to your blog overall. Say you started a post with something like, "I'm so happy to be back from vacation," but your blog is about cooking and sharing recipes.

When writing meta descriptions, be sure to use relevant keywords and keep the description to 150 characters. A meta description can be longer, but search engines show only a certain number of characters and then show an ellipsis to note there is more.

In Blogger, you can add a meta description for your entire blog by going to Settings⇨Search Preferences⇨Meta Tags⇨Description, and then clicking Edit to enter your description. To change the meta description for individual posts or pages, go to your Post Editor and then click Search Description under Post Settings.

As for WordPress.org, the default installation doesn't include meta description data. If you don't want to add a meta description directly into your HTML files, the easiest way to add a meta description for your overall blog and for individual posts is to use a theme that has settings for meta descriptions or to use a plug-in.

For example, in the Genesis theme, you can add your blog's meta description under SEO Settings. (Read more about themes in Chapter 5.) Genesis adds a Theme SEO Settings section under each post and page so that you can enter those meta descriptions.

If your theme doesn't come with SEO options, check out these three popular (and free) WordPress SEO plug-ins:

- **WordPress SEO plug-in by Yoast**

    `http://wordpress.org/extend/plugins/wordpress-seo`

- **WordPress All-in-One SEO Pack**

    `http://wordpress.org/extend/plugins/all-in-one-seo-pack`

- **SEO Ultimate**

    `http://wordpress.org/extend/plugins/seo-ultimate`

These plug-ins all make it easy for you to optimize your site and your posts. In Figure 10-7, you can see how the plug-in WordPress SEO (by Yoast) makes it easy for you to optimize your blog posts for SEO by showing you a Snippet Preview and giving you character counts for SEO Title (title tag) and meta description.

WordPress SEO by Yoast

General | Page Analysis | Advanced | Social

Snippet Preview: Title Tag - momcomm.com
demo.momcomm.com/146/
Ponderum sapientem et pro. Nam ei diam possim, sit nemore mentitum id. Equidem
inimicus has ei, tegere consectetuer duo ne, eam doming noster ne. Diceret no ...

Focus Keyword:

What is the main keyword or key phrase this page should be   Find related keywords
found for?

SEO Title:

Title display in search engines is limited to 70 chars, 47 chars left.   Generate SEO title
If the SEO Title is empty, the preview shows what the plugin generates based on your title
template.

Meta Description:

The meta description will be limited to 156 chars, 156 chars left.

If the meta description is empty, the preview shows what the plugin generates based on your meta description template.

Figure 10-7: Optimize SEO for a blog post.

If you don't care about optimizing certain posts (like a post about your birth-day), don't worry about adding meta descriptions to those posts. Optimize the ones with search engine ranking potential.

Making permalinks friendly

Just as your blog design should be clean, so should the URLs for all your pages and posts. These URLs — *permalinks* — link directly to a page or post instead of your blog's main URL. Search engines use the words within a per-malink to help classify your page, so the better optimized your permalink is, the more quality visitors your page attracts.

The permalink structure options for your blog posts depend upon the blog platform. For Blogger, the default permalink structure uses the post date like so:

```
http://blogname.blogspot.com/2013/01/blog-post-title.html
```

For WordPress.org, the default structure looks like this:

```
http://www.blogname.com/?p=123
```

Note: The WordPress.org default isn't great from a navigation perspective because the link format says nothing about the post. That means your URL isn't helpful in telling the search engines (or people) about the page's con-tent. Luckily, you have a lot of options in WordPress (check out Figure 10-8).

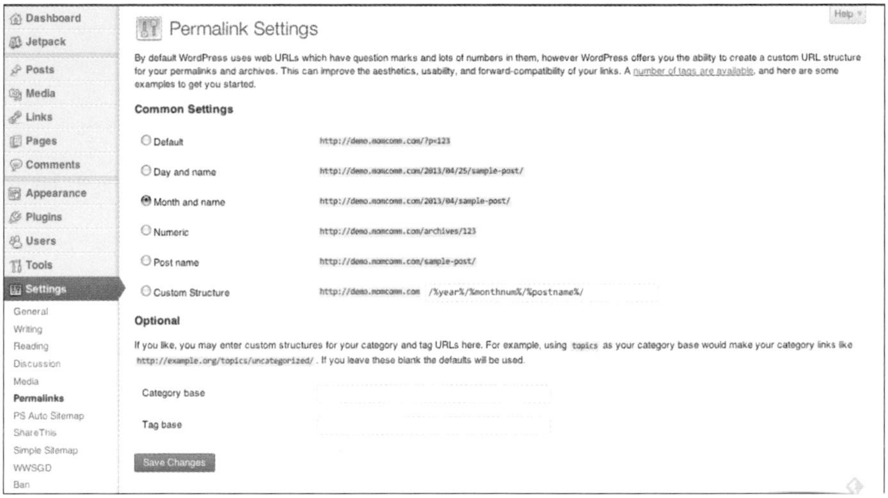

Figure 10-8: Set permalink options here.

To change your permalink settings in WordPress.org, stick to the Post Name option or the slightly longer Month and Name option. Both choices give your reader a descriptive permalink. While Month and Name permalinks are a common choice among bloggers, just note that this format might deter some people from visiting really old posts.

When you change your permalink structure, you need to set up a *301 redirect*, which is a permanent redirect to a new permalink. That way, you don't have to worry about broken links if another website linked to your blog using the structure in place before you changed your permalinks. You can set up the redirect with a WordPress plug-in like Redirection (`http://wordpress. org/extend/plugins/redirection`) or, if you feel like getting into code, by following the instructions from the WordPress.org Codex site (`http:// codex.wordpress.org/Using_Permalinks`).

If another website links to your blog, this external link can help boost your search engine rankings. Search engines assume that the more sites that link to you — your home page, blog post, or page — the more relevant your content is for a particular search term. From an SEO standpoint, a 301 redirect passes between 90 and 99 percent of that page's link power — affectionately called *link juice* — to the new permalink.

If you don't want to change your entire permalink structure, you can change just individual posts and pages when needed. In fact, your blog post or page title and your permalink name don't need to match exactly. For example your About page permalink might include a specific name, like this:

```
blogname.com/about-firstname-lastname
```

That specific name makes the permalink a bit more descriptive than a permalink with only the word *about* at the end, like this:

```
blogname.com/about
```

A more specific permalink is more SEO-friendly for those visitors who might search you by name. If you have a long blog post title, you can adjust the permalink to be more focused on a keyword versus using a full title.

To change a single post or page on Blogger

1. **Create a new post or page.**
2. **Choose Post Settings⇨Permalink.**
3. **Make sure that Custom URL is selected and then enter your custom permalink.**
4. **Click Done when finished.**

When you change a permalink on a Blogger post or page that's already been published, the original link doesn't redirect to your new permalink. For this reason, change only permalinks that are still new (fewer people are aware of the URL) or that haven't been published yet.

To change a single post or page in WordPress.org

1. **Go to the post or page.**
2. **Click Edit beside the permalink (located underneath the Blog Post Title field).**
3. **Make your change in the field and then click OK to save.**

When changing a single previously published URL, Wordpress.org keeps both the old and the new permalink working.

Adding alt attributes and titles to images

alt attributes — alternative text — display as an alternative when an image can't be seen for some reason, such as a slow Internet connection having trouble loading an image. However, `alt` attributes carry even more importance than that from an SEO and navigation design perspective.

Search engines can't see images, so adding an `alt` attribute to each of your images tells the search engine what your image is about. In Figure 10-9, you can see that the Alternative Text field appears when you add an image in WordPress.org.

In the HTML for the image, the `alt` attribute appears in the image tag and looks like this (see the bold text):

Figure 10-9: Blog platforms allow you to easily add an `alt` attribute description.

```
<img
    src="http://www.yoursite.com/images/filename.jpg"
    alt="Costa Rica butterfly"
/>
```

Whether images are part of your blog design or a blog post, include relevant keywords in your `alt` attribute so that search engines can find them easier. Sometimes a search engine user might navigate to your blog by finding an image first and then want to read the post. For example, someone might do an image search for crocheted blankets and then click an image that leads to a blog post with full instructions on how to make the blanket. Other times, the `alt` attribute just gives search engines a bigger picture of what topic is covered on a particular post or page. Bottom line: The more complete the picture that a search engine has about your blog, the more you've convinced the search engine that your blog post or page really covers the topic being searched.

`alt` attributes also aid in navigation by enabling people with blindness or impaired vision to identify what images appear on your site. Assistive devices then read text in the `alt` attribute aloud.

Notice in Figure 10-9 the Title field. When someone hovers over an image, that title description text appears (if the image has one). Although a title description can provide additional information about a photo, that info is more important from a user perspective, not for a search engine.

However, a title description is quite important if your blog readers use Pinterest. When someone pins a post of yours using a PinIt bookmarklet installed on their browser, the bookmarklet pulls up the title description from the image you select to pin. Pinterest uses your image title as the pin description. Without the description, Pinterest pulls the filename of the image, which may not be a helpful description. I talk more about naming images in Chapter 15.

Getting specific using anchor text

Anchor text is a clickable word or phrase within your blog that's hyperlinked to a web page. Say I wrote a blog post and linked to another blog post with the words *Facebook guidelines.* The words *Facebook guidelines* is anchor text.

On the backend, the HTML for a link looks like this (the anchor text is in bold):

```
<a href="http://www.momcomm.com/facebook-guidelines">
           Facebook guidelines</a>
```

Anchor text can help boost how you rank within search engines because search engine spiders use it to determine what your page is about. Anchor text is important to *interlinking,* which occurs when you link to other pages or posts within your own site.

To understand why anchor text is so important, have you ever linked to a post using words like this? (Pretend that the underlined words are links.)

- ✔ I wrote about <u>that here</u>.
- ✔ <u>My last post</u> on crazy hamster tricks.
- ✔ For more information, <u>click here</u>.

Most bloggers have done this at one time or another because it's sometimes the easiest thing to do. However, choosing generic words as the anchor text doesn't help your blog's search engine rankings. That's because generic anchor text doesn't describe the page content. Your blog's navigation design suffers, too, because blog readers need descriptive anchor text that compels them to click through.

Say you wrote a post about making homemade pizza. You write another blog post and want to mention your homemade pizza recipe post. To entice your readers to navigate to your other post, consider which of the following is more compelling:

- ✔ I wrote <u>this great post</u> about making homemade pizza.
- ✔ I wrote this great post about <u>making homemade pizza.</u>

Yup, they are indeed the same sentence, but the second one uses more descriptive anchor text. Not only is using anchor text a good SEO tactic, but it also encourages your readers to actually click the link, which for internal links will give you higher page views and a lower bounce rate. (See Chapter 3 for more about those terms.)

Sometimes you may have to rearrange your sentence to make anchor text work, but for the most part, using anchor text flows naturally in a sentence.

The same rules about anchor text apply when you link to other blogs and websites from your own blog. With more specific anchor text, you can play a part in helping a fellow blogger rank better for a specific term.

Making Your Blog Mobile-Friendly

The Internet is a different place than it was even a few short years ago. According to the Pew Internet & American Life Project, as of 2012, 56 percent of cellphone owners use their device to access the Internet (see `http://pewinternet.org/Commentary/2012/February/Pew-Internet-Mobile.aspx`). This means quite a few of your readers, even first-time visitors, visit your blog on a mobile device.

Because mobile devices have smaller screens than laptop or desktop computers, your blog design may not display on a phone or tablet the same way you see it from your computer. Your visitors may have to scroll back and forth on a small screen to read your content, or your design elements may display incorrectly.

For your blog design to engage visitors on mobile devices, you need to have a mobile-optimized version of your blog. With a mobile-friendly design, your blog's look and feel shines through to your visitor, and visitors can read your blog content easily.

Responsive design

Responsive design is one of the hottest topics in blog design. The name refers to a website or web page's ability to respond to the user's screen size automatically.

Your blog design might not look exactly the same from computer to tablet to mobile device. Even two computers set to different resolutions might not display your blog design the same. However, a *responsive design* adjusts your blog's design and functionality to each device.

Responsive design works by using media queries within a web page's CSS, essentially asking the device about its size and resolution. The web page layout then responds by changing the page layout to best suit that particular device.

In Figure 10-10, you can see an example of responsive design. The design of the blog theme Karma from Theme Forest changes depending upon the device.

```
http://themeforest.net/item/karma-clean-and-modern-
                wordpress-theme/168737
```

 For a blogger, the best way to get a responsive design is to use a theme that has responsive design already built into it. In Chapter 7, I cover some places to get blog themes for both WordPress and Blogger. Some websites, like Theme Forest, offer responsive design themes for both of these blogging platforms.

Figure 10-10: The Karma theme from Theme Forest uses responsive design.

Using a mobile plug-in

If your blog's theme or template doesn't use responsive design, you can use another method to ensure that your blog is easy to view and navigate on a mobile device. Blogger uses a mobile template, and WordPress can do this with a mobile plug-in.

In Blogger, the default setting has the mobile template turned on. To double-check, go to Template. The image under Mobile reads `Disabled` if the mobile template is disabled. To turn it on, click the icon under the mobile image and then select Yes, Show Mobile Template on Mobile Devices. You can also choose from a selection of mobile templates from this window.

Figure 10-11: Viewing a blog that uses the WPtouch plug-in.

In WordPress.org, you can use a mobile-ready theme or choose from many mobile plug-ins. One of the most popular is WPtouch:

```
http://wordpress.org/extend/plugins/wptouch
```

Figure 10-11 shows how my blog looks with the WPtouch plug-in installed and adjusting my blog design for display on an iPhone. (Note that Figure 10-11 shows how my blog displays *before* I customized it. The next section explains how to carry design elements into your mobile design with this plug-in.)

With the basic installation, this plug-in lets readers navigate your blog without having to scroll back and forth, zoom in and out, and so on.

Branding your plug-in

Most WordPress mobile plug-ins allow you to customize your plug-in by changing colors, adding a custom logo icon, and more. WPtouch allows you to brand your plug-in so that it complements your actual blog design and makes your blog easier to navigate. I want to walk you through a few fun ways you can customize your plug-in, like I did in Figure 10-12.

After you have installed the WPtouch plug-in, access your plug-in settings by doing the following:

1. **Go to your WordPress dashboard.**

2. **Go to Settings➪WPtouch.**

    Here you see a host of options to customize your plug-in.

Under General Settings, make the following changes:

Figure 10-12: WPtouch plug-in with some customized touches.

1. **(Optional) Change the site title if needed.**

    Mine read momcomm.com, so I adjusted it to just momcomm.

2. **To change the calendar icons beside your posts, scroll down to Post Listing Options.**

    I chose Post Thumbnails/Featured images, which pulls the featured image set on a blog post. If no featured image had been selected, a generic camera icon appears like that shown in Figure 10-12 on the Hello World! post. Within Post Listing Options, you can also select what information shows below the blog post title.

3. **When complete, scroll to the bottom of the page and click Save Options.**

To adjust colors and fonts, scroll down to Style & Color Options. Here you can change the background and font to one of the options available. More customization options are available in the Pro version.

Under Default & Custom Icon Pool is an array of icons available to use (see Figure 10-13). The last two (bottom row) are custom ones that I added. In this area, you can add custom icons to be used for your logo that displays at the top of the mobile page as well as icons for individual pages.

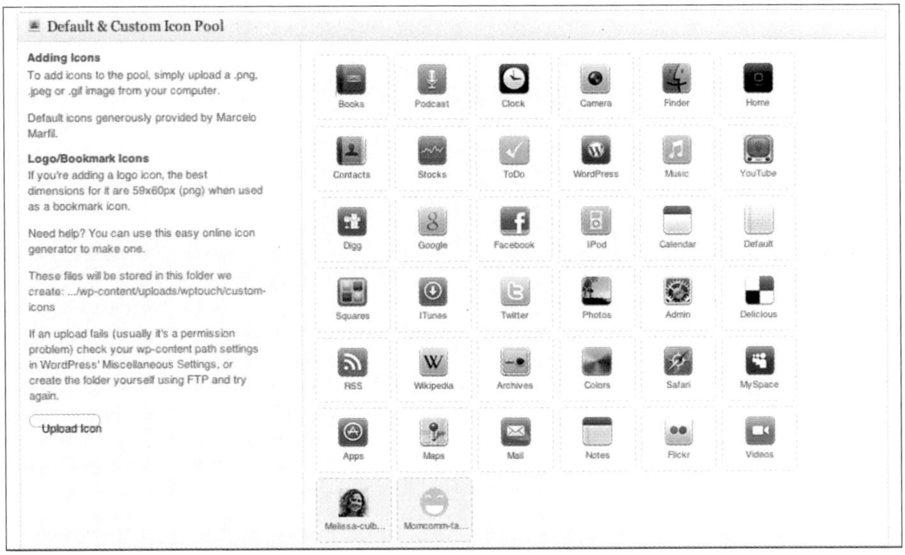

Figure 10-13: Brand your plug-in with icons.

To customize a section with a special icon, scroll to the Logo Icon/Menu Items & Pages Icons section. Be sure to click the Save Options button at the bottom of the page for your change to take effect.

To change your main logo for your design, select the desired icon from the first drop-down menu: Logo & Homescreen Bookmark Icon.

To change an icon for any other page, do the following:

1. **Go to the Pages & Icon section within the Logo Icon//Menu Items & Pages Icons settings.**

2. **Place a check mark beside the page you want to customize.**

3. **Select an icon from the drop-down menu.**

4. **When complete, scroll to the bottom of the page and click Save Options.**

Laying Out Your Navigation Menu and Sidebars

Your navigation menu and your sidebar play a key role in your blog design. They're all about helping your blog visitors navigate somewhere or inviting them to take action — say, visit a social media profile, subscribe to your blog, and then go to an archive page showing your posts in a certain category. The lists goes on.

So although the how-to parts of this chapter pertain to WordPress, this chapter ultimately covers making smart decisions regarding your navigation menu and sidebar. And that applies to every blog, no matter what the platform. In this chapter, I cover how to decide what tabs to put in your navigation menu and what can go in your sidebar. Additionally, I explain how to incorporate your blog design into your menu and sidebar, along with what pitfalls to avoid.

Introducing Important Content with a Navigation Menu

A *navigation menu* is just what it sounds like: a menu of links that guides readers to other key content on your blog. A navigation menu should be prominently displayed on your blog; after all, you defeat the purpose of a navigation menu if a visitor has to search around for it. And although a navigation menu should mesh with your overall blog design, the ultimate goal of your menu is to be functional. A simple bar with plain text is just fine as long the menu serves the main purpose of helping your visitors quickly find information they need.

In these next few sections, I guide you through how to decide on your navigation menu's structure and content.

Deciding what content to include

Determining what content to highlight in your blog's navigation menu ties to what you want to accomplish with your blog. A blogger who wants to work with brands (for product reviews, advertising, or partnerships) should definitely have an Advertising or a PR page in the navigation menu. (I cover what to include in Chapter 14.) Doing so signals to a brand representative that you're interested in hearing from them. If you offer products or services, you want to call attention to that in your navigation menu. If you have key categories of content that you don't want new visitors to miss, those could go in your navigation menu, too.

Here's an example of what I mean. The Young House Love (www.young houselove.com) navigation menu, displayed in Figure 11-1, showcases large buckets of content that guide both new and returning visitors to some of the blog's most popular content as well as a link to their personal blog.

© John & Sherry Petersik, Young House Love

Figure 11-1: This navigation menu includes an About Us page and content they want readers to find easily.

To guide you along with the decision of what to include, start by evaluating the pages, categories, and content you already have (or plan to create). Then ask yourself two questions:

- ✔ What content and information might visitors want to access quickly?
- ✔ What content do I want readers to discover?

There's no magic number as to how many menu items to include, but offering too many choices may overwhelm the reader. If you think you have too many, consider using secondary navigation or drop-down menus. You can even invite some friends to look at your blog and get their opinions on whether you have too many.

Try using index cards (yes, little paper index cards) to aid with deciding on your navigation menu content, especially if you're a larger blog or have varying types of content. Write down content topics and then start organizing them into a navigation menu structure.

Hint: Resist filling your navigation menu with less appealing pages, like a privacy policy or disclosure. Save those for your blog's footer, secondary navigation, or elsewhere within your blog design.

Exploring whether you need secondary navigation

Creating a navigation menu for your blog design starts off as an easy enough task, but after you start really thinking about what to include, you may end up with more menu items than you have room for. This especially holds true if you have a lot of content.

That's when you need to use a *secondary navigation menu,* which contains content that (although important) doesn't serve the primary goal of your blog.

If your content can't be contained within a single menu, decide which menu items should go in the primary navigation and which should go in the secondary. Use the secondary navigation for the more general links, like your About page and Contact page.

Figure 11-2 shows one way to incorporate secondary navigation. The blog No Meat Athlete (www.nomeatathlete.com) splits the navigation by saving the primary navigation for key topics that interest the blog's target audience. The secondary menu is still easy to find, but the design signifies its lesser role by being tucked in the upper part of the page and using smaller text than the main navigation menu.

© No Meat Athlete®, blog design by Charlie Pabst of Charfish Design

Figure 11-2: This blog uses two levels of navigation to help readers find content.

Naming your tabs

Bloggers love to get clever — and clever "rules" unless it's on your navigation menu. Then *sorta clever* and *just plain* rule.

A mistake that many bloggers make is to create menu items that are just too clever. Visitors are unofficially trained to spot pages like About Me. So, if you get a little "creative" and name your About page something like The Lone Tomato, no one is going to know what on earth you're talking about.

A navigation menu's ultimate goal is to guide visitors throughout your blog, so stick to names that make sense.

Now, that doesn't mean you have to be super-plain either. If using just vanilla "About" is too bland for you, you might try one of these titles instead:

- Who's *name*?
- Hi! I'm *name*
- Meet *name*
- About Me
- About *blog name*

In addition, people love to see your personality shine through, so go ahead and have a little fun with your navigation menu names. Just don't go too off-the-wall. Whatever a menu's title, the wording should cause the reader to pause and try to figure out your meaning. For example, Buy Awesome Stuff obviously leads to a shop of some sort.

You can also get clever through using subtitles for your navigation menu items. In Figure 11-3, you see that Geraldine from The Everywhereist (www.everywhereist.com) sticks with simple titles but shows her personality through playful subtitles, such as *About, How I got roped into this blogging mess. And how to contact me.*

© The Everywhereist, blog design by Kimberly Coles, www.kimberlycoles.com

Figure 11-3: Navigation menus can use subtitles to add some character.

Putting Together Your Navigation Menu

After you decide what to include in your navigation menu, you're ready to design the menu to become a part of your overall blog design. This section walks you through to design your menu.

Selecting colors and fonts

In Chapter 6, I give you all the ins and outs of selecting colors and fonts for your overall blog design. When it comes to your navigation menu, the colors and font you select shouldn't hinder the menu's ability to aid in navigating a visitor to elsewhere in your blog.

The blog Simply Vintagegirl (`http://www.simplyvintagegirl.com`) uses a single-colored navigation menu along with Times New Roman font (see Figure 11-4). The yellow bar signifies a division from the header and the content, while the font choice makes the menu easy to read.

© Emily Rose Brookshire, SimplyVintagegirl.com

Figure 11-4: Use a colored navigation menu bar.

When selecting a color or colors to use for your menu bar, choose ones that complement your overall design. This might mean using a color you used within a certain design element or going with a neutral color like gray. Even no color at all might work if you want a simple look.

For each menu item, make sure the text and the background contrast so that the titles are legible. For example, using light green titles on a white background might not contrast enough, but dark green titles on a light green background might look just perfect.

When selecting fonts, simple works better. Here are two common mistakes in navigation menu fonts:

- ✔ **Too thin:** A really thin font makes the words hard to read, especially because navigation menus often use smaller font sizes. Choose fonts that don't disappear into your background. Sometimes a thin font can still work if the background color provides enough contrast.

- ✔ **Too fancy:** A heavily scripted font or a font with lots of flair can be overbearing on a navigation menu. You want your menu to be readable but not take away the focus of your header or blog content. No matter the type of font, make sure it's easy to read in smaller font sizes.

Aside from font and color, watch that your navigation menu titles don't run together and confuse your visitors. In the Figure 11-5, notice the confusing spacing between the words. Is it *About* and *My Photos,* or *About My Photos?* Adjust the padding between menu items to fix this problem. (Chapter 9 explains what you need to know about padding.)

Figure 11-5: Improper spacing between navigation menu items can lead to confusion.

To change your fonts and colors, you can often amend your theme or template's settings. If not, you can make these changes, as well as adjust the padding, in your `style.css` file. Chapter 9 introduces how to edit your CSS.

To find the exact code to adjust your menu and the code's location, use Firebug like I talk about in Chapter 9. You can also play around with color and font changes before you actually make them.

Adding a simple menu

If you use WordPress.org, adding menu items — *tabs* — to your basic navigation menu can easily be done. Just follow these steps, which may vary slightly depending to your theme:

1. **Go into your WordPress dashboard.**

2. **Choose Appearance⇨Menus.**

   You may have a message saying your theme doesn't support menus. Nearly all themes have Menu options by default, but if yours doesn't, visit the WordPress.org Codex site to walk through the process of adding this functionality.

   ```
   http://codex.wordpress.org/Navigation_Menus
   ```

3. **To start building a menu, enter a name in the Menu Name field and then select Create Menu.**

   Depending on your WordPress theme, you may have to select the plus (+) tab to create a new menu.

4. **In the Theme Locations box, select your new navigation menu from the drop-down menu. Then click Save.**

   Now your new menu will display on your blog instead of the default menu.

5. **In the Pages box, place a check mark beside the pages you want to add to your navigation menu. When done making selections, click Add to Menu.**

   This adds the selected page(s) to the Menu area on the right side. Each page you select becomes a separate tab in the menu.

6. **In the Categories box, place a check mark beside the categories you want to include in your navigation menu. When you're done making selections, click Add to Menu.**

   This adds the selected pages to the Menu area on the right side and creates a tab in your menu that navigates your reader to the archive page for that category. An *archive page* shows your blog posts in that category, starting with the most recent.

   You don't need to select every category for your navigation menu (or any category at all, for that matter). You have many other options within your blog design to navigate readers to these archive pages. I go over these options in more detail later in this chapter and in Chapter 12.

7. **Click Save Menu to save your changes.**

   Visit your blog to see your new navigation menu. You may have to refresh the page if you already have it open in a browser window.

To change the order of your tabs, simply drag a page name above or below another page in the Menus screen. To create a drop-down menu for any navigation menu tab, drag the menu item slightly to the right underneath the menu item you want it to be a drop-down option for (see in Figure 11-6). The menu items that are indented make up the drop-down menu.

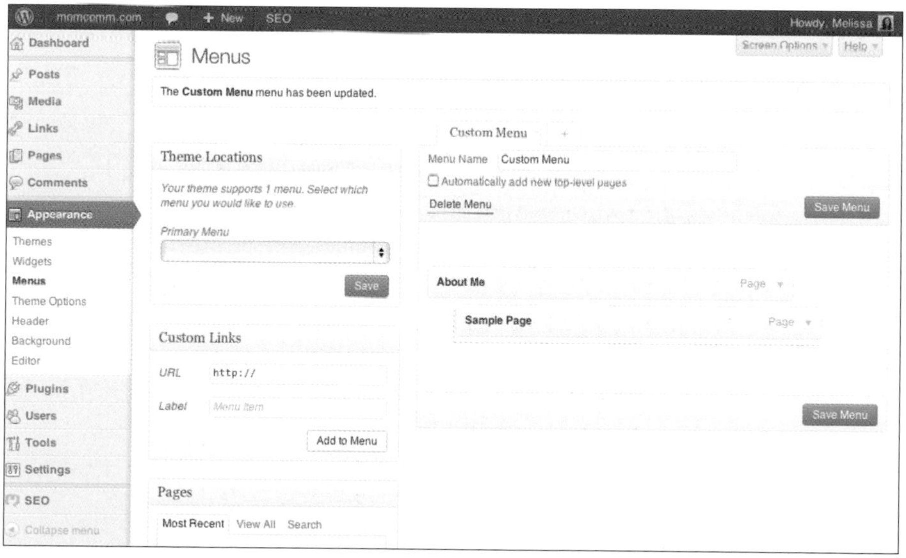

![Screenshot of the WordPress Menus screen showing the dashboard sidebar, Theme Locations, Custom Links, and Custom Menu areas with About Me and Sample Page menu items.]

Figure 11-6: Create a drop-down menu by dragging a menu item to the right underneath another menu item.

Adding images to your menu

When done effectively, adding images to your navigation menu can add flair to your blog design. Sometimes using a little image to the left of each menu tab simply becomes another place to tie in your overall blog branding — in other words, simply for good looks! However, images can also play a more functional role by adding more context to a menu item title. For example, an image of a plane beside a Where to Go tab helps readers better understand where that link takes them.

You can create your image in any photo-editing or illustration program. I created the star you see in Figure 11-7 by using Adobe Illustrator and then saving it as a PNG file with a transparent background. Saving the file this way ensures there's no white box around the star. For more on choosing file formats, refer to Chapter 15.

★ About Me   ★ Menu Item 1   ★ Menu Item 2   ★ Contact

Figure 11-7: Dress up a navigation menu with images beside each tab.

Although there's more than one way to add images to your menu, I want to show you how to do this in WordPress without getting too heavy into coding. Before you start the following steps, make sure your image is uploaded onto your server. You can add images as you build a new menu (like I describe in the following steps) or add images to a menu you already created (start with Step 6).

These steps walk you through adding an image to your About Me tab:

1. **Go into your WordPress dashboard.**

2. **Choose Appearance⇨Menus.**

3. **To start building a menu, enter a name in the Menu Name field and then select Create Menu.**

   Depending on your WordPress theme, you may have to select the plus (+) tab to create a new menu.

4. **In the Theme Locations box, select your new navigation menu from the drop-down menu and then click Save.**

   Your new menu will display on your blog instead of the default menu.

5. **In the Pages box, place a check mark beside your About or About Me page.**

   This adds your page to the Menu area on the right side.

6. **In the Menu area box, click the drop-down arrow beside your About page button.**

New fields appear underneath the About page button. The two you need to work with are the Navigation Label and Title Attribute.

7. **In the Navigation Label field, add the following code, replacing the background image URL with your image's URL and replacing the *Tab Name* with the title you want to show up in your navigation menu (see Figure 11-8).**

```
<div style=
    "background-image: url('http://www.yourblog.com/
        imagelocation/image.png');
    background-repeat: no-repeat;
    display: inline;
    margin: 0;
    padding: 0 0 0 25px;">
Tab Name
</div>
```

8. **In the Title Attribute field, enter the title here as well.**

This attribute is the alternative (`alt`) text that a visitor sees when they mouse over the menu item. For more on `alt` text used with images, see Chapter 9.

9. **When finished, click the Save Menu button.**

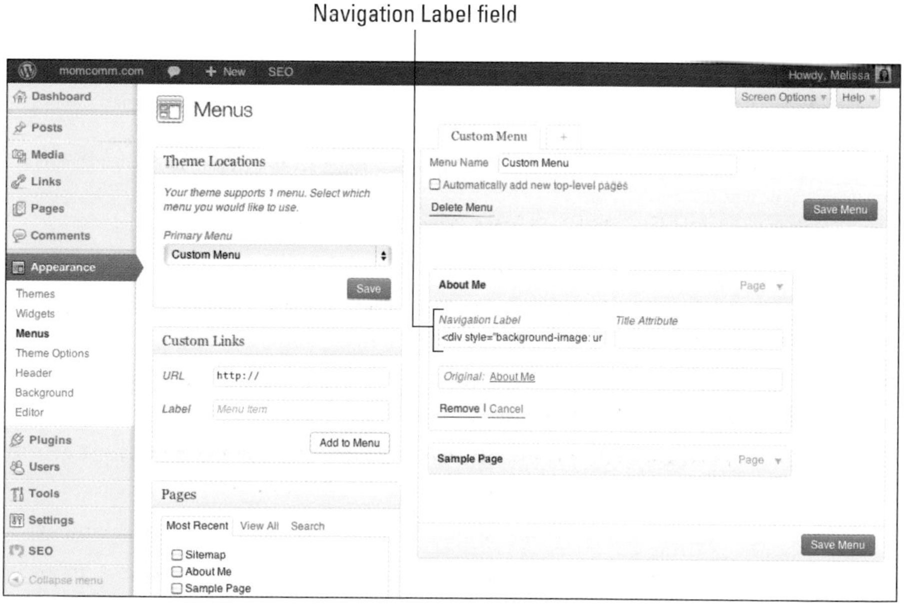

Navigation Label field

Figure 11-8: Code pasted into Navigation Label field.

Showcasing Key Information with a Sidebar

When it comes to your overall blog design, sidebars are prime real estate. Sidebars showcase important things that you want readers to see, actions you want them to take, and places you want them to navigate. Your sidebar design helps the reader understand what awesomeness your blog has to offer. Sidebars can also drive subscriptions, sales, and social media followers. Sidebars pack quite a mighty punch!

The rest of this chapter lays out many ideas for items to include in your sidebar (and some advice on how not to go overboard).

Many of the sidebar components that I talk about would also work well in your blog footer. See Chapter 8 for ideas on how to incorporate content into your footer.

Tying placement back to blog goals

When it comes to your sidebar area, you don't want to add content or design elements haphazardly. Instead, remember those blog goals that I show you how to define in Chapter 3. Keeping those goals in mind help you decide how to prioritize what goes higher up above the *fold* (before a reader has to scroll down your page), what goes in the middle section, and what gets placed at the end of your sidebars.

For example, someone trying to build a larger presence on Pinterest might have a widget that pulls thumbnails of their latest pins, while another blogger might include an e-mail subscription box higher on the page.

In Figure 11-9, you see that Rachel from In Spaces Between (`http://inspaces between.com`) features her newsletter subscription box at the top of her sidebar where readers can see it right away.

Keeping the same look and tone

Think about a brand you love. Now think about how deep that branding goes into every aspect of their presence. For example, every inch of an Apple store looks and feels like the brand. Even the product packaging has Apple's signature touch of simplistic design. Another example is the website for the e-mail service provider MailChimp (`http://mailchimp.com`); from the homepage to a Save button, the site has a conversational, humorous tone.

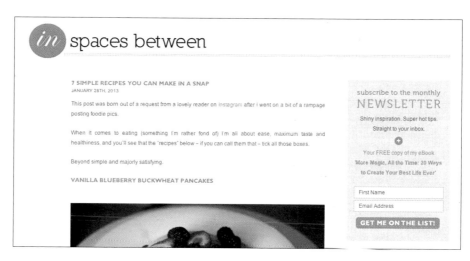

Figure 11-9: A subscription box that stands out drives more subscribers.

Your sidebars should reflect your overall branding, too, by picking up design cues from the rest of your blog design. The tone of the sidebar text is also part of your branding. When you write the sidebar section titles or other content, pull in the tone and personality of your blog to give the sidebar a polished touch.

In Figure 11-10, the blog How to Be a Dad (www.howtobeadad.com) infuses a personality in a sidebar element called "Connect-o-matic," which highlights ways to connect through social media.

Figure 11-10: This blog shows personality in its sidebar.

Identifying Elements to Build a Sidebar

Whether you're filling up a sidebar from scratch or evaluating what you currently have, the possibilities are truly endless when it comes to adding things to your sidebar. In these next sections, I want to give you an idea of how much variety exists in terms of items to add to your sidebar. However, don't feel like you have to add all these! Instead, be judicious and make sure that each element you add serves a purpose and makes sense for your blog.

Introducing your social profiles

As you probably know by now, blogging encompasses more than just blogging. As a blogger, you want to connect with your readers not only on your blog, but also in places they already hang out — Twitter, Facebook, and Pinterest just to name a few.

I can't stress this enough: If there is one element you should have in your blog design, it's a group of social media buttons that link to your profiles. Most readers won't search you out on each separate platform, so having icons that link to your profiles makes it easy for them to connect with you.

The best place for your social media profile icons is toward the top of your sidebar or within your blog header. When you place these icons too far down into your sidebar, visitors must search your blog to find them. Because most people expect to see your social media profile icons toward the top of your sidebar, follow the status quo to ease navigation.

I have heard the argument to leave your social media icons off your blog in order to increase e-mail subscriptions. Well, doing that probably does increase your e-mail subscriptions — but only because you don't give readers any other option. Some visitors might subscribe with a tinge of frustration from having no other alternative, and others might not be bothered by the lack of icons at all. Ultimately, whether you include them is up to you.

Finding social media icons to use is as simple as searching for "social media icons" on any search engine. You'll find a slew of options for icons that might fit your brand, or you can create your own icons to perfectly match your design. In Figure 11-11, you see that Patty from Deep Space Sparkle (www. deepspacesparkle.com) created art-like social media icons that complement her overall blog design.

You can get most logos for the various social media platforms from their respective websites or by searching for "social media platform + logo".

Include only those buttons for social media platforms that you actually use regularly. Re-evaluate your buttons from time to time to ensure you stay relevant.

Providing ways to subscribe

Many people visit all sorts of blogs and websites over the course of a day. At some point, they may start to become a blur, and your blog can easily get lost in the shuffle. So, offering your readers a way to subscribe to your blog can turn a casual blog visitor into a regular reader.

© www.deepspacesparkle.com: Site Design: Darcy Milder. Graphically Designing: Social Media Illustrations: Patty Palmer

Figure 11-11: These social media icons tie into the overall blog design.

Bloggers may offer two ways to subscribe to a blog: via e-mail or through an RSS feed. Subscribing through e-mail delivers the latest blog posts straight to someone's inbox. Blog readers who subscribe via RSS feed typically read your blog through an RSS reader, such as Feedly (www.feedly.com).

Getting folks to subscribe to your blog means that they'll receive your content regardless of whether they go to your blog. To get a blog reader to take action and actually subscribe, make your subscription area obvious and easy to use. You can do this by distinguishing your subscription area from the rest of your sidebar to attract attention.

In Figure 11-12, you see that the subscription area on Everyday Bright (http://everydaybright.com) uses a dark gray and blue to stand out against the rest of the blog. In addition, this section establishes a hierarchy, highlighting e-mail subscription as the most important and the smaller icons below as other ways to follow the blog.

Sharing a brief biography

People enjoy connecting to other people, especially in the blogging world. Consider using some space in your sidebar design to welcome your first-time visitors with a short intro about you and your blog.

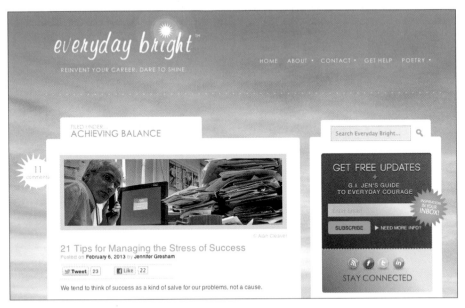

© Everyday Bright, LLC at www.everydaybright.com, Design by Luis Cortés of Well Versed Creative

Figure 11-12: This blog makes it easy for readers to subscribe by making the subscription area stand out and just asking for an e-mail address.

Many successful blogs do fine without including this info, but including a little blurb like this greets someone at your virtual front door. From a blog design perspective, this overview actually connects the personality of your design to an actual person (with a personality). Also, including a picture of yourself can give your readers a visual connection to the face behind the blog. However, it's really up to your comfort level with showing your face online.

You don't need to spill all about your blog's greatness here. Save that for your About page. In a sidebar blurb, try the following:

- ✒ **A sentence about you**
- ✒ **A mention of your name (real, nickname, or pen name)**

    Whether you use your real name or a pseudonym, people need a name to connect and know how to address you.

- ✒ **A sentence about what your blog offers to your readers**

Depending on the type of blog you write, you may just stick with telling visitors about what your blog offers them. No right or wrong here.

When creating this introduction, ask yourself, *What's In It For Me?* (WIIFM). In the marketing world, the *me* in WIIFM is the consumer, and you ask this question to put yourself in the consumer's shoes and ensure that content stays focused on the consumer. As a blogger, put yourself in your readers' shoes. Your sidebar is a key place in your blog design to entice readers to stick around, so tell them how they will benefit from reading your blog. Will they be inspired? Will they learn? What do you offer your readers? Why should they come back?

To show you what I mean about WIIFM, put on your blog-reader shoes:

✔ Say you read a blog about couponing and living on a budget. WIIFM? The blogger gives you hope that you can save that much, too — or motivation to start clipping coupons.

✔ Say you read a humor blog. WIIFM? This blogger's stories entertain you. He makes you laugh even on your worst days.

✔ Say you read a blog about writing. WIIFM? This blogger provides value because you improve your own writing by applying what you learn.

See how these are really about the reader? So instead of writing something like, "I write daily about saving money," opt for something like, "You'll receive daily tips that save you money."

Use this overview as a place to pull in your blog design as well as support it by really showcasing your voice. Notice how Yuliya from She Suggests (www. shesuggests.com) accomplishes this (see Figure 11-13). The circle and font design elements tie into her header design. As for what she wrote, you learn more about her and her blog as well as get a sense of her personality.

You can also use this blurb as a teaser to get a visitor to navigate to your About page. Or simply just end it here as Yuliya did.

Highlighting credibility

If your blog (or you for that matter) has been mentioned or profiled on a popular website or in a really cool publication, then share this with your followers. Highlight places that have shouted your praises by including their logos in your sidebar layout. They catch a reader's attention because the publications or websites are often a well-recognized logo. Plus, they can help build your credibility as a blogger who really knows your stuff.

The same idea also goes for highlighting awards you've received as a blogger by including awards buttons. If you were nominated to a top blogger list for your niche or won a blog-related award, flaunt it. You deserve it!

Avoid those awards where you receive an award but have to post about it and nominate other bloggers. Those aren't true awards but are more like chain-letters. Skip highlighting those altogether.

© Yuliya Patsay, She Suggests; blog design by Freckled Nest Design

Figure 11-13: This About blurb in the sidebar complements the design and highlights the blogger's personality.

Adding great social media widgets

Widgets are little applications that can be installed and executed within a website. WordPress comes with many built-in widgets to do things like display your recent posts, search form, or a drop-down of categories. (Blogger calls them *gadgets.*) However, widgets can also be used to highlight your activity on social media platforms. They add a design element to your sidebar while showing readers a glimpse of your wider online presence. It's a win-win!

In Figure 11-14, you can see a widget for the popular social media platform Instagram. Using SnapWidget (`http://snapwidget.com`), I created this widget to pull in my latest Instagram photos onto my blog.

The great thing about social media widgets is that they can be used for any blogging platform. All it takes is selecting a few settings and then copying and pasting code into your blog. I walk you through creating and installing some popular social media widgets in Chapter 13.

Including relevant buttons or badges

A blog button — *badge* — is a graphic that you place in your sidebar and typically links to another site. A badge tells your readers a little more about you and what you're up to. For example, a conference badge tells your readers that you're attending an upcoming conference. Another blogger's badge can highlight that you're a fan of that blog. An awards badge can build credibility to showcase an award you won.

Choose only those buttons and badges that are relevant to your blog. Otherwise, you run the risk of cluttering up your sidebar design. For example, if you never blog about reading, you don't need a widget that displays your favorite books. Also, whichever badges you decide to display, keep them up to date, especially ones that say you're going to a particular conference. It's easy to forget about them.

Incorporating advertising

For bloggers looking to earn an income from their blog, advertising typically gets woven into the sidebar (and elsewhere on the site, too). Within your sidebar layout, determine the priority that your ads take over other sidebar design elements. Based on priority, decide where in your sidebar you want to display your ads.

Figure 11-14: Instagram widget in a sidebar.

Ads often earn you more money when placed toward the top of your sidebar, so many bloggers place one larger ad at the top and then place smaller ads further down in the sidebar. Other bloggers save the top of their sidebar for other elements, displaying ads only lower in the sidebar and elsewhere on their blog. However, you decide to incorporate advertising, make sure your overall sidebar layout doesn't get overtaken by them.

In Chapter 7, I talk in detail about how to incorporate advertising into your overall blog design.

Deciding how to showcase categories and archives

Space in your sidebar is valuable because your sidebar guides readers to your content! Your sidebar design should showcase your blog content by offering important options within this compact space.

On your blog, these options likely include categories and archives (as well as tags, popular posts, and most recent posts, all of which I cover in more detail in Chapter 12). In this section, you focus on ways to display categories and archives in your sidebar:

- **Drop-down lists:** These menus, when clicked, "drop down" (open) into a list for someone to make a selection. Using drop-down lists save valuable sidebar space.

- **Lists:** Lists show your categories or archives going vertically down a sidebar. If you don't have a lot of categories, using a list might be a good choice. However, use caution when displaying archives this way. Most readers aren't going to read through four years' worth of blog posts that you listed all down your sidebar. Display archives in a drop-down or on a separate blog page.

- **Tag clouds:** Most blog platforms offer the ability to showcase your blog's tags into a visual cloud that displays words you used to tag your posts. The more frequently used the word, the larger the word. If you are consistent about the tags you use, using a tag cloud is an option. However, for the most part, tag clouds take up a lot of space without much value. It's easier for the reader to make a selection through a list than a cloud of randomly placed words.

- **Images:** Images can really liven up your sidebar and draw attention to your categories. I talk more about using images in the upcoming section, "Including Visual Design within Your Sidebar."

Saving space with a tabbed sidebar element

A *tabbed sidebar widget* is an element for your blog's sidebar design that contains content separated by tabs.

The blog Musings of a Housewife (www.musingsofahousewife.com) uses a tabbed sidebar widget to combine three elements — a search box, categories, and archives (see Figure 11-15).

Figure 11-15: A tabbed widget design.

A tabbed sidebar widget has two advantages: It saves space in the overall sidebar design and groups ways to discover content all in one area for easy accessibility.

You can create this design element easily with a plug-in on WordPress. Here are a few options:

- **Tabber Widget (free)**

    http://wordpress.org/extend/plugins/tabber-widget

- **Easy Tab Widget ($9)**

    http://codecanyon.net/item/easy-tab-wordpress-widget/
         full_screen_preview/3756359

- **Hello Tabs WordPress Widget ($12)**

    http://codecanyon.net/item/hello-tabs-wordpress-widget/
         3212734

Some themes include the functionality to create a tabbed widget as well. You can look through a list of places to find themes in Chapter 7.

Including Visual Design within Your Sidebar

Because sidebars hold a lot of content, you can easily bog it down with links and text. Spice it up! Create a sidebar that leaves a lasting impression by adding design elements from the rest of your blog design.

Adding interest with color

Pops of color can be an easy addition to your sidebar's visual oomph. Not only does color liven up your sidebar, but it also pulls a readers' eye to the content.

Change the entire background of your sidebar, use colored text for your section headings, or something else altogether. You have lots of possibilities!

Creating section dividers

To provide structure to your sidebar's overall design, organize your sidebar into sections that organize content into logical groups. Place advertisers in one area, popular posts in another, ways to find content in another, and so on. Using section dividers provides an opportunity to incorporate design into your sidebar and aids blog visitors in navigating around your sidebar layout.

Rage Against the Minivan (www.rageagainsttheminivan.com) uses section headers that look like strips of paper safety-pinned to a board (see Figure 11-16). These section headers stand out visually and give readers navigation cues so they know what each section is about.

© Kristen Howerton, Author – www.rageagainsttheminivan.com

Figure 11-16: Green section dividers in the sidebar bring in design from the blog header.

Here are a couple of ways to create section dividers:

- ✔ **Style clickable text** by editing your style.css file. Chapter 9 introduces how this works.

- ✔ **Create an image for each divider** and insert these images into the sidebar by using a Text widget (WordPress) or HTML/JavaScript (Blogger). Just be sure to use alt attributes for your images like I talk about in Chapter 10.

Showcasing key content through images

One way to visually draw attention to a section of your sidebar is through using images. Use images for important sidebar items, such as popular posts, categories, or a link to a page like a Product page.

The blog Oh My Veggies (`http://ohmyveggies.com`) does a wonderful job of highlighting content with images (see Figure 11-17). Recipe categories in the sidebar are displayed with colorful buttons that link to each category. Because photos are such a big driver when it comes to recipes, the Recent Posts section of the sidebar shows wide, cropped images of the most recent recipes.

Figure 11-17: Use illustrations and photos in sidebar design.

Using images can backfire if they look too much like ads. Make sure that your images are branded to fit your blog design. When images match your blog's branding and design, readers can immediately identify images that lead to blog content, like the images shown in Figure 11-17.

Staying Clear of Sidebar Distractions

Because your sidebar is a blank slate, you may find it easy to fill it up with content (especially with all the ideas I gave you). But wait! Adding certain sidebar content can really distract your readers from your main goals and your actual blog posts. You want to choose sidebar items that are useful for the reader and helpful to you, too. These next few sections go over some distractions and how to avoid them.

Eliminating visual clutter

Too much content can clutter your sidebar, and thus overwhelm the reader. Your key defenses against sidebar clutter are the tips and tools that keep sidebar content organized and easy to navigate. (For example, the drop-down menus, tabs, and widgets in the earlier section "Identifying Elements to Build a Sidebar.") But those tools get you only so far if you have too much sidebar content to begin with.

As you design your sidebar, keep an eye out for the following culprits, which often indicate that your sidebar has too much content:

- **Long lists:** Whether you list categories, archives, blogs you like, or some-thing else altogether, long lists in your sidebar take up valuable space. Plus, a long list becomes a blur to your visitor. When you offer too many options, your reader can't focus on any of them and options can all look the same. Keep your lists short or convert a list to a drop-down list, and visitors will be more likely to read them. Refer to the section "Deciding how to showcase categories and archives" for more on drop-down lists.

  Although there are no hard-and-fast rules, evaluate any list with more than ten items to make sure the list focuses the reader on the most important options.

- **Blog badges:** Blog awards, conferences, other blog badges, yada yada. Blog badges clutter your site quickly and give the impression that you have nothing else to put in your sidebar. Choose badges wisely. Read about how to judiciously choose them, earlier in this chapter.

- **Excessive advertising:** There's nothing wrong with having ads on your blog. However, be wary of burying your content with too much of it. Chapter 7 describes the ins and outs of advertising in more detail.

- **Lots of blinking, flashing images:** Whether it's an advertisement or just a button of some sort, beware of using too many moving images on your blog. They distract visitors from your content and, well, can be down-right annoying.

✔ **Metadata:** Some WordPress themes automatically add a metadata section to your sidebar that includes administrative links like a link to your login URL (see Figure 11-18). Be sure to remove this and just bookmark your URL to log into your blog. Administrative links are for you, not your readers. Save your sidebar space for reader-centric content.

Thinking about your blog goals helps you prioritize your content and how to present it. A few clearly defined goals also help you decide what *not* to include.

META
- Site Admin
- Log out
- Entries RSS
- Comments RSS
- WordPress.org

Figure 11-18: WordPress metadata.

Avoiding auto-playing media

Most people tell you the design is subjective, which is definitely true. However, I'm about to tell you to *never* do something.

Having sound or video that automatically plays when someone lands on your blog is a big no-no. No, it does not add to the ambience of your blog. People surfing the Internet expect to see a blog or website, not hear it.

If you put yourself in the reader's shoes, you can see why this is a bad idea. What if someone was visiting your blog at work with the speakers up? What if your blog visitor was a mom who just got her baby to sleep?

Few things make visitors click the Back button faster, so avoid using auto-playing song playlists or video ads that start automatically.

Limiting your counting widgets

Counting widgets display various blog stats, such as RSS feed subscribers, your blog's Google PageRank, or your number of Twitter followers (see examples in Figure 11-19). You can find most of these widgets by a simple Google search and then customize them to show your numbers.

These counting widgets can serve as social proof that you are a credible, influential blogger although numbers don't always equal someone being truly influential. However, using too many of them can appear egotistical and look junky as well. Stick with the ones that are really important to you, if any, and ditch the rest.

Figure 11-19: Different types of counting widgets.

Removing user behavior or location widgets

Some widgets "watch" people, displaying specific information about a visitor like where they're from or what they're reading. You often see it as a live traffic feed that reads something like *Someone from Raleigh, NC read "Why Puppies Are Awesome."*

It feels a little creepy being watched, don't you think? Obviously, I know how much information someone can learn from web analytics, but that's private: Your reader doesn't see that. Widgets like this are right in the reader's face, and although they may not bother everyone, they may scare off others.

If you want to track what posts readers visit, use an analytics program like Google Analytics or StatCounter. Only you see this information, rather than anyone who visits your blog. See Chapter 5 for an introduction to analytics.

Making Content Easy to Find

*A*t the heart of blog design lies your content, but what good is an awesome blog design if it doesn't drive visitors to your content? Sure, finding your latest blog post on your home page should be pretty easy, but consider navigating readers beyond that. Incorporating navigation design is integral to any good blog design.

This chapter gets you thinking about ways visitors might want to find your content. I offer ways for you to help your visitors find your old content as well as discover content they weren't even looking for — but will certainly be glad to find. You also read about categories and tags and why they're important in content discovery.

Giving Visitors the Opportunity to Explore

Someone landed on your blog for one reason or another: Someone either came to a particular post through a link from another site or found you through a search engine. Maybe the visitor heard about your blog from a friend or clicked a link shared on Facebook. Regardless, visitors come because something about your blog interests them.

So after a visitor arrives at your site, you want to incorporate paths to other content within your blog design. People explore sites differently, so offer a few options to get visitors clicking around your blog to soak up your killer content. To make getting to know your blog easy and effortless, have ways for your visitors to do the following:

✔ Explore categories.

✔ See what other readers like.

✔ See posts similar to the one they're reading.

Making Sure Visitors Find What They're After

Think about a good online shopping experience you've had. Although you probably went to that site originally because you liked those products, your overall shopping experience has kept you a fan. Maybe the company made it easy to find the right size or perhaps suggested other complementary products to help you complete an outfit.

Your blog's navigation design works the same way. Anticipate your visitor's needs by thinking about your blog like a store, and your blog posts are the products:

✔ **Popular and recent posts:** End caps on aisles and displays at the front of the store give you suggestions of things that are hot. On your blog, having a Popular Posts or Recent Posts list bring those blog posts to the forefront for readers to find your greatest and your latest.

✔ **Related posts:** When you're in a store, you've seen strategic product placement: placing related products beside each other. Perhaps you went to pick up peanut butter but then saw jelly and decided you needed that, too. The same with placing batteries in the toy section. Related posts are like this. Your reader came to read a particular post, and you help them discover more by suggesting similar posts.

✔ **Categories:** If you're in a new grocery store, you probably rely on the aisle signage that displays which main product categories are in each aisle. Your blog categories guide readers the same way.

✔ **Search box:** Having a search box as part of your blog design is like asking a store associate to help you find something in particular. You can find what you're after right away.

On the blog What I Wore (http://whatiwore.tumblr.com), Jessica anticipates her readers desire to find certain outfits. On her sidebar, she includes a Find Your Way Around section of different outfit types, a Recent Outfit Posts section with full-length photos, and even a cool grid of colors to find outfits by colors (like that shown in Figure 12-1).

© Jessica Quirk, What I Wore

Figure 12-1: This blog makes sure readers can easily find what they're looking for.

Organizing with Categories and Tags

Bloggers often don't think too much about how categories and tags apply to their navigation design. When writing a post that doesn't exactly fit into a category, you might just start a new category. Or maybe you don't quite understand tags, so you just use them endlessly for a blog post — or don't use them at all. These next two sections help you properly organize your blog posts once and for all. Not only does using good organization make things easier on you, but your readers will appreciate being able to find posts easily, to sort through them, or to discover new ones. In addition, using categories and tags effectively help with your search engine optimization (SEO).

Grouping with categories

A *category* is a broad classification of a topic that you write about. Although most platforms call these categories, in Blogger, these are called *Labels*. Blog platforms require that a post be included in at least one category, even if it's the Uncategorized category. On my blog, some of my categories are Blogging, Social Media, and Writing (see Figure 12-2). Using categories give your visitors a way to quickly find information that interests them.

To organize your blog posts effectively, keep your number of categories to a minimum.

Earlier in this chapter, I compare your blog's categories to aisle signs in a grocery store. Wouldn't you be overwhelmed if each aisle sign listed 20 product categories? Your readers feel the same. They'd rather choose from 7 categories than a list of 50, so try to stick with using no more than 10 categories. If you have years of creating lots of categories, you may have a little work to do paring down your categories! (Hang in there and take it a little at a time.)

Figure 12-2: Categories organize your posts.

Readers consider your blog more relevant in a topic if you have 30 posts in one category versus five posts in six different categories.

You can display categories in many different ways, from drop-down menus to images. A drop-down leaves you room in your sidebar for other important stuff and lets your readers read posts based on what topic interests them most. Read through Chapter 11 for some ideas.

If you're having a hard time reducing your categories, you can also use subcategories to narrow down your topics without committing to full categories. For example, a category on social media might have subcategories for Facebook, Twitter, Pinterest, and so on.

If you decide to use subcategories, make sure that the URLs to your blog posts don't include a category and subcategory. Otherwise, you end up with long URLs like

```
www.blogname.com/category/subcategory/blog-post-title
```

To fix this, change your permalink settings, as I mention in Chapter 10.

Describing with tags

Tags get a little deeper than a category. A *tag* is a word or phrase that describes a blog post more specifically than a category. Tags are like micro categories. And selecting a category is required, but including tags is optional.

If the difference between categories and tags hasn't quite clicked, check out Table 12-1. Notice how tags and categories work together to describe a blog post.

Table 12-1	How Tags and Categories Work Together
Category	*Tags*
Recipes	chicken soup, low-fat, slow cooker
Photography	lens, Nikon, review, camera equipment
Hiking	mountain trails, Smoky Mountain National Park, day trip
Museums	kid museums, Raleigh, North Carolina, tourist attraction

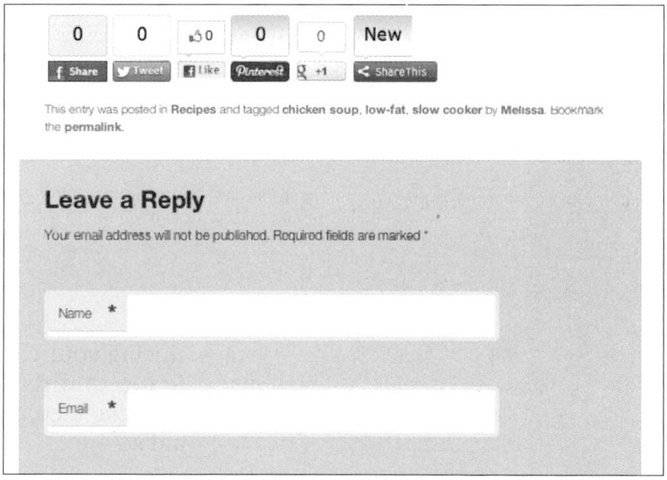

Most blog platforms like WordPress (both .org and .com) show tags at the bottom of a blog post like you see in Figure 12-3. Displaying tags on a blog post helps visitors find similar content within an entire category. Clicking a tag takes you to a page of excerpts from blog posts tagged with that same word or phrase. When you assign tags to your blog post, follow these tips:

Figure 12-3: On WordPress, categories and tags display before the comment fields.

✔ **Use tags that you think you'll use again.** This way, tags can better assist your readers by giving them more blog posts rather than just that one post you tagged "awesome places in NY."

> ✔ **Don't get carried away.** Using too many tags might overwhelm your readers with options. Instead, stick with just a few.
>
> ✔ **Eliminate similar tags.** If your category is Exercise, you don't need both running and jogging. Stick with one convention so readers can look for just one tag to find more content on that topic.

If you're on Wordpress.org and have a lot of categories you want to convert to tags (or vice versa), you can use the Categories and Tags Converter found from your Dashboard under Tools⇨Import.

Helping Readers Find Old Content

As a blogger, you write and post, write and post, write and post. Your most recent content gets all the fanfare while older posts are forgotten. However, older content can still have some glory! After all, many posts you write are still as relevant as they were the day you published them. Providing easy ways to find your past content saves readers from fruitless scanning of blog post after blog post.

Adding a search box

Some readers may return to your blog in search of a blog post they've read. Other readers may want to find any blog posts you have about a particular topic. Whatever the reason, having a search box on your blog is a must-have.

Some themes already come with a search box added to your blog design layout. (Read all about themes in Chapter 7.) If not, you can usually add this popular feature to your blog via your blog's administrator dashboard. For example, WordPress.org offers a search box as a widget within your WordPress admin area. To add a search box to your sidebar using WordPress, follow these steps:

1. **Go to your WordPress.org dashboard.**

2. **Choose Appearance⇨Widgets.**

   The Search widget is available under Available Widgets.

3. **Add the Search widget to your sidebar by either clicking the Add button or by dragging the widget to your sidebar.**

   The option you use depends on the theme. The Twenty Eleven theme uses the Add button (see Figure 12-4). After the widget is in the desired location, you can adjust the title of the Search widget.

You can always add a touch of personality to your search box's title or tie the title to the topics you write about. For example, a food blogger could title a search box *Search for Deliciousness.*

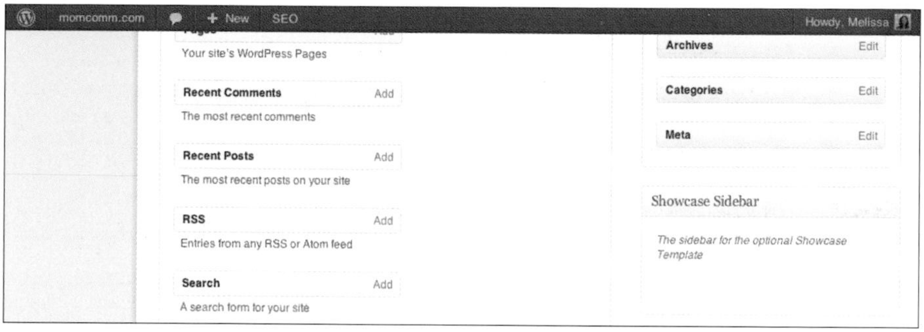

Figure 12-4: Add a search box widget to your sidebar.

To customize the search box in the Twenty Eleven theme, find the following code in your `style.css` file:

```
input#s {
    background: url(images/search.png) no-repeat 5px 6px;
    -moz-border-radius: 2px;
    border-radius: 2px;
    font-size: 14px;
    height: 22px;
    line-height: 1.2em;
    padding: 4px 10px 4px 28px;
}
```

How to customize your search box really depends on your design preferences. You might want to change the search box height or change the font size. In addition to adjusting this code, you can also add to it. For example, adding `background-color: gray` before the closing bracket (}) makes the inside of the search box gray. See Chapter 9 for an introduction to basic HTML and CSS that every blogger should know and to learn how to access your `style.css` file.

If your blog is brand new, consider not adding a search box until you have a few blog posts under your belt. Otherwise, you might leave visitors underwhelmed when search after search returns no content.

Creating an archive page

Archive pages aren't the sexiest piece of your navigation design, but they can prove helpful for visitors to search through old content to navigate to various places on your blog.

This type of archive page is different than the default archive pages you might see when you click the month from the WordPress Archive widget. With those, you go to a page containing that month's posts. The archive page

I'm referring to here is more like a sitemap on a traditional website. Sitemaps typically show major categories of information and pages of a website all on one page. An archives page can do that, too.

Some WordPress themes come with an Archives template, but others don't. Without getting into too much code, you can create an archives page by using a plug-in like one of these:

✔ **Smart Archives Reloaded**

```
http://wordpress.org/extend/plugins/smart-archives-
        reloaded
```

✔ **Snazzy Archives**

```
http://wordpress.org/extend/plugins/snazzy-archives
```

I created my blog archives from the Genesis Framework's archive page template (see Figure 12-5). As you may have noticed, an archive page doesn't have to be anything fancy. Most people who visit an archive page just want to scan through a big overview of your blog to find what they want.

Figure 12-5: A basic archive page.

If you're using WordPress and want to create an archive template without using a plug-in, you can visit the WordPress Codex page for how to do this:

```
http://codex.wordpress.org/Creating_an_Archive_Index
```

Increasing Reach by Highlighting Your Blog Posts

One important way to help readers around your blog is to plant navigation seeds within your blog design. The power of suggestion is, well, powerful. Showing readers popular posts, relevant posts, and links to other posts aid the reader in finding out more about your blog's content in a way that's fluid and natural rather than disruptive.

Showing popular posts

The great thing about popular posts is that everyone has them (if you have a blog already, that is). When you have a list or page of popular posts as part of your blog design, this page becomes your personal promoter of sorts. If a new reader stumbles onto your blog, two things might happen that could make a popular posts section beneficial.

- Visitors may love the first blog post of yours they read and want more, more, more! Having a popular posts section puts all your golden posts at their fingertips and propels them further into your content.

- On the flip side, maybe someone read a post of yours that was either underwhelming or maybe just an announcement-type post, like telling readers you'll be on vacation. Having a popular posts section gives this visitor direct access to what your blog *can* offer them.

Either way, including popular posts as part of your navigation design could be the difference between someone subscribing to your blog or just walking away (figuratively, of course). One way to add a popular posts list to your sidebar is on WordPress through a plug-in or on Blogger by using a widget. On WordPress, two popular (no pun intended) options are (the aptly named)

- **Popular Posts plug-in**

  ```
  http://wordpress.org/extend/plugins/
          wordpress-popular-posts
  ```

- **nRelate Most Popular plug-in**

  ```
  http://nrelate.com/products/most-popular
  ```

These plug-ins give you a lot of customization options such as how many posts to display, how far back in time to go, and which categories to exclude — which will also force you to improve the categorization of your posts.

In Figure 12-6, you see that Sarah from Real Life (`http://www.reallife blog.net`) draws attention to posts that are current favorites among her readers. She uses the setting built into the WordPress Jetpack plug-in:

```
http://wordpress.org/extend/plugins/jetpack
```

Highlighting related posts

In effective navigation design, one goal is to keep readers engaged with your content. If visitors like the blog post they're currently reading, they may want to read more about that particular topic. Using a plug-in or widget like LinkWithin (`www.link within.com`) or nRelate Related Content (`http://nrelate.com/ products/related-content`) automatically pulls up posts similar to the one a visitor is currently reading. Both LinkWithin and nRelate Related Content are available for WordPress and Blogger.

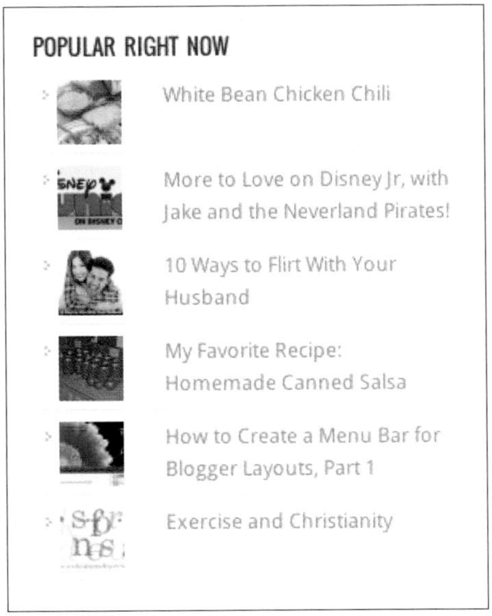

You can see one way to display related posts in Figure 12-7. Using LinkWithin, I display the three related post titles and thumbnails under my Adventuroo blog posts.

Linking to other pages

One simple navigation design trick is to make your blog's content easy to find through *interlinking*, which simply means linking to older posts or pages from within another page or post. You can see what I mean in Figure 12-8.

Interlinking gives readers more relevant content to read, all from within the blog post or page they're currently reading.

POPULAR RIGHT NOW

> White Bean Chicken Chili

> More to Love on Disney Jr, with Jake and the Neverland Pirates!

> 10 Ways to Flirt With Your Husband

> My Favorite Recipe: Homemade Canned Salsa

> How to Create a Menu Bar for Blogger Layouts, Part 1

> Exercise and Christianity

© Sarah Pinnix, sarahpinnix.net

Figure 12-6: Thumbnails add a visual touch to the popular posts listing.

You might also like:

When Nature Calls... in Nature

Five and Two Years Ago

Preschool for Working Mamas (and the Struggle to Have It ...

LinkWithin

Figure 12-7: Use LinkWithin to highlight posts similar to the post being displayed.

My Post about Puppies

This post is about puppies. It reminds me of when I wrote another post about taking care of puppies. In this post, I'm talking about teaching a puppy to shake but I shared my simple trick to teach a puppy to sit last week.

Figure 12-8: Linking to other posts is interlinking.

Notice in Figure 12-8 that when I linked to another post, I didn't say "that post I wrote about here" or "click here." The reason is two-fold:

- First, which phrase sounds more specific: "click here" or "taking care of puppies"? Of course, "taking care of puppies" is more specific. This phrase — *anchor text* — makes it more clear to readers that the link navigates them to a place relevant to their interest.

- Second, linking to other posts also helps with your search engine optimization (SEO, which I talk about in Chapter 10) — that is, if you use proper anchor text.

Thinking in terms of SEO, "click here" isn't a keyword someone might look up in a search engine. However, "taking care of puppies" is.

Building a sneeze page

Building a sneeze page is another great way to propel readers into your content through great navigation. The term *sneeze page,* coined by Darren Rowse from Problogger (www.problogger.net), refers to a page that directs readers to multiple posts within your blog.

These pages take many forms. You could have a page that highlights popular posts, posts around a specific topic, or posts that were part of a series. In Figure 12-9, you can see a sneeze page I created for a five-part series I wrote on blogger business cards.

Figure 12-9: Use a sneeze page to direct readers to posts on your blog.

To build a sneeze page, create a new page in your blog platform and pull together the links you need to use on the page. Then use color, formatting, and images to help readers navigate deeper into your blog. See Chapter 14 for ideas on how to lay out blog pages.

Increasing Ability to Share and Interact

*B*logging isn't merely about writing content that people read. Blogging also means having conversations with readers. You and your readers may converse in the comments under a blog post, in a community forum, or on a social media platform outside of your actual blog. Blogging is also about sharing content. Sharing includes giving readers a way to share your content with their friends, family, fans, or followers via social media. A good blog design incorporates the ability for readers to interact with you (and even fellow readers) and spread the word of your awesomeness by sharing your content to a wider audience.

This chapter covers how to make content easier to share by using plug-ins that do the heavy lifting for you. I also tackle managing your blog comments so you encourage interaction rather than unintentionally discourage it. Finally, this chapter includes ideas for calling attention to your most active social media channels.

On WordPress.org, using too many plug-ins can slow down your blog's loading time, so choose only those plug-ins you really need and deactivate or delete ones you aren't using any longer.

By making content easy to share, more readers see your blog posts, and you increase your blog traffic. And when your content rocks, your readers will want to comment and share your posts with their networks.

The takeaway? Designing your blog to make sharing and interacting as easy as possible benefits your readers (they don't leave in frustration). You benefit by growing traffic and reaching into social media networks. And making your content easy to share involves making just small changes and adjustments to your blog. Minimal work with maximum benefit — a win-win!

Exploring Sharing Buttons for Your Blog Posts

If you want others to spread your awesomeness, you have to make sharing your blog posts part of your blog design. Without an easy way to share your blog posts on Facebook, Twitter, or another platform, many readers won't bother to take the time to do it themselves.

For example, if a reader wanted to share a blog post on Twitter, but your post doesn't have a sharing button, that person would have to copy the blog post's URL, go into Twitter, paste the URL, copy or retype the post title, find your Twitter name to acknowl-

Figure 13-1: Sharing buttons count how many times a post is shared.

edge you in the tweet, and then tweet it. Whew! Adding sharing buttons like the ones you see in Figure 13-1 makes this much easier on your readers, because a sharing button does most of that work for them.

You have many options to include sharing buttons within your blog design. You can add the supporting code to your blog; however, most bloggers use some sort of sharing plug-in to display sharing buttons within their blog design. And many of these plug-ins aren't WordPress-only, either! Here are a few popular choices:

- **AddThis**

    www.addthis.com
- **Digg Digg** (WordPress.org only)

    http://wordpress.org/extend/plugins/digg-digg

- **Really Simple Facebook Twitter Share Buttons** (WordPress.org only; displays more than just Facebook and Twitter)

    http://wordpress.org/extend/plugins/really-simple-
        facebook-twitter-share-buttons
- **Shareaholic**

    https://shareaholic.com/publishers/sharing
- **ShareThis**

    http://sharethis.com

✔ **Simple Social Buttons** (WordPress.org only)

```
http://wordpress.org/extend/plugins/simple-
        social-buttons
```

However, you can't just install a social media plug-in and be done! The next two sections walk through customizing your plug-in to simplify sharing.

Blogger does have some built-in sharing capabilities, but consider using one of the plug-ins in the preceding list for more customization options.

Deciding what social media platforms to include

Plug-ins have to cater to many audiences, so they often come with options to include more than just the most well-known social media platforms. You can then pick and choose the platforms you want to display and the ones you don't. For example, in addition to Facebook and Twitter, a plug-in might offer the ability to share to sites like Bebo, FriendFeed, Diigo, Orkut, Myspace, or Twackle. You need to pare down those offering for your readers.

Hand-selecting what social media platforms have sharing buttons on your blog has a few benefits:

✔ **Limiting readers' choices actu-ally increases the likelihood they will take action:** I explain the thinking behind this behav-ior in Chapter 10. In Figure 13-2, notice how cluttered the first set of icons looks with so many choices. Reader have to spend time searching for the icon they want to click. The second set gives a reader a choice without being over-whelming.

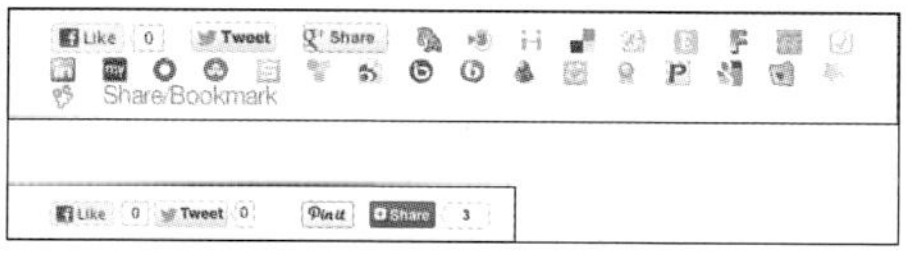

Figure 13-2: Providing readers with fewer choices is less likely to confuse them.

✔ **Choosing only a few platforms helps you cultivate your blog's com-munity:** If you stick with the platforms that you use and most of your community uses, keeping up with your readers becomes much more manageable. You want to be able to follow what readers are saying when they share a post via social media and join in on the conversation. But if you include too many social sharing buttons below each post, readers (especially newer ones) won't know where the conversation is really happening.

When deciding which platforms to include, I can't tell you to only include three options. Or four. Or five. Instead, make the decision by asking yourself these two questions:

✔ Is this social media platform where my audience is?

✔ Is this where I want to grow my audience?

If you live in a country where a certain social media platform is really popular or if your audience is big on a certain platform, add that platform into the mix! Also, check your analytics and see where your referring traffic comes from. Then ditch the rest.

Avoid multiple sharing plug-ins. It's confusing. Your readers don't need five different ways to Like a post on Facebook. A reader might get confused as to which one to use and just not use any of them.

Customizing your plug-in for effective sharing

Adding a plug-in to your blog can be a great asset to your blog design, but you may end up with some unexpected surprises if you don't customize your plug-in options. For example, have you ever clicked a Tweet button on someone's blog only to have it read `via @share this` instead of that blogger's Twitter handle (see Figure 13-3)?

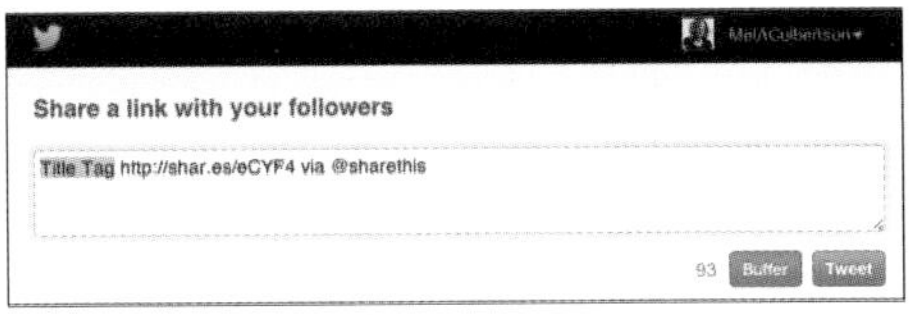

Figure 13-3: Without changing your settings, the ShareThis Twitter name gets tweeted instead of yours.

I don't know about you, but I like giving credit where credit is due. So do your readers. They want to mention *you* in the tweet, not `@sharethis` — or worse, no one at all. That is one of the surprises I'm talking about.

All the plug-ins I mention earlier in this chapter can be customized. In the following steps, I walk you through some key settings to adjust in the ShareThis plug-in so your readers can share your posts without frustration.

After you download and install the plug-in, start in your WordPress dashboard, and then follow these instructions:

1. **Go to Settings⇨ShareThis.**

2. **Choose from one of seven display options.**

These styles range from showing the buttons as Large Icons to horizontal counting buttons that display how many times a post has been tweeted, shared on Facebook, and so on. The default buttons are a Facebook Share, Tweet, Email, and ShareThis button. The ShareThis button displays more sharing options when clicked.

3. **Add a Facebook Like, Google +1, Pinterest, or Instagram button to the default buttons.**

   By default, all these are selected. To remove any, simply clear them.

4. **Choose which version of the sharing widget you want to see.**

   This choice is only for the green ShareThis button shown in Figure 13-1. I selected Multi-Post instead of Classic because Multi-Post allows a user to share to many social media platforms from a pop-up on your blog rather than leave your blog (see Figure 13-4).

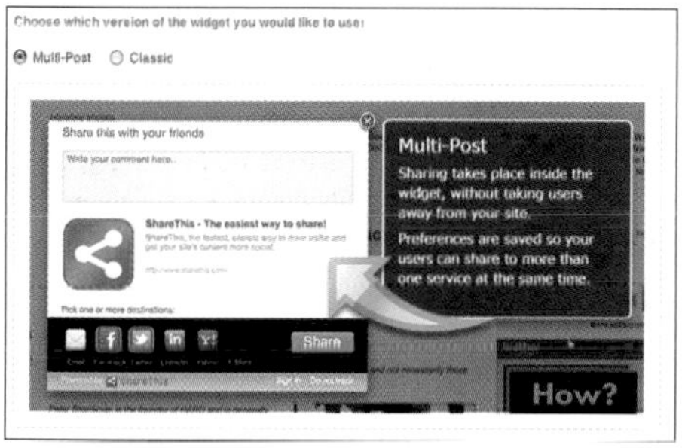

   Figure 13-4: The Multi-Post option in ShareThis.

5. **Change the order of your buttons by clicking the Click to Change Order of Social Buttons or Modify List of Buttons link.**

   This brings up a field with the names of all the buttons you're currently using. Arrange the names into the order you want to display them. If you want to remove any of the original four default buttons, just delete the names of them here.

6. **Customize the Twitter sharing by clicking the Click to Add Extra Twitter Options link.**

   Within this section, you have two options to customize. As I mention earlier, you want to get visibility when people tweet your blog post. In the first field, enter your Twitter name so that it automatically adds `via @NAME` at the end of the tweet. Leaving it blank results in `via @share this` being added (refer to Figure 13-3), so be sure to fill this in.

   By entering your Twitter name in the second field in this section, a page comes up after someone tweets with a suggestion to follow you. If you don't add your name to this field, your readers are prompted to follow the ShareThis Twitter account (see Figure 13-5).

   Figure 13-5: Make sure your Twitter name shows up as a suggestion to follow, instead of ShareThis.

Don't add the @ in front of your Twitter name for either of these fields. The plug-in already adds this for you.

7. **Save your changes by clicking the Update ShareThis Options button.**

Managing Comments

Whether readers leave you praise, a reaction, an opinion, a question, or even an answer, you probably love comments on your blog. Comments are part of what makes a blog social! But you also need to manage them.

When you think of managing comments, you probably think of deleting spam, but, managing comments also means organizing the commenting process as part of your overall blog design. Pay particular attention to the following:

✔ First, take a look at one of your posts. How easy is it to find the place to comment? If you display full blog posts on your home page, be sure you have a link to leave a comment at the bottom of the post. Readers are most likely to leave a comment after they actually read your blog post. You can also display the number of comments at the top of your posts with a link to comment; after all, lots of comments instantly suggests that your blog post is worth reading. Still, make sure that your comment link shows at the bottom, too. Showing that your readers are engaged through commenting provides social proof to new visitors, meaning that you get a boost in credibility right away.

✔ Next, consider adding the capability to notify a commenter when someone replies to his or her comment. This becomes helpful if you (or someone else) replies to someone's question. Above all, these e-mail notifications increase the potential for even more interaction because that person may continue the conversation by commenting again.

For WordPress, you can use a plug-in like Comment Reply Notification:

```
http://wordpress.org/extend/plugins/comment-reply-
          notification
```

For WordPress and other platforms, you can also use a third-party commenting system, which I discuss later in this chapter.

For certain blog pages — for example, an About page, Contact page, and other types of pages — I strongly recommend turning off comments. On these types of pages, I've seen everything from a comment from a personal friend (not a Facebook Friend) — "Happy to see your blog is up!" — to random questions that make your page look dated — "Are you going to the conference next week?" It's also one more place to watch for spammy comments.

Capturing spam

At some point in your blogging adventures, you're going to get a spammy comment. *Comment spam* is any irrelevant comment on your blog left with the intent of artificially increasing another website's search engine rankings. When spammers leave a comment on your blog, they also leave a link to a website, hoping that the link helps build their search engine rankings.

As a blogger, dealing with comment spam on the backend of the blog can be difficult to manage without the right tools. On the front end of your blog — the part your readers see — a lot of spammy comments on your blog posts or pages can make even the most well-designed blog look unmonitored and less credible.

Many blog platforms have some built-in spam prevention, but you might need to take extra steps to combat spam. On WordPress, you can try these plug-ins:

- ✔ **Akismet (Free for personal use)**

  ```
  http://wordpress.org/extend/plugins/akismet
  ```

  Just about every WordPress blogger has Akismet installed. If you don't, then make this one of the first plug-ins you install. Akismet catches a great deal of spam and may be the only spam-fighting plug-in you need.

- ✔ **WP-Ban (Free)**

  ```
  http://wordpress.org/extend/plugins/wp-ban
  ```

  WP-Ban is a great plug-in when you're having problems with certain IP addresses spamming your blog. In your WordPress comment tools, copy the IP address beside a problematic comment, and then input it into the WP Ban settings to prevent future spam, as shown in Figure 13-6.

- ✔ **Growmap**

  ```
  http://wordpress.org/extend/plugins/
           growmap-anti-spambot-plugin
  ```

  If you install Akismet and WP-Ban yet still have problems, try Growmap. Growmap asks readers to mark a check box to say they aren't a spammer. Because many spam comments are automated, they don't take the added step of checking a box. I like that you can customize the message default message `Confirm you are NOT a spammer`, giving you another place to infuse a little personality into your blog design. For example, you could say `Please let me know you aren't an evil spammer by checking this box`.

Many plug-ins on WordPress — too many — can slow down how quickly your blog loads. Start with Akismet and then add other spam-fighting plug-ins only when necessary.

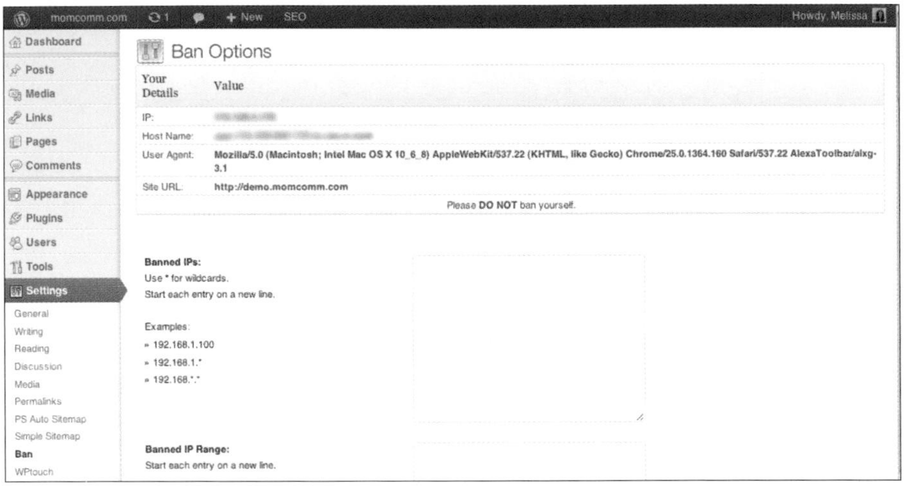

Figure 13-6: Settings for the WP Ban plug-in.

TIP

If spam is a large problem for your blog, turning off commenting on older posts — even just specific older posts that seem to be targets — can help combat spam. On an older post, the real commenters are likely done with the conversation around that particular post. Turning off commenting won't remove the conversation that's already happened but will keep out the spambots.

Using word verification and moderation

To prevent spammers, some bloggers use a word CAPTCHA, moderate their comments, or both. CAPTCHA stands for Completely Automated Public Turing test to tell Computers and Humans Apart. Who knew? Unless you have a really compelling reason to do so, though, consider taking CAPTCHA and comment moderation off your comments. A well-designed blog should be as easy as to use as possible. CAPTCHA and moderation create a barrier to interaction between you and your readers.

A CAPTCHA displays a series of distorted characters or a simple math problem to solve. A reader has to enter that word or the problem solution into a field. This is supposed to prove the commenter is human because automated spam doesn't have the cognitive ability to determine the correct answer (see Figure 13-7).

WARNING!

Word verification isn't inherently bad so don't think you should never, ever use it. For example, if you have a registration form for an online course, you could add word verification there. Having said that, using word verification can annoy people, especially if a reader needs to leave multiple comments (like leaving comments with entries to enter a giveaway). A potential commenter might leave your blog out of frustration.

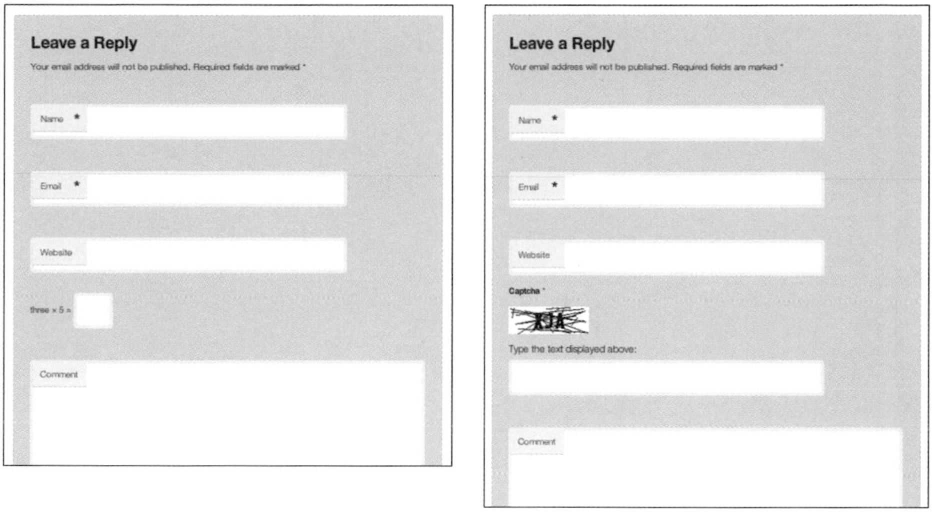

Leave a Reply

Your email address will not be published. Required fields are marked *

Name *

Email *

Website

three × 5 =

Comment

Leave a Reply

Your email address will not be published. Required fields are marked *

Name *

Email *

Website

Captcha *

Type the text displayed above:

Comment

Figure 13-7: Two common types of CAPTCHAs: a math problem and word verification.

Comment moderation means that you don't let comments publish to your blog instantly. Instead, the comments go into a queue for you to approve.

If you want to design your blog for interaction, skip comment moderation. After all, interaction can't happen until you approve each comment, which means your blog might be silent for hours. People like the instant gratification of being able to see a comment post immediately, which implies that you trust them. Plus, seeing comments by others encourages new visitors to that blog post to comment.

After comments are published to your blog, then of course delete any spam that makes it through or delete posts that you deem inappropriate. If a lot of spam goes through, consider using the plug-ins I suggest in the previous section.

If you moderate comments because you're worried about not getting notified of new comments without moderation, there's a way to do this! For Blogger users, go to Settings and click the Comments tab from your Dashboard. At the bottom of that page, in the Comment Notification Email field, enter your e-mail address and *voila!* For WordPress users, go to Settings⇨Discussion and then select the check box to be notified. You should now get e-mail notification when someone comments, without having to moderate them.

Visitors might want to comment on many blog posts and often leave comments on blog after blog. They expect to be able to comment quickly and easily, so help them.

Blogger commenting options

If you're on Blogger you should know that by default new blogs are set to allow comments only from registered users. Registered users are those with WordPress.com, LiveJournal, TypePad, AIM, OpenID, or Google Blogger accounts. If you want to receive comments from WordPress.org users — and anyone else for that matter — you must change your settings so that anyone can comment. To change this, start at your Blogger Dashboard. Go to Settings➪Post and Comments and select Anyone from the Who Can Comment setting.

This allows readers to comment by entering a Name and URL. This does mean that you have to allow anonymous comments, too, but you probably won't get that many. Plus, you want to make commenting easy on your readers. I can't tell you how many bloggers I know who have left a Blogger blog without commenting because this option wasn't available!

Choosing a third-party commenting system

Many bloggers stick with their blog platform's native commenting system. After all, every blog platform has the ability to leave comments. However, bloggers sometimes look for more functionality in their commenting system — and that's when a third-party commenting system comes into play.

A third-party commenting system can increase sharing and interaction because most offer the ability to post the comment not only on your blog, but on a social media channel as well. For example, when visitors leave a comment on your blog, they have the option to post it to their Facebook profile. This can bring new readers to your blog by extending your community to new eyes.

The downside to using commenting systems like these is that some readers complain about having to log in. Fellow bloggers might not mind because they're probably already logged in via one of these systems. However, if you have a lot of readers who aren't bloggers, they might not want to log in, even if they can log in by actually signing into Facebook or Google account through the commenting system. And even though the Disqus and IntenseDebate commenting systems allow you to log in as a guest, the options presented might confuse visitors into thinking that they have to log in.

See Table 13-1 for the most common third-party commenting systems, supported blogging platforms, and ways to log into the system.

Table 13-1	Third-Party Commenting Systems	
Commenting System	*Supported Blogging Platforms*	*Ways to Log In*
Disqus http://disqus.com	WordPress, Blogger, Tumblr, Typepad	Disqus, Facebook, Twitter, Google, Name/E-mail (if you don't have a Disqus account)
Intense Debate http://intense debate.com	WordPress, Blogger, Tumblr, TypePad	Intense Debate, Facebook, Twitter, Guest (if you don't have an IntenseDebate account)
Livefyre www.livefyre.com	WordPress, Tumblr, Blogger (coming soon)	Livefyre, Facebook, Twitter, Google, LinkedIn, OpenID

In Figure 13-8, you can see how the Disqus commenting system looks within a blog.

Figure 13-8: The Disqus commenting system.

Highlighting Social Media Profiles

Building a great blog design means inviting readers to easily become immersed in your blog community. Think of your blog as the hub of your community and the social media channels as spokes.

In Chapter 11, I describe how including buttons that link to social media profiles allows your readers to follow or connect with you with little effort on their part. This section covers how to add sidebar buttons that link to your social media profiles. In addition, this section covers social media widgets that infuse parts of those communities into your blog design. By doing so, you highlight your involvement in a greater community that extends outside your blog, which leads to more interaction within those social media platforms.

Adding social media buttons to your blog

Including social media buttons in your sidebar gives readers links to your key profiles in one place. After you find or create social media buttons that complement your overall blog design, placing them on your blog involves simply adding a little HTML code to your sidebar. You may even want to display the social media buttons again in your footer because a visitor might scroll down your blog to where your sidebar's buttons are no longer visible.

A quick Internet search for *social media buttons* or *social media icons* gives you many pre-made options to choose from. You can also design your own buttons using social media logos and a design program like Adobe Illustrator, Adobe Photoshop, or PicMonkey (www.picmonkey.com). Do a search for *social media vectors* or *silhouettes* to find the logos needed to create your buttons.

To add a social media button to your sidebar, you first want to upload the button images onto your blog. Then, after your social media icons are uploaded to your blog, you can add them to your sidebar. In the following steps, I use a Twitter button as an example. Copy the URL of the image you uploaded, and then take the following steps in WordPress:

1. **Open your WordPress dashboard.**

2. **Navigate to Appearance⇨Widgets.**

3. **Under Available Widgets, find the one named Text.**

4. **Click the Text button and then drag it to the right column into the Main Sidebar area.**

   The exact title of this area may vary, depending on your blog's theme.

5. **Add the following code into the Text box (see Figure 13-9).**

```
<a href="http://twitter.com/NAME" target="_blank">
    <img src="http://www.NAME.com/Images/twitter-icon.
        png">
</a>
```

In Step 5, the bold and italicized text indicates a placeholder. Be sure to replace the placeholders with, respectively, the actual name that appears in your Twitter URL and the actual location of the image that you want to link to your Twitter page. If you need help remembering what this code means, see Chapter 9. You can also add a title to this sidebar section if you'd like.

6. **Click Save.**

Be sure to visit your blog after you save it to make sure the icons look okay and the links work correctly.

Widget Text

Title:

```
<a href="http://twitter.com/NAME" target="_blank"><img
src="http://www.NAME.com/Images/twitter-icon.png"></a>
```

☐ Automatically add paragraphs

Figure 13-9: Adding HTML to a text box in the Twenty Eleven theme.

Enhancing your blog with social media widgets

Social media widgets bring your extended online community straight to your blog by giving readers a glimpse of your involvement in that particular social media platform. Some bloggers like to add a widget or two into their blog design, either in a sidebar or a footer.

By showcasing pictures, posts, or tweets right on your blog, you encourage readers to become involved by piquing their interest in those communities. Just know that every widget invites readers to click away from your blog. For that reason, just stick to using one or two within your blog design; you don't need a widget for every single social media platform you're on.

Here are some popular social media widgets you can add to your blog design:

✔ **Facebook Like box**

```
http://developers.facebook.com/docs/reference/plugins/
         like-box
```

Add a Like box to your blog. The box displays a reader's friends who follow you, your latest Facebook fan page posts, or both.

✔ **Twitter**

```
https://twitter.com/login?redirect_after_login
        =%2Fsettings%2Fwidgets
```

You can show tweets from your full timeline or limit the tweets shown to those that you mark as a Favorite or include in a list or those that contain a keyword or hashtag.

✔ **Pinterest Button and Widget Builder**

```
http://business.pinterest.com/widget-builder
```

Display your latest pins or highlight pins from a particular board.

✔ **Instagram SnapWidget**

```
http://snapwidget.com
```

✔ **Instagram Widget**

```
www.instagme.com
```

Show off all your Instagram pics, or pics from a certain hashtag.

If you're on WordPress.org, you can also find plug-ins for all these, but remember that using too many plug-ins can slow down your blog's loading time. Using widgets that create HTML code for you to place into your blog's sidebar or footer avoids the use of plug-ins.

Because Facebook is the most popular social media platform, I want to walk you through customizing a Facebook Like Box widget and putting it on your blog.

To create a Facebook Like Box, follow these steps:

1. **Visit the Like Box Developers page:**

   ```
   http://developers.facebook.com/docs/reference/
           plugins/like-box
   ```

   In the center of the page, you see a sample Find Us on Facebook box.

2. **Type your Facebook page's URL into the first field.**

   When you press Tab to go to the next field, the sample box changes to your own page's feed.

3. **Customize the box, using the fields shown in Figure 13-10.**

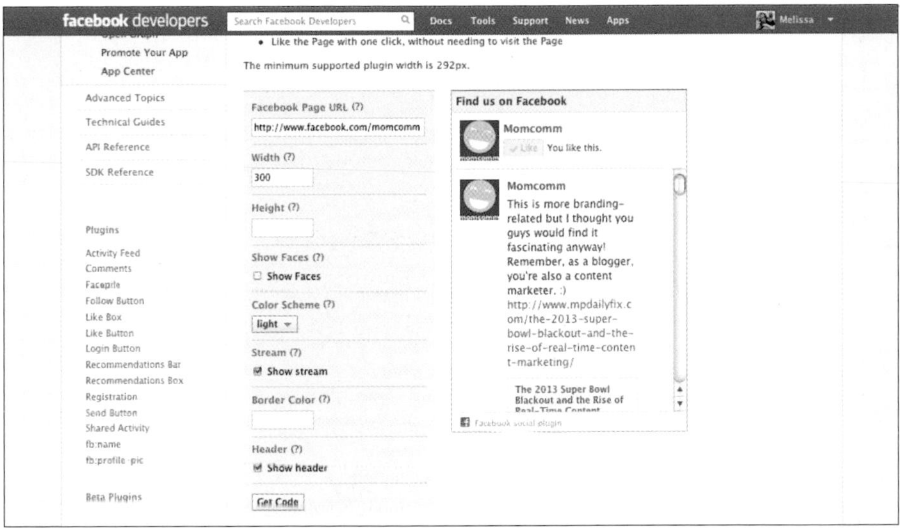

Figure 13-10: Facebook Like Box settings.

You have a few fields to select your preferences:

- *Width and Height:* The width is typically set to the width of your sidebar. Select a height as well if you want to constrain the box to a certain height; otherwise, the height is determined automatically.

- *Show Faces:* Leaving this setting checked shows the faces of a visitor's friends who also like your Facebook page. This can help build your credibility because if their friends like your page, then they may be missing out!

- *Color Scheme:* Select either light or dark.

- *Show Stream:* This shows your latest Facebook posts, and a visitor can scroll through them right from your blog page (although they can't comment, Like, or share them). Displaying this can pique curiosity and drive more Likes.

- *Border Color:* Enter this value as a hex color code (#xxxxxx) or by writing in a common color name (red, blue, and so on). For more on hex codes, see Chapter 6.

- *Show Header:* Deselecting this makes the Find Us on Facebook header disappear.

4. **Click Get Code.**

   This brings you a box with various types of code to copy and paste into your own blog.

5. **Click the IFrame tab; then copy and paste the code.**

6. **Add a widget for Text (WordPress) or gadget for HTML/JavaScript (Blogger) to your sidebar.**

7. **Paste the content into the HTML field.**

8. **Save your changes.**

   If you visit your home page, you see your customized Facebook Like box in your sidebar.

To prevent your sidebar from becoming overwhelmed with too many social media widgets, select the ones that are the most important to you. You can also use them in your blog footer as well, which I talk about in Chapter 8.

Part IV
Creating Design-Friendly Content

Learn ways to draw attention to your blog's special pages at www.dummies.com/extras/blogdesign.

In this part. . .

- ✔ Explore ways to integrate your blog's branding into your blog posts.

- ✔ Discover ideas for working design and navigation into your blog pages.

- ✔ Learn the basics of choosing and editing images for your blog as well how to work with illustrations.

- ✔ Decide how to showcase multiple images within your blog posts.

- ✔ Find the secrets to making your content easy to read by banishing long blocks of text.

Designing Main Pages of Content

*W*hen designing or redesigning a blog, you often find that you focus so much on your overall design — the header, sidebars, and layout — that your main pages of content becomes an afterthought. However, incorporating blog design into main pages of content gives you more opportunities to showcase your awesome blog design and make your content shine.

This chapter walks you through six common blog page types, giving you ways to design these pages from both a visual and navigation standpoint.

For tips on formatting your actual blog content for easy readability, check out Chapter 16.

Incorporating Design into Your Blog Posts

Working in a few simple design elements can attract a reader's eyes to your blog posts. The next few sections walk through strategies for jazzing up the elements in a blog post.

Customizing blog post titles

Blog post titles are quite likely the most repeated design element on your entire blog. This makes blog post titles an easy place to pull in something from your overall blog design into your main content area.

Here are some ideas for customizing your blog post titles:

- ✔ Custom font (See Chapter 6)

- ✔ Special color (See Chapter 6)

- ✔ Another color that displays when someone hovers over your title (See Chapter 9)

- ✔ Small design element or graphic before each title (See Chapter 11)

In Figure 14-1, you can see that my blog post titles use my custom font as well as two viewer-activated colors. The blue shows when someone hovers over the title.

Figure 14-1: Use blog post titles with custom font and color to match overall design.

Identifying what to include in your byline

Even if you're never heard the term *byline,* you've surely noticed one. A *byline* is technically the display of a blog post's author, but it often refers to a wider net of information at the top of the post, such as the author name, date, time, categories, and so on. In WordPress, you might hear it referred to as *post metadata*.

This area of your blog posts doesn't have to be fancy from a design perspective. However, using a different byline font style than your blog post title and content helps give the byline a subtle, yet informative place within your blog page design. Many bloggers use small caps or italics for a byline.

Good blog design also means providing some information that provides context around your blog post. Of course, deciding what information to display depends a lot on your blog theme, but here are some common things to include:

- ✔ **Author name:** If you're the only writer for your blog, make sure your byline doesn't say the highly impersonal, default name "admin." Some themes add byline options in the theme settings. In WordPress, go to Users➪Your Profile and then check whether the Display Name Publicly As field shows the name you want to display.

  If you want a guest blogger's name to show in the byline without making them a user of your blog, consider using a WordPress plug-in like Custom Author Byline:

```
http://wordpress.org/extend/plugins/custom-author-
    byline
```

- ✔ **Categories:** Displaying the category you assigned to a blog post can make it easy for your reader to navigate to an archive of posts in that particular category. It also gives the reader a clue as to what your blog post is about. (Read more about categories in Chapter 12.)

- ✔ **Link to comments:** Depending on your theme, a link to blog post comments shows up either at the top or bottom of your post. A visitor simply clicks the link and is directed to an area to leave a comment. See Chapter 13 for more about managing comments.

- ✔ **Tags:** Many bloggers prefer to list tags at the bottom of a post or not to list them at all. Because you might use a lot of tags for one post, this keeps the top of your blog post from being too cluttered. (Read more about tags in Chapter 12.)

Styling block quotations for visual interest

Within your blog posts, you've probably emphasized a bit of text before by using the block quote (or block quotation) feature in your visual editor. (Figure 14-2 shows the block quote icon in WordPress.) Depending on your blog theme's settings, the emphasized text might display with a box around it, such as the simple block quote design from my blog, Momcomm, shown in Figure 14-3. Another theme might use large quotation marks to set off the block quote, or some other visual element.

Block Quote icon

Blog Post Title

Figure 14-2: Create a block quote in WordPress.

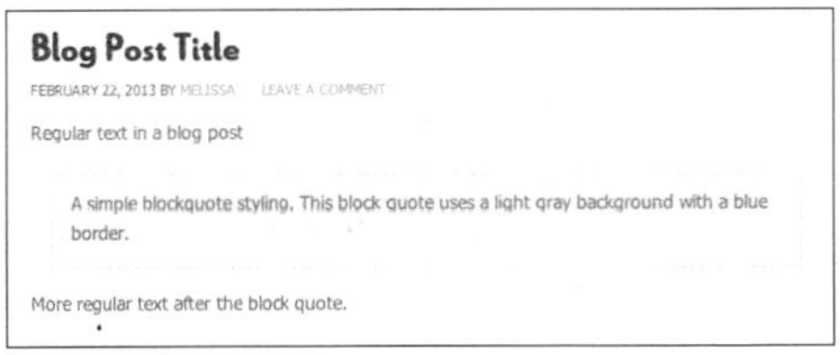

Blog Post Title

Figure 14-3: Even simple block quote styling stands out within a blog post.

Block quotations are used to highlight a quote from a person or another source. In other words, use block quotations solely for quotes — a famous quote, a quote from an article, a definition cited from a dictionary, and so on. Block quotations are also characterized by the fact that the quoted text isn't mentioned elsewhere within the article (which differs from a *pull quote,* where text is pulled from the article and emphasized in a styled quote).

As I mentioned in Chapter 2, readers tend to scan content on the web. Block quotations provide a way to draw attention to quotes more than just using simple quotation marks.

Block quotations shouldn't be used to simply make part of your own writing stand out within a blog post. If you want to highlight other parts of your content, then use indentation or other methods I describe in Chapter 16.

You can customize your block quotes to complement your overall blog design. To do so, you need to dig into your blog's `style.css` file. If you're not comfortable editing code, this may seem daunting, but just look for the word `blockquote` in the `style.css` file. (That's the CSS selector that styles text in a `<blockquote>` tag in your HTML, as I explain in Chapter 9.) After you find the `blockquote` selector, you can see where to play with the CSS code.

Bloggers often style eye-catching block quotes in one or more of the following ways:

- Changing the color or size of the text
- Adding a box or border around the text
- Applying a background image within the CSS that displays the quote within a talk bubble, with a large quotation mark to the left of the quote, or another visual element
- Indenting the text
- Adding a vertical line to the left of the text

Sharing Your Story with an About Page

Aside from your home page, your About page is the single most important page on your blog, because an About page is the first place someone goes to find out more about you and your blog.

The About page is also one of the hardest pages to write because it's hard to talk about ourselves! Moreover, the About page can leave you stumped as to how to incorporate design into the page. You probably don't think much about adding design elements other than a picture of yourself.

This section gives you ways to make your About page more meaningful to your reader through both visual appeal and navigation.

Breaking up areas through visual design

With an About page, you can get so wrapped up in what you want to say that your page ends up mostly being a large wall of text. However, just like a blog post, an About page needs some visual elements that align with your overall blog design and catch the readers' attention.

Here are some ideas to break up your page with design elements:

- **Single photographs:** People like to see a picture of the person behind the blog. If you blog anonymously, this still applies to you! Take a fun picture with your back to the camera or use a good illustration so you don't have to reveal yourself. Also, consider including pictures relevant to your blog or that give someone a better picture of who you are. These images could be a famous monument if you're a travel blogger or a picture of your family for a personal blog.

- **Photo collages or strips:** Another way to include photos is by using collages or even a ribbon of thumbnail photos (similar to a strip of film). These images liven up the page and provide visual information about the topics on your blog.

- **Subheadings:** Images are the only visual element on an About page. Subheadings also break up long blocks of text. (Read more about this technique in Chapter 16.) They give the reader a place to pause and can entice readers to read further.

- **Bullets and numbered lists:** Organizing your content into bullets or numbered lists gives readers a visual break and emphasizes key things you want the reader to know.

- **Testimonials:** If your blog is more product-oriented, try including a testimonial to break up the text. Use the block quote treatment so the testimonial visually stands out, which I cover earlier in this chapter.

- **Call to action area:** Use your About page as a chance to capture a small piece of information, like an e-mail address for a newsletter. If you add this near the bottom of your page, you can even repeat the same subscription box from your sidebar, especially because the reader may have scrolled past the sidebar subscription box and it's now out of sight.

- **Social media icons:** At the end of an About page, offer a way to connect with you by including social media icons for your profiles.

One of the best About pages on the web is from Kiersten at Oh My Veggies (http://ohmyveggies.com). She mixes the right blend of personal details and information about her blog in a way that's both fun and visually awesome. Figure 14-4 shows a few of the elements she includes on her About page.

© Oh My Veggies – Design by Shay Bocks

Figure 14-4: Design elements on an About page can really liven up the page.

Including navigational cues

If you use visual elements to pull your blog design into your About page, don't let navigational design go to the wayside. An About page's purpose is to tell the reader more about you and your blog, but you can include only so much information without the page becoming overwhelming.

An About page should always give the reader something to do next or somewhere to go next. You can do this through the following three navigational cues:

- ✒ **Interlinking:** Interlinking puts other content on your blog within easy reach by linking to it within the text of your About page. A visitor who's reading your About page is clearly interested in you and your blog. Entice this reader into becoming a regular blog visitor by pointing him or her to some hand-selected examples of your content.

   In Chapter 12, I go into some more detail about interlinking. Instead of linking within your text, you can direct readers to posts visually, by linking image thumbnails and post titles.

- ✒ **Links to other sites:** Instead of just showing a list of sites you contribute to, projects you've been a part of, or places you've been featured, include a link to them as well. Doing this saves the reader from having to find those links on their own (most won't bother), with the added benefit of boosting your credibility. Just keep in mind you don't want too many links that navigate away from your blog so do this in moderation.

- ✒ **Contact information:** Yes, you should have a separate Contact page, but put it in easy reach by linking to that page within your About page.

Even better? Include an e-mail address right on your About page so that readers don't even have to click over unless they want more details or a contact form to fill out. If you're interested in working with brands (for product reviews, advertising, or partnerships), many brand reps visit blog after blog. They'll be grateful to save a little time by having the contact information handy.

In Figure 14-5, notice that Jo-Lynne from Musings of a Housewife (`www.musingsofahousewife.com`) does a good job of linking to places both on and off of her blog. She also provides images along with the links to lead readers deeper into her blog.

© Jo-Lynne Shane's Musings of a Housewife

Figure 14-5: This blog provides navigation options throughout the About page.

Laying Out the Basics with a Start Here Page

When it comes to new visitors navigating your blog, you want them to magically understand exactly what your blog is all about, subscribe or follow the blog on social media, and start reading your content — in just one visit. With a Start Here as part of your blog design, you have a better chance of making that magic happen.

Blog visitors often need a little extra guidance in navigating your site for the first time, even if you think your site describes itself through your design and content. Time is scarce, so the easier you make it for visitors to get a crystal clear picture of your blog, the more grateful they'll be.

A Start Here page tells your readers how they can benefit from your blog and highlights some of your best content to prove it.

From a content standpoint, your Start Here page shouldn't rehash your About page. Instead, focus mainly on your readers and describe who your blog is for and why they should read it. From a design standpoint, follow some of the visual element suggestions I mention in the About section: things like adding images, subheadings, and bullets.

Showing off your best stuff

This Start Here page can really make or break your new reader's opinion of your blog. This means you have to share your absolute best content that really gives a clear snapshot of what your blog is about. (No pressure, right?)

Although your About page may have covered some of your best content, the Start Here page uses your great content to convince the reader your blog is the place for them. Make that content visually interesting with thumbnails, images, graphical elements, or even a touch of color.

Including a link on your About page to your Start Here page gets readers navigating to a place to learn even more specific information about your blog.

A Start Here page doesn't have to literally say *Start Here,* nor do you have to begin the page describing exactly what your blog is about. The blog How to Be a Dad (www.howtobeadad.com) calls this page the New Here? page. Bloggers Charlie and Andy start off by dispelling the idea that their blog is serious advice about how to be a dad. They make it clear from the start what their blog is *not*, and then feed visitors their best content.

As you see in Figure 14-6, they visually show off their popular Notebook and Instructional Diagrams with a short section introduction, thumbnail images, and blog post titles to guide the reader to some of their best stuff.

© Andy Herald and Charlie Capen, How to Be a Dad

Figure 14-6: How to Be a Dad's *New Here?* Page.

Asking your reader to take action

New readers navigate to your Start Here page because they want a course of action. Showing your best content should convince the reader whether your blog is the place for them. If they like what they see, the next logical step for the visitor is to take action by subscribing to your newsletter, signing up for a course, or following you in social media.

Whichever action you want your visitor to take, make that section visually distinct from the rest of the page. The section should draw readers' eyes straight to it so they can't miss it.

Distinguish your call-to-action section by using a different color or different design element not used elsewhere on the page. Within that design element, stick to a simple action statement, which is easier to digest than a wordy one. In Figure 14-7, you see the last section of the Smart Passive Income blog (www.smartpassiveincome.com) Getting Started page. Pat uses the same section design as the rest of this page but grabs attention with a product image (that's free!) and a to-the-point subscription box.

© Smart Passive Income

Figure 14-7: This Getting Started page ends in a clear, visual call to action.

Encouraging a Sale with a Product Page

Bloggers don't often start out offering products on their blog but sometimes stumble into selling products as their content and audience grows. An effective design and layout on a product page can be the difference between a sale and, well, no sale!

The products you sell as a blogger might be virtual or physical ones. Now or in the future, you might sell items like the following:

- E-books
- Online courses
- Printables (craft templates, tutorials, checklists)
- Branded items (t-shirts, stickers, mugs)
- Related products
- Handmade products

Whether you're designing a product page as a single page or as part of an ecommerce store, this section gives you tips for a well-designed page that commands attention and encourages a sale.

See Chapter 17 for some ideas on extending your brand to virtual products, such as printables and e-books.

Piquing interest through quality imagery

When it comes to selling products on your blog, imagery within your product page design can make or break a sale. High-quality imagery conveys professionalism and credibility. Whether you're selling an e-book or a knitted hat, create a page design that includes appealing imagery.

If you sell physical products, make sure the products are taken in good light and without distracting backgrounds. Consider using close-up images in addition to the main product images to show product details. See Chapter 15 for tips on what makes a good-quality image.

If you sell virtual products on your blog, you don't have product photographs to work with. However, you do have lots of possibilities when it comes to visually showcasing your virtual product, such as the following:

- ✔ **E-covers:** An *e-cover* is an image or set of images designed to look like a physical book, disc, or other representation of a physical product. For example, if you sell an e-book, you might have an e-cover created that looks like an actual book. You can find e-cover creator software online or create them yourself if you're graphically savvy. Just be careful that your image doesn't mislead the visitor (like showing a really thick e-book graphic for a 20-page e-book). One online e-cover creator you can try is MyEcoverMaker (www.myecovermaker.com/ecover-design), who lets you pay per e-cover download or by month.

- ✔ **Sample image:** Show a sample page or image from your virtual product to give visitors a glimpse of what they'll receive. In Figure 14-8, you see that Christina from the blog Hair Romance (www.hairromance.com) showcases her 30 Braids in 30 Days e-book cover and an image that highlights a page from the e-book.

- ✔ **Supporting graphics:** Aside from showing the actual product, consider using colored graphical elements to pull the visitor down through the product page. This could be a light border between sections on a long page, the logo of your product, or another graphical image. Just be careful not to overdo it.

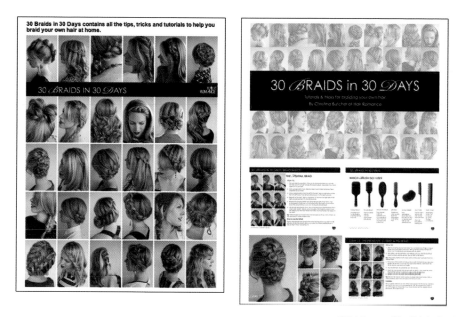

© Hair Romance™ by Christina Butcher

Figure 14-8: These two Product page images shows the reader just how much valuable content the e-book includes.

Interesting your prospects with appealing testimonials

Testimonials aren't just a way to build trust. They can also provide a visual break within your product page design. Testimonials help a potential buyer overcome skepticism and doubt, so you want them to get noticed. Just displaying them as plain text in the body of your content won't cut it.

Make testimonials stand out visually by adding color (text, background, border), using the block quote function (see the earlier section, "Styling block quotations for visual interest"), or displaying a headshot of the person giving the testimonial.

In Figure 14-9, notice how the testimonials on the blog No Meat Athlete (www. nomeatathlete.com) stand out from the rest of the page's content. Each one uses a subtle background color and bolded text at the top to highlight a quote pulled from the full testimonial. Some also include headshots to personalize the testimonial.

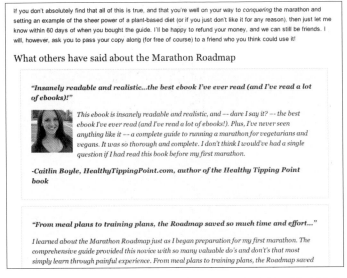

Figure 14-9: One way to highlight testimonials on a Product page.

Styling the testimonial can be done within the content itself or use a plug-in that formats testimonials for you, like the Testimonials Widget for WordPress:

```
http://wordpress.org/extend/plugins/testimonials-widget/
        screenshots
```

You can also create a quote in a photo-editing program and use it on your page as an image. Just make sure to use an effective image title (see Chapter 15) and an `alt` attribute (see Chapter 10).

Closing the deal with a distinct call to action

You've probably heard the phrase "Ask for the sale" before. On your blog's product page, this doesn't necessarily mean asking a question. It means asking the visitor to do something. In the marketing world, this request is known as a *call to action.* Your call to action can be something like Add to Cart, Get Started, or Download Now. Feel free to get even more creative with it! A call to action on your product page is most effective when it's done within a graphical element of some sort.

In Chapter 2, I talk about contrast being a core principle of good design. A call to action that contrasts with the rest of the page draws the reader's attention and thus increases the chance of making a sale. Add contrast by using color, size, font, and so on. In Figure 14-10, you see two effective examples of call-to-action buttons: a Download It Now button from Hair Romance and an Add to Cart button from No Meat Athlete.

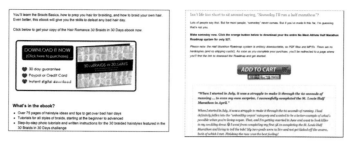

© Hair Romance™ by Christina Butcher (left) © No Meat Athlete®, blog design by Charlie Pabst of Charfish Design (right)

Figure 14-10: These call-to-action buttons stand out by contrasting with the rest of the page.

Building an Enticing Resource Page

A Resource page contains links to articles and websites around a specific topic. This type of page improves the usability of your blog by providing a one-stop place to find the content you deem most relevant around a particular topic. If you blog about blogging, the page could include links to your host, the place where you buy domain names, and plug-ins that you use. If you blog about travel, perhaps the page includes your favorite website to buy airline tickets or your must-have travel apps for a smart phone.

Because a Resource page is just that — resources — the page design has a tendency to be quite boring. This section gives you some ideas to spruce up the page design and improve its appeal.

Part of a good blog design means your blog should always be as easy to use as possible. Because this page is full of awesome resources, people will want to share the page on social media sites. Make this easy for them by adding sharing buttons that enable your readers to easily share the page with their social media networks. See Chapter 13 for more on using sharing buttons.

Grouping related content

In Chapter 2, I talk about grouping related blog design elements to provide structure for the reader. The same concept applies to large amounts of content in your Resource page.

After you gather the resources you want to feature on your page, resist the impulse to simply list resources in the order you add them to the page or to list resources alphabetically. Instead, organize your resources into groups of similar content. Readers want the simplest navigation possible. When they visit your resources page, they're likely looking for a certain category of information. For example, on a blog about taking photos, a reader might visit the resources page to find the blogger's five favorite websites for buying camera equipment. Whatever your blog's topic, you provide much more value to your reader by grouping links in a way that allow the reader to easily find the desired information.

Avoiding link lists

Many Resource pages start with good intentions but end up being one really long list of links. Ack! I've seen Resource pages with literally 50 links, one right after another. From an ease-of-use perspective, long lists with no visual breaks overwhelm the reader with choice and hinders the ability to focus on any one of them. Breaking up lists on your Resource page design simplifies the choices by giving readers a place to rest between each grouping (even without removing any links).

Visually break up link lists by using subheadings, graphics, or dividers between sections. In Figure 14-11, the blog Leaving Work Behind (www.leavingworkbehind.com) uses subheadings and colored links to make the list of resources organized and easy to follow.

Blogging and Internet Marketing Resources

Since I decided to quit my job in May 2011, I have used an enormous number of products and services related to making money online.

Over the past year or so, I have explored everything from WordPress plugins, to books, to hosting providers. So I thought it might be useful to recommend the highest-quality products that I have come across.

My aim with this resources page is to make you better informed, so that you can make the right decisions.

There are affiliate links on this page. If you purchase a product through one of them, I will receive a commission. It will cost you nothing extra. **I only ever endorse products that I have personally used and tested extensively.** Thank you!

Freelance Writing

- **Successful Freelance Writing Online**: This is my guide to making a full time living in part time hours from freelance blogging, which is what enabled me to quit my job in 2011. I would thoroughly recommend it to anyone interested in making money online.

Building a Blog or Website

- **WordPress**: In my opinion, the best content management system for bloggers (and for the vast majority of websites in general). You can start blogging with WordPress at no cost by **clicking here**, but I would strongly recommend that you invest in a self-hosted site (the WordPress software is free, but a domain and hosting will set you back a few bucks).

© Leaving Work Behind, www.leavingworkbehind.com

Figure 14-11: Using subheadings and color solves the issue of long link lists.

Creating an Informative Advertising Page

Some bloggers never try to make money from their blog. If that's you, then by all means, skip this section! However, if you want to make money from your blog through advertising or working on projects with companies, then having an Advertising page as part of your blog design is a must. Otherwise, how's a company representative supposed to know you're potentially interested in working with that company?

Of course, you can call this page something other than the Advertising page (Advertising/PR, Work with Me, Sponsorships, and so on); just make sure the name is obvious to the potential advertiser. You don't want someone to have to search your site to find it. Creating an informative Advertising page means making your blog's opportunities clear and your page design easy to navigate.

Showcasing your blog's opportunities

Some bloggers prefer to include a lot of details on their Advertising page. Others prefer to keep it short and then direct visitors to contact them for more info. How much or little you include really boils down to personal preference.

You can showcase opportunities on your Advertising page through visual or navigation design. The following examples illustrate how you might add helpful images or links on your advertising page:

- **Ads in your blog or newsletter:** Help the visitor visualize advertising opportunities by showing graphical representations of the ad sizes you offer.

- **Reviews or giveaways:** Display thumbnail images and titles that link to past posts or simply provide a link with a short description.

The blog Musings of a Housewife (www.musingsofahousewife.com) has a great example of a robust Advertising page. This Media Kit page uses a mix of subheadings, links, images, and even video to highlight a range of opportunities (see Figure 14-12).

Advertisers are also typically interested in your blog stats like your page views, number of Facebook fans, and other relevant statistics that demonstrate your blog's reach. How much detail you provide on your Advertising page is your call. Some bloggers prefer to show a lot of detail, while others prefer to save details for a media kit that they e-mail to a potential advertiser upon request.

© Jo-Lynne Shane's Musings of a Housewife

Figure 14-12: This page attracts potential advertisers by showing a wide range of opportunities.

If you include statistics on your Advertising page, make the data easy to scan. You could also liven up your page by using graphical elements or symbols to accompany the statistics (like a Twitter icon beside your number of Twitter followers).

Selling ad space directly from your blog

For some bloggers, selling ads directly from your Advertising page makes sense as a great, hassle-free option. Instead of managing the advertising process manually — e-mailing advertisers back and forth, managing payments, and placing the ads on your blog — you sell ads through an application that handles the advertising for you. Incorporating this into your Advertising page design lets your potential advertiser easily purchase an ad from your site with less administration from you.

Setting up a way to sell ads directly from your Advertising page is easier than you might think. Two options to consider are

- **Skyscraper:** www.skyscraper.io
- **Passionfruit:** https://app.passionfruitads.com

They work on any blog platform, from WordPress to Blogger to Tumblr, and take a fee each time you sell an ad on your blog.

As you can see in Figure 14-13, Passionfruit Ads let you set up a professional-looking shop for advertisers to purchase ads on your blog. Choose how many ads you want, provide descriptions for each one, and set advertising terms like how long the ads run. To display Passionfruit Ads on your Advertising page, you simply paste the code that Passionfruit provides into your page, and the advertising shop displays on your blog. On WordPress.org, go to edit the page in which you want to add the advertising shop, click the Text tab, and paste the code into the page's content area. On Blogger, click the HTML button from the post editing page, and then paste the code into the page's content area.

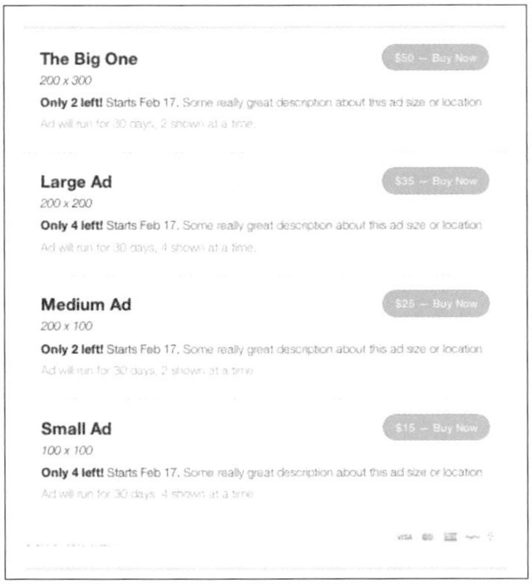

Figure 14-13: Use an advertising shop to run your ads.

If you decide to use an app like this to sell advertising for your blog, take a few minutes to customize the colors to match the rest of your blog. Refer to your blog's style guide (see Chapter 4) to get the color hex codes for your blog design colors.

Making Yourself Available with a Contact Page

A Contact page provides a place for someone to get directly in touch with you. Most bloggers include a Contact page in a navigation menu although sometimes you might find it in a footer, more like a typical company website.

After your About page, adding a Contact page to your blog design should be your next priority — it's that important.

Although visual design can add a great branded touch to your Contact page, your page design should focus on usability. After all, you want to make getting in touch with you easy-peasy. This section walks you through a couple of things to consider when putting together your Contact page design.

Providing multiple ways to contact you

You might wonder who will actually use your Contact page to communicate with you. Your readers may want to tell you how much they adore you, ask you a question, or give you feedback on something. A company brand or PR representative may want to see whether you'll work with them on a new campaign. A reporter may even want to see whether you're available to interview for a story. With so many different people to consider, it helps to include at least a couple of ways to contact you within your Contact page design.

The most common options to offer are an e-mail address and a contact form. When using an e-mail address, enhance the navigation design by making it an active link. That way, a visitor can just click the e-mail address, and it opens a new message in their e-mail application.

You can do this by clicking the hyperlink button in your blog post's Visual Editor and writing `mailto:name@email.com` instead of listing a URL.

For contact forms, you have many options, from plug-ins for WordPress to apps for just about any blogging platform. Here are a few choices:

- **Wufoo:** free and paid versions; most platforms

    www.wufoo.com

- **Kontactr:** free; most platforms

    http://kontactr.com

- **Google Forms:** `drive.google.com/forms` free; any platform

    http://drive.google.com/forms

- **Contact Form 7:** free; WordPress

    http://wordpress.org/extend/plugins/contact-form-7

- **Fast Secure Contact Form:** free; WordPress

    http://wordpress.org/extend/plugins/si-contact-form

- **Gravity Forms:** $39/year and up; WordPress

    www.gravityforms.com

In Figure 14-14, you can see that Tom from the blog Leaving Work Behind (`www.leavingworkbehind.com`) uses an e-mail address and a contact form as well as links to a Facebook page and Twitter profile. He gives the reader plenty of options to contact him without making the choices too overwhelming.

© Leaving Work Behind, www.leavingworkbehind.com

Figure 14-14: Use a clean, effective Contact page.

Minimizing distractions to encourage communication

A Contact page's primary purpose is to give someone an easy, obvious way to contact you. Resist the urge to clutter up the space or making things overly fancy from a design standpoint.

If you include a contact form, try not to ask for too much information lest you deter someone from filling it out. You might even remove the sidebar from your Contact page so a visitor can concentrate fully on contacting you.

Good blog design means making your blog easy to use and functional.

On the opposite end of the spectrum, don't use create a Contact page with just one sentence. This makes the page look too vacant from a design standpoint and can give the impression you're indifferent about readers contacting you.

Jennifer from Everyday Bright (`http://everydaybright.com`) keeps her Contact page free from distractions (see Figure 14-15). Her social media communication channels are at the top, and her contact form sits underneath.

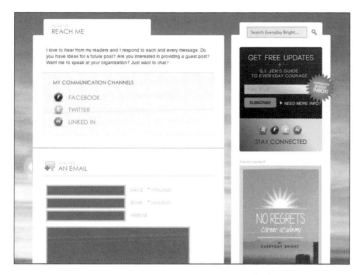

© Everyday Bright, LLC at www.everydaybright.com, Design by Luis Cortés of Well Versed Creative

Figure 14-15: This well-organized Contact page has the right dose of design.

15
Working with Images

*P*eople's time — and thus attention — is so fragmented these days. People bounce from blog to blog and social media network to network, not to mention spending time online to do product research, check their bank account, or find their closest gym.

In the online world, you'll often hear, "Content is king." Images are content too. They play a huge role in grabbing a reader's attention and should play a huge role in your blog design. Images can support your opinion, illustrate a how-to explanation, or fuel your story with emotion. Strong images also help build your blog brand's look and feel and guide readers through your site.

Think about it. Would you flip through a magazine if there were no images? Probably not. Like magazines, blogs come alive with images.

Images aren't just important when someone is actually *on* your blog. With the rise of social media platforms like Pinterest and Instagram, and reading apps like Flipboard, great imagery that gets shared from your blog posts also gives you a chance to capture someone's attention *outside* the realm of your blog.

Of course, working with the images you want to use in your blog design does take time — sometimes a great deal of time. In this chapter, I walk you through the ins and outs of choosing images for your blog, including websites that offer a great selection. I also tell you about the various software tools available for working with images and making simple edits. I even touch on using vector images. So enough with the words. Get ready to find out about images.

Finding Photos for Your Blog

Finding quality photos you can actually use on your blog isn't always easy. In fact, I'd say that many bloggers know photos are important but don't include as many as they could just because finding and prepping photos can be so time-consuming.

Having a few go-to resources for photos helps tremendously. Whether your blog design calls for using a photo for a blog post or elsewhere on your blog, this section walks you through options for finding photos and how to make sure you're using them with proper permission.

Knowing the anatomy of a good photo

A high-quality photo enhances your blog design. Conversely, a poor-quality photo detracts from your design. Even if you're sourcing the photo rather than using your own, it's important to recognize quality. (See the sidebar, "Avoiding poor photo quality.")

In the following list, I share the basic elements of a great photo:

- ✔ **Good composition:** *Composition* refers to how elements within a photo are set up. Sometimes you plan the composition: for example, when you photograph a plate of mouth-watering food. Other times, you resort to lightning-fast composition, such as when snapping a great shot of a running toddler.

Figure 15-1: The elephant's face hits around one of the grid intersections.

Use photographic elements like lines, patterns, and balance to create interesting photos. One of the most tried-and-true ways to compose a photograph for greater visual interest is the *Rule of Thirds*. In this method of composition, you imagine the image divided into thirds, both horizontally and vertically. When taking a photo (or finding one to use), ensure the point of interest lands at the intersection of one of the thirds, as shown in Figure 15-1.

- ✔ **Good lighting:** When you use a built-in flash or shoot photos in low light conditions, your photos can lack the oomph that your blog design needs. A well-lit photograph keeps the focus on its subject and doesn't distract blog readers from the point of the image. Harsh shadows or overlit sections of a photograph can often make or break your ability to entice the readers, make an emotional connection, or aid in a tutorial.

Take a look at the two images in Figure 15-2 for an example. Which food would you rather eat?

If you take your own images, try to take images in early morning or early evening, when the natural light is best. If you're indoors, look for a natural light source, such as a window. Try not to use your built-in flash indoors, even in low light. They're notorious for overlighting your photo or giving people the dreaded red eyes. Because low light requires that the camera's shutter stay open longer to let in more light, try setting up a tripod or place your camera on a flat surface. Then, use a self-timer to take the photo, which prevents camera shake that can occur when you're holding your camera (or even pressing down the shutter button), helping you take a crisper shot.

✐ **Emphasis on the subject:** Who or what is the subject of your photograph? What is the story you're trying to tell? If your subject is your dog, then get close to minimize a distracting background. However, if you want to show how your dog loves nature, step back so you can show him trotting down a hiking trail. No matter what you write about, your blog posts are where you tell stories, educate, inspire, and more. Make sure your photos align to that purpose.

© Amanda Padgett, EverydayElementsOnline.com

Figure 15-2: The poorly lit food on the left just doesn't make your mouth water.

Beyond what I've covered here, other, more technical factors come into play when you're talking about good photographs such as focus and exposure. For more details on composing great photographs, check out *Digital Photography For Dummies,* 7th Edition by Julie Adair King.

Using your own photos

Using your own photos is the easiest choice, especially if you have a lifestyle or memoir-type blog. Getting photos this way is free (minus the camera equipment), you don't have to worry about copyright issues, and you can get precisely the images you want. (***Important:*** Read more about copyright issues in the upcoming section, "Understanding permissions.") Hundreds of people could be using that photo you just downloaded from Flickr, so perhaps the biggest benefit of using your own photo is that your photo is unique.

Avoiding poor photo quality

Photos help bring your blog to life, but using poor quality photos can be worse than having none at all. Good images show professionalism and strengthen branding for your design. Bad images have the opposite effect.

Poor-quality images can occur because of the way the picture was manipulated in image editing software. Here are two frequently seen mistakes:

✔ **Pixilation/blurriness:** *Pixels* are all the tiny dots that make up an image. When you make an image smaller, the photo quality remains because photo-editing programs know which pixels to throw away. However, if you make a picture larger than the original, photo-editing programs just add pixels to fill in the spaces. If you increase the image too much, pixels start to look blurry or like squares, as in this image — and that's *pixilation.*

In some cases, you can actually use pixilation on purpose if you're trying to blur part of a photograph, such as nudity or someone who wants to be anonymous in your photo. In that case, you can easily tell the pixilation is used for an effect, instead of a mistake. The simplest fix is to keep images within the confines of the original size by going smaller. If you must go larger, keep a close eye on the image to ensure the quality doesn't diminish too far from the original.

✔ **Distortion:** When manipulating an image, you may accidentally "stretch it," making the objects in the image disproportional. Sometimes this occurs when editing an image in a photo-editing program. However, distortion can also occur if you place an image into a space that isn't proportional to your image size, such as trying to fit a square image into a wide and narrow header. Distortion always looks the worst with people, stretching them as if they're standing in front of a funhouse mirror. Distorted images look amateurish, so always maintain proportions when resizing an image. In many programs, you can maintain the image's proportions by holding down the Shift key as you drag the corner of an image when resizing it.

Even if you use your own photos, image quality still needs to be top notch. To accomplish this, you don't need a fancy, expensive dSLR camera. You can take great photos on a basic point-and-shoot camera, or even on a built-in camera on your phone. For example, Elan Morgan takes wonderful pictures from her iPhone to use on her blog Schmutzie (www.schmutzie.com), shown in Figure 15-3. See the sidebar "Avoiding poor photo quality" for more about photo quality.

© Elan Morgan of Schmutzie.com and Ninjamatics

Figure 15-3: You can use an inexpensive camera for your blog images.

Using images from other sources

Using your own images doesn't always make sense for a blog post. For example, if you're writing about a Twitter tip, taking a relevant photo might be a challenge. You also might decide that you're not the best photographer and would rather use an image from someone else. Whatever the reason, the Internet is full of places to find stock images that you can legitimately use on your blog.

A *stock image* is a photograph licensed for public or commercial use. You find stock images in online databases that users can search by keyword, category, and so on to locate the right image. Some stock images are free, and some you have to pay to use.

The biggest benefit of free images is, well, they're free. Having said that, many come with a requirement to attribute the image in some way, such as linking back to the owner. Although you should never skimp on doing so, you may not find this situation ideal if you're trying to use an image in your blog header or if you want your page to feel more branded. In that case, there's the option to pay for images.

Purchasing images often means you receive a higher-quality image (but not always). In addition, although you may not be the only person using that image, chances are that fewer people are using it (than if it were a free photo).

On my blog, I use a mix of both. I typically start by searching for a free image. Then, if I don't find what I'm looking for rather quickly, I move to paying for a small image size for web use.

Here are some popular sites for free images:

- ✔ **Stock.XCHNG:** www.sxc.hu
- ✔ **Flickr Creative Commons:** www.flickr.com/creativecommons
- ✔ **Image Base:** http://www.imagebase.net
- ✔ **FreeFoto:** www.freefoto.com/index.jsp
- ✔ **Stock Free Images:** www.stockfreeimages.com

When purchasing images, some sites require you to buy credits instead of purchasing images individually. You purchase a minimum amount of credits, and then each size of an image costs a different number of credits. The more credits you buy at a time, the less expensive each image becomes. Here are some popular sites for purchasing images:

- ✔ **iStockphoto:** www.istockphoto.com

  See Figure 15-4.
- ✔ **Veer:** www.veer.com
- ✔ **Bigstock:** www.bigstock.com
- ✔ **PhotoXpress:** www.photoxpress.com
- ✔ **Fotolia:** http://us.fotolia.com

All these paid sites have advanced search options so you can search by keyword, image orientation, and more. For example, the iStockphoto advanced search options let you search by hex code or by marking where you want to place text on a photo. Read more about hex codes in Chapter 6.

If you're on the WordPress.org platform, take advantage of photo-finding plug-ins. These plug-ins find relevant images based on your keyword, and then add them to your blog post while automatically linking to the source. Some of the more popular ones include Photo Dropper, Zemanta, and Flickr Photo Post.

Figure 15-4: Fee-based stock photo houses are another option for obtaining images.

Understanding permissions

Just because an image is on the Internet doesn't mean you have free reign to use however you wish. All images are copyrighted, so when using the paid and free options for finding images, you need to understand what permission you have to use the work.

A *copyright* legally protects original works of authorship. That could be a photo, graphic design, writing, piece of music, or other type of creative work. Unlike trademarks or patents, copyrights don't require additional paperwork. In the U.S., copyright attaches to a piece of work as soon as you create it.

As a general rule, you can't use a copyrighted work without permission from the owner. This means that you can't just use an image from another website (or a place like Google Images) and then credit that person by linking to them. The same goes for right-clicking an image from a website and saving it to your computer. *Giving credit isn't the same as getting permission.*

With paid images, you generally don't need to attribute back to the owner because you've essentially purchased the right to use the image. However, before you purchase an image or use one for free, you should always read the licensing agreement.

Free images may require you to link to the source of the image, but you may not be able to use a free or paid photo for commercial use. If you want to purchase an image to use in your blog header design but you also want to make t-shirts to sell with your blog header on them, you might need an extended license. There are a myriad of other potential requirements, so read the license agreement before you use a particular image.

Editing Photos

Photos are rarely perfect right out of the camera. In fact, you'd probably be surprised to see unedited versions of some of your favorite photos.

To get the most out of your pictures, you'll want to edit them in some small (or big) way. Editing photos can range from simple things like removing clutter by cropping, to more advanced techniques like adding creative effects. I'm certainly no photo-editing professional, but I often find that just a small tweak can make a photo go from mediocre to awesome. For the more adventurous, you can find many *For Dummies* books on digital photography, cameras, and photo-editing programs. Visit www.dummies.com.

Choosing photo-editing software

When it comes to making a choice for photo-editing software, you have quite a few options that vary widely in price and learning curve. What you choose ultimately boils down to how much you want to spend and how much editing you plan to do.

If you're looking for basic features — say, resizing, cropping, and adjusting contrast or balance — you can probably get by with a free or almost free program. If you're looking for (or are eager to learn) more advanced features — creating paths, using masks, and working in layers — you'll need more complex software with a higher price tag.

Many bloggers might not want to invest in pricey software, so I cover the free web-based software PicMonkey (www.picmonkey.com) in this book (see Figure 15-5). PicMonkey describes itself as "the world's friendliest photo editor," which might be true! (Many bloggers moved to PicMonkey when Google's Picnik went the way of the dodo bird.) There's no software to install because PicMonkey is web-based. Just browse to the PicMonkey web page, upload a photo, and get to work.

Figure 15-5: PicMonkey is an easy-to-use photo-editing option for bloggers.

Of course, they are many, many other choices aside from PicMonkey. Here are just a few:

- **Adobe Photoshop**

  www.adobe.com/products/photoshop.html

  Mac and PC. Photoshop is the industry standard in photo-editing software and is ideal for professional photographers or serious amateurs. Along with the myriad of features that come built in, you can also add brushes, plug ins, patterns, and color swatches for even greater functionality. There's a definite learning curve, but Photoshop can do just about everything you'd want it to.

- **Adobe Photoshop Elements**

  www.adobe.com/products/photoshop-elements.html

  Mac and PC. According to the NPD Group/Retail Tracking Service, this program is the best-selling consumer photo-editing software in the United States. This program has many features similar to the more expensive Photoshop but is geared more for someone who doesn't need advanced features. It does have a learning curve, although not as steep as full-fledged Photoshop, so Photoshop Elements is a good stepping stone from basic to high-end software.

- **Corel PaintShop Photo Pro X5**

  www.corel.com/corel/product/index.jsp?pid=prod4900067

  PC only. PaintShop Photo Pro X5 is a rival to Photoshop but at a lower price point. It has less image-processing power and fewer features, but some users consider this program more user-friendly than Photoshop. It's also more geared toward the average consumer.

✔ **Picasa**

```
http://picasa.google.com
```

Mac and PC. Picasa is a Google photo-editing application. You can do basic editing or apply effects in an easy-to-use interface. You might also find this program good for organizing your photos and using as a photo-sharing tool.

✔ **GIMP**

```
www.gimp.org
```

Mac. GIMP (GNU Image Manipulation Program) enables you do many of the same things as Photoshop but isn't as user-friendly to use. GIMP is a popular choice for those who don't want to invest in Photoshop, but it's hard to compare the two given that GIMP is free, and Photoshop is among the more expensive image-editing programs available.

Choosing the right file format

No matter what program you use to create blog design elements, at some point you have to save them in a file format that can be displayed on the web. When it comes to web graphics, you only need to worry about three file formats: JPEG, PNG, and GIF. Each of them serve different roles, so this section explains when you should use each of them and why.

Before I get to that, you need to understand two data compression techniques:

✔ *Lossy compression* reduces file size by getting rid of (losing) some of the file's data. JPEGs use lossy compression. For example, if you resize a photo from 500 x 500 pixels down to 200 x 200 pixels, the compression throws out data to make the file smaller. If you try to change that 200-x-200-pixel image back to its original size, the image quality won't be the same, because data from the original file is now gone.

✔ *Lossless compression* reduces file size without getting rid of any file data. Because no data is thrown out, a file is typically larger than its JPG equivalent. PNGs and GIFs use lossless compression. For example, if you resize a 500-x-500-pixel illustration down to 200 x 200 pixels, you can then change the size back without any change in quality. The data can be reconstructed exactly as it was.

Table 15-1 lists each file format, the compression type, and when to use that particular file format. If you're ever unsure what format in which to save your design, just flip to this table.

Table 15-1	File Formats for the Web	
File format	*Compression type*	*Best Uses*
JPEG (Joint Photographic Experts Group)	Lossy	Photographs
PNG (Portable Network Graphics)	Lossless	Screenshots, graphics, illustrations, text-heavy images
GIF (Graphics Interchange Format)	Lossless	Graphics with few colors (GIFs are limited to only 256 colors)

Large file sizes increase your blog's loading time. If you need to further reduce the size of a JPEG, PNG, or GIF, try Puny PNG (`http://punypng.com`), a free web optimization tool that reduces image file size without any loss in quality.

Resizing photos

When you download photos from your camera to your computer, the photos are almost always too big to use on your blog, because they're taken at a resolution suitable for printing. The screens people use to view images on the web need a much lower resolution than print. Also, large images slow down your blog's loading time. So, before you upload photos to your blog, you need to resize them.

To resize a photo in PicMonkey, follow these steps:

1. **Go to the PicMonkey website (`www.picmonkey.com`).**

2. **Click the text that reads Edit a Photo (at the top of the interface).**

   A window pops up to let you select the photo you want to use.

3. **Select a photo and click Open.**

4. **On the menu of Basic Edits, select Resize at the bottom of the list.**

   The numbers that populate in the Change Size To fields are the current width and height of your image in pixels.

5. **Type new pixel numbers in the Change Size To field.**

   You have two additional options to adjust the size of your image, as shown in Figure 15-6:

   - *Use Percentages:* Select this check box to change the units from pixels to percentages. You can resize from there.

   - *Keep Proportions:* Selecting this option allows you to enter an amount for width or for height, and the other amount will automatically adjust to maintain the proportion of the image.

Figure 15-6: PicMonkey allows you to resize images in proportion.

6. **When you get the image to the size you'd like, click the Apply button.**

7. **Click Save (above the image) and save the image to your computer.**

   Be sure not to close your browser window before you save the image, or you'll lose all your edits.

To save time, resize images for your posts in batches. Although you can't do this in PicMonkey, you can try a free resizing tool such as Fotosizer (www.fotosizer.com). If you use a program like Adobe Photoshop, you can create an Action that will automatically resize images to a size that you select.

Cropping photos

Cropping means trimming unnecessary portions of an image's outer area. Cropping is one of the easiest ways to enhance an image. You may want to crop an image to

✔ Remove clutter in the background.

✔ Fit an image into a space with different proportions, such as placing a rectangular image into a square.

✔ Showcase a particular portion of that image.

Follow these simple steps to crop an image in PicMonkey:

1. **Go to the PicMonkey website (**www.picmonkey.com**).**

2. **Click the text that reads Edit a Photo (at the top of the interface).**

   A window pops up to let you select the photo you want to use.

3. **Select the photo you want to crop and click Open.**

   The photo opens, ready for editing.

4. **Select the Crop tool from the list of options.**

   A cropping box automatically appears with four circles at each corner, as shown in Figure 15-7.

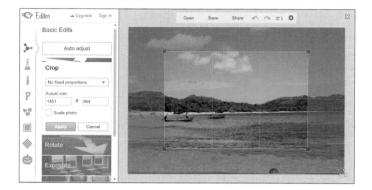

Figure 15-7: The cropping box shows you how the image will look before you crop it.

5. **Choose your proportions.**

   Here are a few of the options you'll see:

   - *No Fixed Proportions* allows you to enlarge or shrink the cropping box without being confined to a certain shape. As you adjust the box, the image dimensions shown in the Actual Size fields change automatically.

   - *Original Proportions* confines the image you're cropping to the original file proportions even though the actual image size gets smaller.

   - *Facebook Timeline* sets the cropping box to proportions that will fit as a Facebook Timeline cover photo.

   You even have settings for common desktop screen sizes and iPhone screens. Sweet!

6. **Select the area you want to keep.**

   You can select this area in two ways:

   - Click any corner of the cropping box and move in any direction.

   - Click anywhere on the inside of the cropping box to move the entire box.

After you make your selection, the area you want to crop from your image becomes shaded. If you need to undo the area you selected to crop, click the left-pointing arrow above the image or readjust using either of the preceding techniques.

7. **Click the Apply button to crop your image.**

8. **Click Save to save the image onto your computer.**

In Figure 15-8, you can see the cropped version of this image. The cropping changed the orientation from landscape to portrait and removed someone's head from the bottom edge to improve the image composition.

Figure 15-8: Cropping this image removed background clutter that didn't help tell this photo's story.

Using Images in Your Blog Posts

You can place images just about anywhere on your blog: a special blog page, header, sidebar, and so on. Aside from the prominent blog header, the heart of imagery in your blog design lies within your blog posts.

As I mention in Chapter 2, images serve to grab the readers' attention. As you include imagery throughout your post, they pull readers deeper into your content. Images also make your blog post more memorable because people visualize imagery more easily than text.

Whatever images you use should be relevant to your blog post, but they don't have to be blatant to be effective. For example, a blog post sharing marathon running tips could feature a close-up image of a finish line instead of someone actually running a marathon.

Images in your blog posts also help drive traffic from social networking sites. When readers share your posts on sites like Pinterest or Facebook, those sites let your readers select an image to display with the link to your post. An image relevant to your post will garner more traffic than just your blog's logo or header.

Deciding where to place images within a post

Deciding where images should go within your blog posts plays an important role in your overall blog design. When a new reader lands on your blog, you need a point in your post that can immediately catch their eye. To do that, always try to place one image above the *fold* of your blog design, which is the point where the visitor must scroll down to see more. An image above the fold of your design becomes a teaser of sorts, enticing the reader to scroll down to see (and read) more past the blog post title.

If the only image that can potentially be seen above the fold is your blog header, your header size might be too large. Refer to Chapter 7 where I talk about effective header sizes and offer tips on a well-sized blog header.

As the story or purpose of your post develops in the text, images should reinforce the information the text conveys and break up the text as readers continue through your post. Images deeper within a post create a visual path through your posts in a way that text alone just can't do.

Images also provide clarity to your readers. For example, if you're working through a how-to explanation, such as a craft or software tutorial, showing images of steps along the way (as shown in Figure 15-9) makes each step much easier to understand than just showing the end result.

Don't go overboard with images. Maybe only one image is enough for your post. If that's the case, just format your text in a way that easily moves readers through your post. I give you all sorts of ways to format blog post text in Chapter 16.

Figure 15-9: Illustrating a step of a craft tutorial can help your readers.

Properly sizing images

When incorporating images into your blog posts, you not only want some visual oomph, but you want to ensure that those images don't slow down your page-loading time.

Before you even insert images into your blog post, edit the image size in your photo-editing software so that the image fits within the column of your blog post. If your column width is 600 pixels (px) but your original image is 800 px, the image stretches into another column, like what you can see in Figure 15-10.

As a fix, you could resize large images within your blog post — but, you affect your blog's loading time because you still uploaded the original size. Only

Figure 15-10: Having a picture stretch into the sidebar looks messy, covering up elements in the sidebar.

make small sizing adjustments within your blog. You can adjust image sizes outside your blog by following the steps in the section "Resizing photos."

As a starting point, I typically size my photos to the width of my blog post. I can then resize as needed, such as for portrait-oriented photos. For example, if the shorter side of a portrait-oriented photo runs the entire blog width, the photo would be gigantic. So I know to always resize those.

On the other end of the spectrum, bloggers often makes the mistake of using teeny-tiny images in their blog posts, which detract from your overall blog design and decrease the image's ability to make a statement. Your readers actually want to see your images, so make them large enough to see!

Some bloggers prefer to wrap text around their images, as shown in Figure 15-11. This comes in handy if you want to show a smaller image like a headshot as part of a bio or an icon that should accompany a piece of text. Whether you do that for your other images is really just a matter of preference.

Figure 15-11: Wrap text around an image for visual appeal.

In most blogging platforms, wrapping text simply involves selecting an available wrapping style when placing an image into a post. You (or your designer) can adjust how much space to use between the image border and the text by making adjustments within your cascading style sheet (CSS).

Avoid wrapping text around images in a way that produces a jarring effect. For example, when two images in close proximity wrap on different sides of your blog post (see Figure 15-12), content can become cramped between the images, making your blog post hard to read.

I recommend keeping images within your post further apart or aligning images to a certain side. Check your blog post layout in preview mode before you publish to ensure that your images don't hinder readability.

Naming image files

Have you ever used an image on your blog with a totally unhelpful filename like `DSC001.jpg` or `image01.png`? Well, this section is for you! Get onboard because properly naming images helps with blog navigation design, search engine optimization (SEO), and more.

Lorem ipsum dolor sit amet, iusto veniam ut sea, mea at utinam essent debitis. Sit sumo voluptaria eu, nec ea stet impetus. Veri illum nominati ei eos, ea wisi labitur eam. Et choro eripuit pertinacia vel, in democritum persequeris quo, ne usu iisque accumsan.

Ut unum labore vim, harum nullam ocurreret ad eum. Mei in omnis vocibus accumsan.

No saepe putent forensibus nam. Pri stet nobis platonem no, eum falli tantas epicuri no. Sit option complectitur ad. Dicam aperiam imperdiet an pro. Sea ad scripserit consectetuer. Nam te vidisse consulatu. Quem idque quaeque ei mel. Cu cum dicit sadipscing, ad impedit civibus mel, no affert volutpat usu. Ne vel legimus pertinax eloquentiam, autem interesset est at.

Ponderum sapientem et pro. Nam ei diam possim, sit nemore mentitum id. Equidem inimicus has ei, legere consectetuer duo ne, eam doming noster ne. Diceret nostrum intellegat vim in, pro ad bonorum percipit, sed eu quem copiosae. Ut audire periculis mei, ei nonumy intellegam eum. Pri stet nobis platonem no, eum falli tantas epicuri no.

Veri illum nominati ei eos, ea wisi labitur eam. Et choro eripuit pertinacia vel, in democritum persequeris quo, ne usu iisque accumsan.

Figure 15-12: Too many images can look awkward and interrupt word flow.

for you! Get onboard because properly naming images helps with blog navigation design, search engine optimization (SEO), and more.

When working in the back end of your blog, you can more easily find an image you're looking for when the image has a descriptive name. In addition, you end up with shorter, cleaner image URLs.

For SEO, using good file names become critical. In a search engine's eyes, a name like `DSC001.jpg` says nothing about what the image really contains.

Search engines can't see pictures, but they can see filenames.

And image names don't just matter for search engines and your blog. Sites like Pinterest can be a huge drivers of traffic, depending on the type of content you produce. If someone pins your image to their Pinterest board,

Pinterest might automatically pull the image name into the pin description. People like to pin quickly and might not bother to change DSC001.jpg to something more descriptive and helpful. You could lose out on some mega traffic from a simple oversight.

Naming your images the right way doesn't have to be difficult though. Here are my tips:

- ✒ Name your files using a keyword that's related to the content of your image or blog post. Don't get spammy, though, and stuff your image name with lots of keywords. For example, if you wrote a blog post on puppy training and you have an image of a dog shaking your hand, then the file name puppy-training-shaking-hands.jpg is better than puppy-training-dog-training-tricks-shaking-hands.jpg.

- ✒ Keep filenames relatively short. That way, they're easier to remember or to copy and paste them elsewhere.

- ✒ Use hyphens between words to make the image name easier to read.

- ✒ Stick with naming the file with just words (or a mix of words and numbers) rather than including special characters or using only numbers.

- ✒ Avoid using spaces in your image names. The link to an image named homemade apple pie.jpg will show up as /homemade%20apple%20 pie.jpg, which is not as easy to read.

If you don't share certain personal information on your blog — such as kids' names, your last name, or the city you're from — leave that out of your filename, too. Otherwise, that information is visible to anyone.

Showcasing Multiple Images within a Post

People love images. Blog readers love images (after all, they're people). But how do you decide how many to include? And when you've figured that out, how can you showcase them in a visually appealing way?

Deciding how many images to include

More images in your blog post doesn't always equal better. Few people want to scroll and scroll through image after image of your latest vacation, no matter how spectacular your vacation was. However, when the images are your own, you might have a hard time deciding which images to cut out.

When narrowing down photos from an event, consider removing photos that include unflattering facial expressions, show distracting clutter (that can't be cropped out), or appear too similar to another photo. Instead, select images that capture emotion, are well focused, and best help tell your story.

When deciding how many photos to include in a post about something else, my best advice is to include as many images as it takes to get your point across. For example, a 20-step tutorial may not need an image for every step, but a review of five top gifts for kids might need an image to showcase each product.

After you narrow down your images, you may have the right balance of images and text for your blog post. If you still have too many images, consider displaying a group together in a collage or photo gallery.

Creating a photo collage

A *photo collage* is basically just a composition of many photos. On a blog, a collage allows you to present more images in a smaller space than they'd take up if you inserted them one after another in a blog post. Collages can also make looking a multiple images more enticing, whether they're in your blog post or elsewhere in your blog's design.

Like just about anything design-related, you have oodles of options for creating a collage. You can create one in a program like Picasa or Photoshop. However, I default again to PicMonkey (it must be that cute monkey). Here's how to create a collage using PicMonkey:

1. **Go to PicMonkey (**www.picmonkey.com**).**

2. **Click the text that reads Create Collage (at the top of the interface).**

3. **Select Upload Photos to choose your photos.**

   At this point, a window will open where you can select the images that you want to use in your collage. Select multiple images at once by holding down Shift if they're grouped together. If they aren't grouped together, simply hold down the Ctrl key on a PC or the Command key on a Mac while you click to select files.

4. **Select a collage layout by clicking the Layouts tab on the far left of your screen, as shown in Figure 15-13.**

   You have many types of options here with fun names, such as Biggie Smalls and L-egant. Move your cursor over one of the options, and a sample of the layout appears. Clicking a selection shows you a number of options with that type of layout.

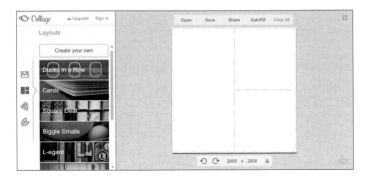

Figure 15-13: PicMonkey gives you many collage template options as a starting point.

5. **Select your template.**

6. **Adjust the collage dimensions to a size that fits within your blog post.**

   You can find the dimension directly underneath the collage area. Be sure to input the number as pixels.

7. **Add one of your images to the collage by simply dragging the image from the Images tab into a frame within the template and dropping it in.**

   After you place the image, you can move around the image within that frame. You just can't zoom into the image at all to create a tighter crop.

   If you want PicMonkey to take a stab at laying out your collage, select the Autofill feature, sit back, and let the monkey do the work. You may just save yourself some time!

8. **(Optional) If you fill in all the frames with images and decide you want to add another image, drag that image to a place of white space where you'd like the photo to be placed — but not on top of an existing image.**

   When you do this, two lines appear to denote the image will be placed in that spot, as shown in Figure 15-14. Release the mouse to let go of the image, and it drops into the collage and resizes all the other images to make room.

9. **After you build your collage to your liking, click the Save button (above the collage).**

   Then you can name the collage, and select a file type and image quality. Save it somewhere on your computer that you'll remember, and you're done! Figure 15-15 shows a finished collage created in PicMonkey.

Insertion point

Figure 15-14: Drag and add an image into the collage.

Adding a gallery

Sometimes you might want to display your images more dynamically than a collage. That's where galleries come in. A *gallery* is a way to showcase multiple pictures, where each image can be clicked. Clicking that image can show a larger version of the image or can direct someone to another part of your blog. You can include a gallery as part of your overall blog design, within a blog post, or even within special pages, such as a resource or recipe page.

WordPress has a very simple built-in gallery feature for blog posts. However, most people want more than the built-in gallery. That's where the following options come in.

Figure 15-15: A finished collage, ready to place into your blog post.

I present a lot of choices because, well, you have many free and premium options. WordPress.org will give you the majority of choices, but the first option lets bloggers on any platform create galleries from Facebook albums, Flickr, or Picasa.

- ✔ **QuickGallery (free, not solely for WordPress):** www.quickgallery.com
- ✔ **NextGEN (free):** http://wordpress.org/extend/plugins/next gen-gallery

- ✔ **CataBlog (free):** `http://wordpress.org/extend/plugins/catablog`
- ✔ **TouchCarousel (premium):** `http://codecanyon.net/item/touchcarousel-posts-content-slider-for-word-press/1479088`
- ✔ **PhotoMosaic (premium):** `http://codecanyon.net/item/photomosaic-for-wordpress/243422`
- ✔ **Fancy Gallery (premium):** `http://codecanyon.net/item/fancy-gallery-wordpress-plugin/400535`

Not every gallery plug-in works nicely on smart phones, so be sure to check the plug-in details for specifics.

Working with Illustrations

For most of this chapter, I focus (ha!) on photos because every blogger uses (or should use) photos. But what about illustrations?

You might think you need to be artistic to work illustrations into your blog design. Not true! For example, I'm more comfortable manipulating illustrations rather than designing them from scratch. I purchase illustrations and then combine them into a design, like I did on my blog header for Adventuroo (see Figure 15-16). I designed this blog header using two sets of illustrations. I then adjusted colors, removed trees, added animals, and overlaid it with text to create a custom look.

Figure 15-16: I made this blog header by combining and manipulating two sets of illustrations.

With illustrations, you can make custom social media buttons, abstract patterns or backgrounds, icons, and more. This section will give you a basic overview of illustrations, also known as *vector images*.

Getting to know vector images

Vector images are decidedly *not* photographs. *Vector images* are illustrations with lines and points. Think about how you draw something on paper. You wouldn't create a star using hundreds of tiny dots, like a photo has. You draw the star using lines and points. When it comes to computer graphics, that's a vector.

And you know how photographs can get fuzzy when you increase their size too much from the original? That doesn't happen with vector-based images because they're defined by math rather than pixels, so you can scale them up (or down) without any quality loss. Bonus: Vector images also are smaller file sizes than files made up of pixels.

Because of this scalability, quality logos are always done as vectors. They can be easily edited without affecting the quality. For example, if you have only an image of your logo in JPEG format, you can't change the color, increase the font size, or anything else. With a vector, though, you can — and then export the image into a JPEG for web use.

Here are some common file formats you'll see for vectors:

- Encapsulated Post Script (EPS)
- Adobe Illustrator (AI)
- CorelDRAW (CDR)
- Scalable Vector Graphics (SVG)

Vector files need to be opened in vector-based software. That means you'll need to convert a vector image to a rasterized file (that is, one with pixels, like a JPEG) in order to use the image on your blog.

Vector images can usually be purchased at the same places you find stock imagery. (See the section, "Using images from other sources.") You can also find them at sites like these:

- **VectorStock:** www.vectorstock.com
- **Vecteezy:** www.vecteezy.com
- **QVectors:** http://qvectors.net

Choosing vector-based software

Vector programs aren't as intuitive to use as some image-editing programs. If you work with a blog designer for your vector-based designs or you want to learn only a few basics, I recommend sticking with a free vector-based software like Inkscape. I should at least tell you about the two most well-known paid vector programs:

✔ **Adobe Illustrator:** The most popular for-fee vector-based program, it's hands-down the standard for vector designs.

    www.adobe.com/products/illustrator.html

✔ **CorelDRAW Graphics Suite X6:** A powerful competitor to Illustrator.

    www.corel.com/corel/product/index.jsp?pid=prod4260069

For those looking for a free solution, Inkscape (http://inkscape.org) is one of your only options. Inkscape allows you to create drawings using pencil, pen, and calligraphy tools; manipulate objects; use paths; and more.

Creating a simple vector graphic

Most people have edited a photograph, but vector graphics are probably strange, new territory, so I want to show you a quick Inkscape example on how to create a cloud icon. Then, you could use an icon to highlight a special section on your blog or to create a social media button by placing a social media logo on top of that cloud within the illustration.

1. **Browse to Inkscape** (http://inkscape.org) **and create a new icon by choosing File⇨New⇨icon_64x64.**

2. **On the toolbar, select the Circle tool.**

   This allows you to create circles and ellipses.

3. **Draw an ellipse shape as shown in Figure 15-17.**

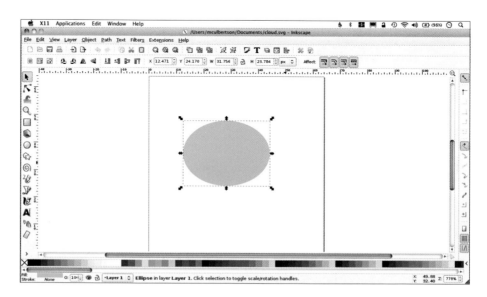

Figure 15-17: An ellipse shape forms the basis for a cloud shape.

4. **Adjust the color and stroke to suit your preference.**

   - *To adjust the color:* Go to Object⇨Fill and Stroke. You can change the color in a variety of ways, from changing RGB values to selecting a color in a color wheel. I kept the color flat but changed it to a blue shade I selected from the Wheel tab.

   - *To adjust the stroke color:* Click the Stroke Paint tab. Adjust the stroke (outlines a shape) color to your liking.

5. **Create new ellipses of different sizes and arrange them to form a cloud shape.**

   Keep all ellipses the same color with the same stroke color. After you create the shape of your cloud, you merge all the shapes so the stroke is visible only on the outside of the cloud shape.

6. **Go to Edit⇨Select All.**

   This selects all the ellipses at once.

7. **Go to Path⇨Union.**

   Union combines the separate ellipses into one single image. In Figure 15-18, you can see how the shapes merge into a simple cloud shape.

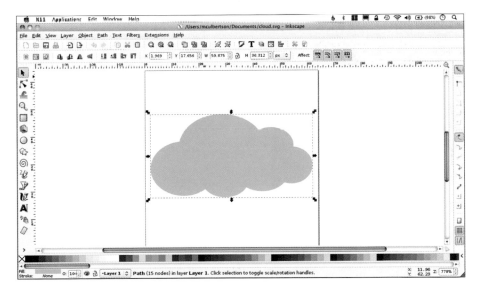

Figure 15-18: Separate shapes transformed into a cloud using the Union feature.

8. **Save illustration by choosing File⇨Save.**

9. **To convert the icon to a format suitable for web use, choose File⇨Export Bitmap.**

   This saves the image as a PNG image, which will prevent the image from having a white box around the cloud.

For more about creating vector artwork in Inkscape, try The Inkscape Tutorials Weblog (`http://inkscapetutorials.wordpress.com`) or Creative Nerds' blog post featuring links to 50 tutorials (`http://creativenerds.co.uk/tutorials/inkscape-tutorials`). If you're looking to get into using Adobe Illustrator, try VectorTuts+ (`http://vector.tutsplus.com`). You can even find a few Inkscape tutorials there, too.

16

Incorporating Design into Your Blog Posts

When it comes to pages of content, readers see one type of page time and time again: your blog posts. Because blogs essentially revolve around those posts, working blog design into your blog posts should be a given. Your blog may have rock star content, but if your blog posts aren't visually inviting, a visitor may skip over the content altogether.

In this chapter, I explore ways in which you can add some of your overall blog design into your blog posts through customizing blog post titles, styling block quotations, and more. This chapter also provides ideas for breaking up your long stretches of text with visual elements.

Banishing Long Blocks of Text

One day on Twitter, I came across a tweet about a tutorial that interested me. I clicked through to the blog post and started to read. While the content really did rock, I actually struggled reading through the entire post because the blogger buried the content into a few, very long paragraphs.

When it comes to blog design, getting rid of long blocks of text doesn't often get the focus. However, your content is the star of your blog. Honor that content of yours by ensuring visitors can easily read each and every word should they choose to do so. Making your content visually easy to digest also benefits those people who might only scan your content. (Chapter 1 dives into more about how people often skim content.)

Whether you're writing a tutorial, recipe, story, or something else altogether, you can get rid of lengthy paragraphs for good, ensuring your blog posts or pages visually guide the reader through your content. The tips in the rest of this chapter show you how.

Breaking Text into Smaller Paragraphs

Publishing a blog post or page with long paragraphs isn't often done purposefully. You might be pinched for time or really excited to get your thoughts on "paper," so you just write and write and write without much thought for how the text will actually look on your blog. The fix is simple (and I apologize if this advice sounds overly simplistic): Split your text into smaller paragraphs.

Keeping paragraphs relatively short gives readers' minds a quick break, letting them soak up your words more easily (or scan through them if they're short on time). In addition, paragraph length can be a powerful way to add emotion to your words without even changing your writing. Try splitting important parts of a story into new single-sentence paragraphs to intensify the emotion. It pulls readers' eyes down to keep reading more.

In Figure 16-1, notice how the text on the left looks denser than the text on the right. I didn't change one single word. I just added visual breaks to the content.

> Writing is one of those things that can be painful. Am I right? You need to write but the words just don't come. You fidget. You get up. Get down. Toggle over to Facebook. Go to Pinterest to pin a few things. Check your email. Next thing you know you've wasted an hour and have MAYBE one good sentence written. I've been there. I know you have too.

> Writing is one of those things that can be painful. Am I right? You need to write but the words just don't come.
>
> You fidget. You get up. Get down. Toggle over to Facebook. Go to Pinterest to pin a few things. Check your email. Next thing you know you've wasted an hour and have MAYBE one good sentence written.
>
> I've been there. I know you have too.

Figure 16-1: Breaking up paragraphs gives content more impact and is easier to read.

Although separating long blocks of text into smaller paragraphs can make your content more readable, having a really long page of super-short paragraphs can also hinder readability by making the content seem choppy. Strike a balance to bring the right flow to your content.

Just looking at your content within your blog platform's visual editor isn't enough to check your post or page's readability. Before you click that Publish button, preview your blog post or page to see how long each paragraph looks on your blog. If you notice long paragraphs, break them up into smaller paragraphs.

Using Subheadings

Subheadings serve as mini-headlines to separate your content into different sections. Breaking up long blocks of text by using subheadings plays a role in blog design, too. Subheadings impact your content's visual design and usability all-in-one as follows:

- **Organizing information:** When you visually separate your blog post or page into sections, you give your readers a mental pause and a chance to digest your content.

- **Creating hierarchy:** Using subheadings provides a visual hierarchy, telling your reader that the subheading is important to read. This helps readers understand the main points of your post, even if they happen to just skim your post.

- **Providing bookmarks:** Subheadings act like bookmarks for your content. Someone returning to your post or re-reading your content can use subheadings as visual bookmarks to get the piece of content they're looking for.

Figure 16-2 shows a blog post with and without subheadings. As you can see, the subheadings visually break up long blocks of text and help the reader better understand the content.

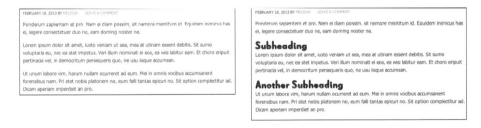

Figure 16-2: Blog content with subheadings is easier to follow.

When talking subheadings, you probably think mostly about one level of subheadings within your blog post. However, if your content has more than one layer to it, divide your content even further by adding one heading level deeper.

In Chapter 10, I offer some tips for styling your subheadings with custom fonts and colors that complement your overall blog design.

Including Images

A picture is worth a thousand words, right? Right! And a picture can also *enhance* a thousand words. Images in your blog posts visually break up your content *and* help illustrate or support your content as well.

As you can see in Figure 16-3, simply adding a couple of photographs gives visual spots for a reader's eye to land, easing readability. The images keep your eyes moving down through a page instead of getting lost in big chunks of text.

If you want to know more about working images into your blog posts and overall blog design, I devote Chapter 15 entirely to images.

Figure 16-3: Use images in your blog posts to keep a reader's interest.

Depending on the topics you write about, images in your blog posts can also take the form of charts, graphs, or infographics. You can create charts and infographics using programs like Microsoft Excel or Adobe Illustrator. Or if simpler programs are more to your liking, check programs like Google Chart Tools (`https://developers.google.com/chart`) and Piktochart (`http://piktochart.com`) for creating infographics.

Applying Indentation and Block Quotes

Another way to apply design elements to your blog posts and break up long blocks of text is to use indentation and block quotes. Both indentation and block quotes can add visual appeal to your content by adding contrast to that particular block of content. However, they each have a distinct use:

- ✔ If your blog post includes a quote that's important to the content of your blog post, use a block quote.
- ✔ If your blog post includes text you want to set off from the body text, such as an important point or example, use the indent feature.

To see the difference between indentation and block quotes, look at Figure 16-4, which shows how the WordPress Twenty Eleven theme displays them both. The text in italics is a block quote, and the second section uses indentation.

Figure 16-4: Block quote and indentation examples.

Indentation and quotes work well to highlight content containing a definition, quote, testimonial, or any other text that you feel warrants emphasis.

To indent text within a blog post or page on WordPress, click the Indent button from within your Visual Editor (see Figure 16-5).

To turn text into a block quote within WordPress, click the Quote button from within your Visual Editor (see Figure 16-5).

Figure 16-5: Set indented and block quote text within the WordPress Visual Editor.

To see how to visually style block quotes, see Chapter 14.

Including Lists

Just as subheadings can visually organize content within your blog post, so can using lists within your blog posts. You can provide focus to listed content by making it visually stand out from the other blocks of text within your post or page.

Within your content, you can display lists that are either bulleted or numbered. In Figure 16-6, take a look at the buttons used to change your text into either list option.

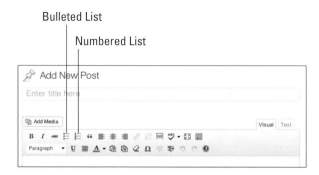

Figure 16-6: Bulleted and numbered list icons within the WordPress Visual Editor.

Sometimes it's okay to include a short list as part of a regular sentence, but displaying content as a list gains more attention when it's visually different from the rest of the content. You might use a list for the following:

- Supplies needed for a project
- A checklist of things to do or accomplish
- Must-haves for a particular topic (fashion accessories, WordPress plug-ins, photography equipment, and so on)
- Wish lists

Lists don't just have to be used for items that fit on just one line. You can also use paragraphs within a list format. Consider adding more visual interest to a list like this by using bold or italics, like I did in Figure 16-7.

Ponderum sapientem et pro. Nam ei diam possim, sit nemore mentitum id. Equidem inimicus has ei, legere consectetuer duo ne, eam doming noster ne. Diceret nostrum intellegat vim in, pro ad bonorum percipit, sed eu quem copiosae. Ut audire periculis mei, ei nonumy intellegam eum. Pri stet nobis platonem no, eum falli tantas epicuri no.

Veri illum nominati ei eos, ea wisi labitur eam. Et choro eripuit pertinacia vel, in democritum persequeris quo, ne usu iisque accumsan.

- **No saepe putent forensibus nam.** Pri stet nobis platonem no, eum falli tantas epicuri no. Sit option complectitur ad.
- **Dicam aperiam imperdiet an pro.** Sea ad scripserit consectetuer. Nam te vidisse consulatu. Ponderum sapientem et pro. Nam ei diam possim, sit nemore mentitum id.
- **Equidem inimicus has ei, legere consectetuer duo ne, eam doming noster ne.** Diceret nostrum intellegat vim in, pro ad bonorum percipit, sed eu quem copiosae. Ut audire periculis mei, ei nonumy intellegam eum. Pri stet nobis platonem no, eum falli tantas epicuri no.

Veri illum nominati ei eos, ea wisi labitur eam. Et choro eripuit pertinacia vel, in democritum persequeris quo, ne usu iisque accumsan.

Figure 16-7: Use lists to organize longer areas of text.

Increasing Space between Paragraphs

When a blog post or page has long blocks of text, the amount of space between paragraphs can almost get lost, adding to what looks like a never-ending paragraph.

Most blog themes are designed to having an adequate amount of space between paragraphs. However, if you begin to customize your blog design by changing fonts, you might need to increase this spacing.

To change the spacing between paragraphs, you have to modify your CSS. (Read more about CSS in Chapter 9.) Typically, you can search for a piece of code in your `style.css` file that starts with p (for paragraph) and then adjust `margin-bottom`. In the WordPress Twenty Eleven theme, it looks like this:

```
p {
    margin-bottom: 1.625em;
}
```

Adjust the spacing by increasing the em size to make a noticeable space between your paragraphs. In Figure 16-8, notice how the text on the left becomes more spaced out after I increased the spacing between paragraphs, as shown on the right. (I explain em sizing in Chapter 9, in the section about adjusting font size properties.)

If you can't find this bit of code, your theme may display it differently. Use Firebug to find the code you need to modify. I give you the run-down on Firebug in Chapter 9.

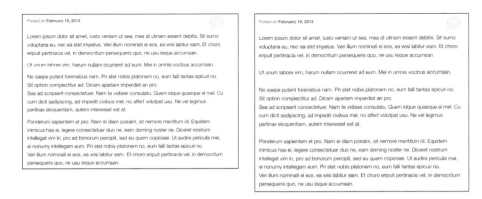

Figure 16-8: Paragraphs are much easier to read with adequate space between them.

Part V
The Part of Tens

 Continue the flow of great design by exploring another Part of Tens list online at www.
dummies.com/extras/blogdesign.

In this part. . .

- ✔ Extend your blog's design into your social media profiles.
- ✔ Create other blog materials that complement your blog design, from a media kit to blog business card.
- ✔ Discover ideas from ten blogs that know how to make readers happy with impressive blog design.
- ✔ See examples of blog design details that give these ten blogs a polished touch.

17

Ten Places to Extend Your Blog's Design

Your blog design doesn't just exist on your blog. You probably have a presence on at least one social media channel, and you may have even ventured elsewhere into activities such as e-books or speaking engagements.

As I mention in Chapter 1, part of building a brand is consistency. Infusing your blog design into other areas of your blogging life connects those things with your blog, building a consistent look across a variety of platforms and mediums.

This chapter offers ten places where you can work in your blog design. From social media to actual printed media, you have many opportunities to showcase that great design of yours!

When working on ideas from this chapter, don't forget to pull out your blog's style guide that I show you how to create in Chapter 4.

Facebook Page

As a blogger, having a great blog design and great content doesn't automatically equate to a huge audience. However, being active in at least one social media channel can help bring traffic to your blog and build a community of readers. Many bloggers start with a Facebook business or community page because Facebook is the largest social media network. Luckily, Facebook offers plenty of ways to brand your blog's Facebook page so that it matches your blog design.

The two main areas of your Facebook page are the large cover photo and the profile picture. Cover photos give you a chance to show imagery that represents your blog, and a profile picture works best as your blog logo or picture of you.

A smaller version of your profile photo displays when you publish a post or comment.

In Figure 17-1, you can see how Cheryl from Tidy Mom (`http://tidymom.net`) uses a Facebook cover photo to highlight an image of her and a little about her blog. The profile picture shows the red Tidy Mom logo that people associate with the blog.

Profile picture   Cover photo

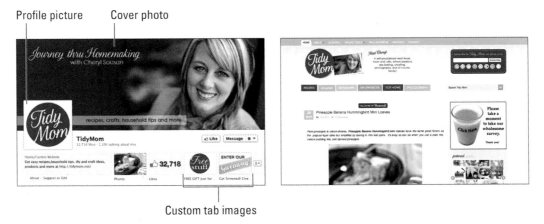

Custom tab images

Figure 17-1: Choose a Facebook cover photo image that represents you or your blog.

Facebook has just one guideline when it comes to cover photos: Cover photos can't contain more than 20 percent text over the entire image. However, they can include the following:

- Price or purchase information
- Contact information, such as a blog address
- References to Facebook features or actions, such a Like or Share
- Calls to action, such as "Buy now" or "Get this offer"

In addition to cover photos and profile pictures, you can also brand your Facebook page using custom tab images. These images direct your Facebook page visitors to special apps or tabs, such as an e-mail subscription page or an Instagram page within Facebook. In Figure 17-1, you can see that the Tidy Mom fan page has one image that leads to a way to get a free gift and another image that leads to a giveaway page. You can even customize the text under the image.

The Photos tab can't be moved or modified.

To prepare these images, you can use any of the photo-editing programs that I mention in Chapter 15. Here are the following dimensions (in pixels) you'll want to use:

- **Cover photo:** 851 x 315 px
- **Profile picture:** 160 x 160 px

  The photo must be uploaded at a slightly higher size, though — 180 x 180 px.
- **Custom tab images:** 111 x 74 px with a maximum file size of 5MB

Twitter

Twitter (`https://twitter.com`) is a social media microblogging platform where users share information in 140 characters or less. Followers (or potential followers) may visit your Twitter profile to learn more about you, so your profile should make a good first impression. Create a Twitter profile that reflects your blog's style and personality.

In Figure 17-2, you can see how Andy and Charlie from How to Be a Dad (`@HowToBeADad`) pull in elements from their blog design while adding a personal touch by showing themselves as well.

Figure 17-2: Twitter gives you a few places to infuse your blog's design.

A Twitter profile has three main visual elements: a small profile picture, a header image, and a background. Along with these visual elements, you can also change the colors of the links shown on your Twitter feed and in the sidebar. Here are the dimensions to create a profile picture and header image. Then I talk a bit about the background.

- **Profile picture:** 81 x 81 px

  However, upload a larger image and let Twitter re-size it. This way, your picture its best when someone clicks the image to see a larger version. Profile pictures can be up to 2MB.

- **Header image:** 1252 x 626 px (Twitter resizes this to 520 x 260 px)

Creating a customized Twitter background can get tricky because what a visitor sees on your background depends on their computer or device's screen size. The actual parts of Twitter that show on top of the background (the sidebar, header, and Twitter stream) amount to 865 pixels wide, which doesn't change with a computer monitor's screen size.

So, to reach as many viewers and followers as possible, I recommend going with the following. Create your background image with a size of 1920 x 1080 px to cover large screen sizes.

Most of your background design should be a graphic, pattern, image, or color, leaving text for the left side of your background design, since this is the part of a background that nearly everyone can see. On the left, consider a width of approximately 66 px your safe zone for placing any key information (like text). Those 66 pixels will be unobstructed for anyone with a screen resolution of 1024 x 768, which amounts to nearly every Twitter user. You could even stretch that dimension as far as 194 px wide, but bear in mind that only

82 percent of Twitter users will be able to see the content. For many Twitter users, the benefit of having more space for content outweighs the chance that someone won't see the content.

Google+

Launched in 2011, Google+ (Google "Plus") is a social network has gained in popularity. Some bloggers use Google+ business pages for their blogs, and others prefer to use their Google+ personal profile. Make your page or profile instantly recognizable by adding elements of your blog design to your Google+ page.

To create graphics for your page or profile, use these dimensions:

- **Cover photo:** 2120 x 1192 px (part of this image runs behind the profile picture)
- **Profile picture:** 250 x 250 px

Google adds a black gradient to the bottom of the cover photo image, displaying the page name, page URL, and number of +1s (or people in your circles on a personal profile). This area is about 160 pixels tall, so don't put text in the bottom 160 pixels of your cover photo.

Pinterest

Pinterest (http://pinterest.com) is a popular social media platform that works like an online pinboard, giving you a place to pin images of recipes, crafts, and more. Pinterest can drive mega traffic to many types of blogs, from food blogs to fashion blogs.

Because Pinterest focuses heavily on images, some bloggers create a Pinterest-friendly image for their blog posts. A Pinterest-friendly image typically includes a title and a graphic like you see in Figure 17-3. From Away (www.fromaway.com) sometimes labels a recipe image, using a font from its blog design and a clean look that doesn't distract from the amazing recipe photos.

Pinnable images may start to look repetitive if you use the same image for every blog post you link to on Pinterest. For Pinterest images, play with your design while still honoring your overall blog design. Consider designing a few templates and base them off part of your blog design. Don't be afraid to go outside your color scheme and use colors that complement your design.

© FromAway.com

Figure 17-3: Use a variety of Pinterest-friendly images that all complement one another.

E-books

Depending on your content, you might end up venturing into creating an *e-book,* which is simply an electronic book that might be in an e-pub format (an electronic publication format that can be read on devices like tablets and smart phones), a Kindle format, or PDF (or even all three).

After downloading your e-book, though, that visitor no longer needs to visit your blog to retrieve it. In fact, if you sell your e-book on another site (such as Amazon), your e-book reader may never even have to visit your blog at all. For this reason, designing your e-book (at the very least, your e-book cover) gives you a change to introduce readers to your blog design so you can connect the e-book with your blog.

In Figure 17-4, Anna from My Life and Kids (http://mylifeandkids.com) pulls her blog's primary font and colors into her e-book cover. The result is an e-book that complements her blog design.

© Anna Luther, My Life and Kids

Figure 17-4: Pull fonts, colors, or imagery from your blog design into your e-book design.

If you sell your e-book in an e-pub and a Kindle format, you won't have as many opportunities to incorporate design into the actual body text of your book. That means you must really make your cover count!

Printables

Printables have become popular in many circles of blogging. A *printable* is typically a PDF that readers can download and print. The PDF content can be anything from a checklist to a craft template to a calendar. Bloggers who create printables typically create them rather frequently as a great way to drive traffic to a blog.

Designing a printable to complement your blog design increases your blog's brand recognition. Including your blog's name and design in the printable also helps if someone forgets from whose blog they actually got the printable.

Rachel from In Spaces Between (www.inspacesbetween.com) offers a free daily planner that keeps the same look and feel as her blog design. The result is a printable that reinforces her blog's recognition for anyone who may download the printable (shown in Figure 17-5).

© www.inspacesbetween.com

Figure 17-5: Use parts of your blog design when creating printables to build blog recognition.

Media Kit

Bloggers who sell advertising on their blog or want to work with brands often create a media kit to give to potential partners. A blogging media kit should be around one to three pages and consist of available opportunities, blog statistics, and rates. You might hand out a media kit to a potential partner at a blog conference or e-mail a PDF version to a potential advertiser.

Your media kit should be specific to your blog's design so that a potential advertiser or partners have that association to your blog in their mind. Plus, matching your media kit to your blog design looks polished and professional versus just having a plain document with text and some links. After all, this is your chance to impress potential advertisers or partners!

Blog Badges

Some bloggers create badges for their blogs so that other bloggers or websites can display the badge on their site and link back to your blog. Think of a badge like a little advertisement for your blog. Your blog badge might be displayed on a fellow blogger's sidebar to show adoration for your blog. You might even use the badge for an ad or at the end of a guest post or contributor post on another website.

Because a blog badge represents your blog, the badge's design should take all its design cues from your overall blog design. Badges are typically 125 x 125 px or slightly larger at 150 x 150 px. You don't have much space to work with, so don't try to cram too much of your design into the badge design. Instead, stick with your blog name, your colors, and maybe a design element of some sort.

In Figure 17-6, you can see the blog badge from No Meat Athlete (`www.nomeatathlete.com`) keeps the font size large and easy to read while tying into the overall blog design.

© No Meat Athlete®, Design by Charlie Pabst at Charfish Design

Figure 17-6: A blog badge should be a small representation of your blog design.

Blog Business Cards

While branding social platforms like your Facebook page may seem obvious, extending your blog design into something that's actual paper may not seem as obvious.

If you attend a conference or other networking event and plan to represent your blog, though, most people expect to exchange blog business cards with you. Use a photo-editing or desktop publishing program to create a custom design to match your blog. As an alternative, if you use a print company's standard business card template, ensure you can customize at least a few pieces of the card. For example, use your blog's main color or add a visual element from your blog's design to the template.

Slides for Videos and Presentations

As a blogger, you might record a video for anything from a product review to an online tutorial. If you get into speaking or online training, you might need to create a presentation. With videos and presentations, creating slides that mimic your blog design can get readers familiar with your blog design before they even visit your blog. Infusing your blog design into videos and presentations is especially important if you publish videos and presentations online but away from your blog, like YouTube for videos and SlideShare (www.slideshare.net) for presentations.

For videos, you can create a title slide and even slides that divide a longer video into sections. Pull colors, fonts, and recognizable design elements into your slides.

For presentations, you can create a design in a photo-editing program and then add images to your master slides in a program like Microsoft PowerPoint. The dimensions for these slides depend on your computer screen resolution and version of PowerPoint.

I've spoken at a few conferences and match my presentation design to my blog design (see Figure 17-7). In doing this, those who may have seen my blog in the past can make a connection to me.

Figure 17-7: Use branded presentation slides to stand out from a sea of standard presentation templates.

Ten Well-Designed Blogs

In the span of writing this book, I looked at literally hundreds of blog designs. And I came across many blogs that cover a range of styles, from subtle elegance to vivid bursts of color. This list isn't meant to be a "top 10" but rather a peek at some great-looking blogs. Each blog in this list stays true to a consistent design, complete with little design details that give each of these blogs that extra wow factor.

Joy the Baker

If you love food, then prepare to get hungry when you visit Joy the Baker (`http://joythebaker.com`). While the majority of Joy Wilson's blog features baked goodness, she also shares fantastic recipes from smoothies to müesli.

The Joy the Baker blog shows you an example of a successful monochromatic blog design. As you can see in Figure 18-1, her blog design features various shades of pink, from pale pinks to pinks that border on purple. The design uses familiar shapes like circles, triangles, lines, and hearts as beautiful design elements throughout the blog. In the sidebar, I love how the triangles serve as arrows to guide the reader through the sidebar.

Under the Explore section, large images of recent recipes entice visitors. When you run your mouse over one, the image fades, and the post title appears.

Triangles guide the reader

© Joy the Baker

Figure 18-1: This blog's clean design lets you focus on the food images.

Go See Write

Go See Write (www.goseewrite.com) is a travel blog written by Michael Hodson. In December 2008, he set off on a trek across the world. Sixteen months later, he succeeded . . . and then kept traveling. Michael's travels have taken him from Ethiopia to Colombia.

Michael's header features a font and illustrations reminiscent of an art deco style (see Figure 18-2). The bold, red circle and blog name in the center of the gives the header a symmetrical look, with modes of transportation and famous landmarks to balance each side. Having a navigation menu within the header graphic adds a nice twist on the typical menu bar. In addition, the large rotating photo gallery moves your attention downward; below the gallery, you see excerpts of his latest blog posts.

Underneath a handful of blog post excerpts, you find five columns of even more content with a category label at the top. The change from the previous excerpts makes these stand out and provides a nice timeline of recent travels.

Figure 18-2: This blog design uses red to make a bold impact.

Nom Nom Paleo

Nom Nom Paleo (http://nomnompaleo.com) is a popular blog in the world of paleo cooking. Blogger Michelle Tam grew up loving food, majored in Nutrition & Food Science at Berkeley, and later earned a doctorate in clinical pharmacy. After first laughing off the paleo(lithic) diet her husband was on, she began seeing his results and decided to go paleo herself in 2010. About six months later, she started her blog and is now considered an expert in all things paleo.

Michelle's blog (see Figure 18-3) forgoes a header at the top of the blog design, instead prominently featuring a logo at the top of the sidebar. The cartoon image of herself appears throughout her blog, adding a recognizable and repetitive element to the design.

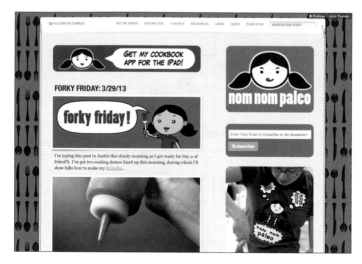

© Nom Nom Paleo, Creators: Michelle Tam and Henry Fong

Figure 18-3: A distinct logo at the sidebar top replaces the need for a blog header.

A blog design goes from great to wow when you add little surprises into your design like Michelle does (see Figure 18-4). When a visitor runs their mouse over certain design elements on the blog, her cartoon self changes expressions. So clever!

Nom Nom Paleo even has an iPhone app that mimics the look of her blog and exudes as much personality as the blog design does.

© Nom Nom Paleo, Creators: Michelle Tam and Henry Fong

Figure 18-4: A few elements of this the Nom Nom Paleo blog design change when you mouse over them.

Say Yes to Hoboken

On the blog Say Yes to Hoboken (`http://sayyestohoboken.com`), Liz Stanley and her team of contributors share tutorials, style ideas, and recipes that make you want to try doing everything. The blog's tagline states "three cheers for stylish & crafty living," and the blog design indeed brings that statement to life.

The header is clean and simple, using bright, cheerful colors to tie into the mission of the blog (see Figure 18-5). The design uses a few different colors but avoids being overwhelming by serving up plenty of white space.

Main navigation in the sidebar

© Blog Design by Christine Hughes of Darling Studio

Figure 18-5: A cheery design perfectly complements this blog's content.

One reason why I love this blog's design is because it proves you don't always have to place the navigation menu at the top to be effective. The main points of navigation are contained within the top of the sidebar. Further down the sidebar, four labels call attention to the blog's main categories, and bright yellow buttons highlight some common menu items many readers expect to see. Below those buttons, four images call out the blog's featured tutorials.

Alex Beadon

Alex Beadon's blog (www.alexbeadonphotography.com) began as a blog for photography but has morphed into a blog that helps small business owners build a successful business and "live life like a boss."

Alex's blog design commands your attention with its vivid colors and impactful font, as shown in Figure 18-6. Each blog post features an eye-popping image with large graphical elements and a picture of Alex.

When you're someone building a brand with your name, frequently using an image of yourself helps reinforce that connection to you.

A bar, an image, and an action statement for each category

© Owner: Alex Beadon www.alexbeadon.com/dummies, Designer: Melissa Love www.melissalove.co.uk

Figure 18-6: Vivid colors add a creative twist to the blog header image.

On the sidebar, each main category is elegantly highlighted using a simple bar at the top, image underneath, with an action statement overlaid on the picture (refer to Figure 18-6). Using the same design treatment on each category helps the reader understand that these are all topics she blogs about. Underneath these, an e-mail subscription area uses a complementary yet different look to distinguish it from the others.

Los Angeles, I'm Yours

Los Angeles, I'm Yours (www.laimyours.com) focuses on the art, design, lifestyle, and culture in the city of Los Angeles as well as showcasing the people who bring artistic passion to a thriving metropolis. Run by Bobby Soloman and Kyle Fitzpatrick, the blog is "a love letter to the city, from the city."

As you can see from its homepage (shown on the left in Figure 18-7), this blog features a minimal design with a vast amount of white space, allowing images to take the spotlight. The design features a large main image of the most recent post with two right sidebars of different widths. The sidebar on the far right highlights a Contact page, a fun LA Drink Map, and a list of categories. That sidebar's content is ideal for the narrow width, saving space for the main sidebar featuring Newsbites that lead to other sites featuring LA-focused content.

When you click a blog post, you're lead to a page, like that shown on the right in Figure 18-7. The first sidebar vanishes to make way for a large main image that sweeps across most of the page, making a big impact. Underneath the image, the space splits into the actual blog post and a conveniently located space to encourage interaction such as leaving a comment, sharing the post, or reading similar posts.

Home page   Blog post page

Figure 18-7: Great blog design doesn't need a lot of design elements to work.

Rage Against the Minivan

A professor of psychology, Kristen Howerton started her blog (www.rage
againsttheminivan.com) back in 2006 as a coping skill for becoming a
mom to four children within four years through birth and adoption. Not only
is the blog name Rage Against the Minivan just brilliant, so is the blog design
(see Figure 18-8).

Kristen's blog features earthy colors, while pops of blue from her family pictures draws your eyes to the header and individual family shots in the sidebar. With a subtle linen texture in the background, the green from her blog
header and blue from her header image stand out even more.

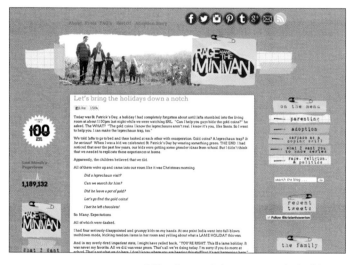

Figure 18-8: Colors stand out because of contrast.

Torn paper strips, crinkled paper, tape, staples, and safety pins all make this
blog feel handmade and welcoming. These embellishments are used throughout the blog, making the blog design consistent no matter which area you're
viewing. You can also see how a hierarchy exists with some of these design
elements. For example, the green pieces of paper all use safety pins and are
reserved for the header and sidebar headings, while the staples are reserved
for the top categories in the sidebar.

What I Wore

Jessica Quirk started posting photos of her daily outfits online in 2007 while she was working in Manhattan and Hong Kong. Those posts grew into the 2008 launch of What I Wore (`http://whatiwore.tumblr.com`) and is now her full-time business.

Jessica's overall blog design, shown on the left in Figure 18-9, features a clean layout with gray design elements. Her blog design mixes a bold all caps font with a simple serif font. The neutral-colored layout places the focus on photos of her daily outfits or photos illustrating other topics like exercise routines. Her outfit photos provide vivid colors that contrast nicely with the neutral background.

© Jessica Quirk, What I Wore

Figure 18-9: Using gray design elements make Jessica's daily outfit photos pack even more of a punch.

For each daily outfit post, Jessica features a few photos of her wearing the outfit and then one photo features a circle design element, a transparent strip, and a tip like you see on the right in Figure 18-9. The consistency lets readers know that they can expect a quick tip in each daily outfit post. Clicking Read More from the homepage takes you to even more details about the outfit.

What I Wore features great, user-friendly ways to find the daily outfits. Check out Chapter 12 to see how Jessica's blog lets you find an outfit by color, recent outfits, and more.

Butter

Butter (`http://mombutter.typepad.com`) is a blog by Jan Livingston Mokhtari that focuses on "rich bites of inspiration" from food to music to style. Jan, a mom living in Los Angeles who grew up in the Midwest, is a creative director for an ad agency and runs a production company with her husband.

Her blog design caught my eye with the bright yellow word Butter against a gray background. The yellow fits with the blog name Butter and pops throughout the design as section headings and lines like you see under each blog post title (see Figure 18-10).

Hand-drawn category buttons

© MomButter.com, blog design by Jan Livingston Mokhtari & FreckledNestDesign.com

Figure 18-10: Pops of yellow make this blog cheery and uplifting.

One of the most endearing qualities about this blog are the hand-drawn buttons for her blog categories. Jan actually drew them herself with a permanent marker and watercolors. I just love how each button complements the others yet remains unique to the topic it represents.

The Everywhereist

The Everywhereist (`www.everywhereist.com`) is a travel blog infused with a healthy dose of humor. Geraldine DeRuiter started the blog in 2009 after she was laid off. Instead of finding another job, she decided to travel the world with her husband who was already traveling extensively for work. On the blog, Geraldine explains that at its core, the blog is a love letter to her husband so he can remember the places they visit, even when he's sometimes stuck inside giving presentations or attending meetings.

When you first arrive on The Everywhereist, the header design draws you in right away with the red blog name and dark gray travel landmarks (see Figure 18-11). The blog design manages to make it clear that this blog is about traveling but without being cliché in its design.

In this blog's design, one of the best aspects is the subtlety of the design elements. The gridded background in the header reminds me of a map, and the icon above the "I" in the blog name is a symbolic reference a pin on a map. Stamp borders outline the navigation menu tabs in the header and the e-mail list field in the footer.

The blog also places valuable links and information directly underneath the header instead of the sidebar. The contrast between the script font and all caps font add visual interest, and the linked images turn blue when you mouse over them.

© The Everywhereist, blog design by Kimberly Coles, www.kimberlycoles.com

Figure 18-11: Subtle design touches like on The Everywhereist strengthen a blog's design.

Index

About the Author

Melissa Culbertson is a marketing communications professional with over 12 years of experience doing everything from writing content and designing marketing materials to overseeing web projects and managing social media. She's worked in various industries and on projects ranging from website redesigns to new product launches.

In 2009, Melissa stepped into the blogging world, writing at her personal blog Adventuroo (www.adventuroo.com). The deeper she got into blogging, the more she realized that bloggers craved knowledge to improve their blogs. She had a light-bulb-flashing moment: Her marketing communications knowledge applies to blogging, too.

Less than two years after hitting Publish on her first blog post, she started Momcomm (www.momcomm.com), where she offers tips on blogging and social media and teaches online blogging courses. On Momcomm, she's critiqued over 100 blogs, offering tips to improve a blogger's design, navigation, and content. Melissa has also spoken at blogger conferences on everything from blog design to increasing reader engagement.

Melissa lives in Raleigh, North Carolina, in a house overrun with boys — her husband, two sons, and the family Labrador Trajan.

Dedication

This book is dedicated to my wonderful husband Daniel, whose support for the work I do never wavers. This book is also for my two boys, Noah and Ethan, who will think it's cool to see my name on the cover and their names in print. I love you all.

Author's Acknowledgments

I've been a *For Dummies* book fan since the early 2000s, when I purchased *Marketing For Dummies*. I already had a young career in marketing but didn't want to miss out on something I was supposed to already know. I also credit *Puppy Training For Dummies* as the sole reason my dog is so well-behaved. I'm honored (and a more than a little giddy) to have my name on the front of one. Thanks to Wiley for giving me this opportunity.

I'd like to thank Amy Fandrei, Becky Huehls, Teresa Artman, and Susie Gardner from the *For Dummies* team for answering my many questions, providing direction, and working so incredibly hard behind the scenes to make sure this book rocks. You ladies have talent!

I'd also like to give props to Andrea Updyke, Brittany Van der Linden, Erin Lane, Fadra Nally, Melanie Nelson, and Heather Rook for being both sounding boards and question takers as I went through the book writing process.

To my family and close friends, thanks for sharing this journey with me (and sorry if I forgot to call you back). I'd like to thank Mom and Dad for always encouraging me to write, whether it was a short story in grade school or an article for the local paper in high school. Thanks also to my sisters Christy and Jennifer for all those childhood coloring sessions. I'm sure they had something to do with the creative spark we each have inside us.

Finally, I'd like to thank all those colleagues I've worked with in the past who taught, mentored, and challenged me throughout my marketing career. I'd like to give huge thanks my blog readers — your desire to learn and your blogging successes inspire me. Thanks also to the bloggers who allowed me to feature them in this book — the book wouldn't be the same without your blogs as examples of great design.

Publisher's Acknowledgments

Acquisitions Editor: Amy Fandrei

Sr. Project Editor: Rebecca Huehls

Sr. Copy Editor: Teresa Artman

Technical Editor: Susannah Gardner

Editorial Assistant: Annie Sullivan

Sr. Editorial Assistant: Cherie Case

Project Coordinator: Katie Crocker

Cover Image: Background © ryccio/iStockphoto; Icons © James Gately/iStockphoto; Laptop © ansonsaw/iStockphoto